MARTYRS AND FANATICS

SOUTH AFRICA AND HUMAN DESTINY

By PETER DREYER

SIMON AND SCHUSTER · NEW YORK

Published by Simon and Schuster
A Division of Gulf & Western Corporation
Simon & Schuster Building
Rockefeller Center
1230 Avenue of the Americas
New York, New York 10020
SIMON AND SCHUSTER and colophon are trademarks of Simon & Schuster
Designed by Christine Swirnoff
Picture editor: Vincent Virga
Manufactured in the United States of America
Printed by The Murray Printing Co.
Bound by The Book Press Inc.
1 2 3 4 5 6 7 8 9 10

Library of Congress Cataloging in Publication Data

Dreyer, Peter,
Martyrs and fanatics.

Includes bibliographical references and index.
1. South Africa—Race relations—Addresses, essays, lectures. 2. South Africa—
Politics and government—Addresses, essays, lectures. 3. Blacks—South Africa—
Race identity—Addresses, essays, lectures. 4. Nationalism—South Africa—
Addresses, essays, lectures.
I. Title
DT763.D7   305.8'00968   80-11659

ISBN 0-671-24428-0

The author gratefully acknowledges permission to quote from the following:

Selected Poems by Ingrid Jonker, translated from the Afrikaans by Jack Cope and
William Plomer. Translation copyright © 1968. Reprinted through the courtesy of
the Estate of Ingrid Jonker, Jack Cope, William Plomer, and Jonathan Cape Ltd.

Murder in the Cathedral by T. S. Eliot. Copyright © 1935 by Harcourt Brace Jova-
novich, Inc.; © 1963 by T. S. Eliot. Reprinted by permission of the publisher.

Skryt: Om 'n sinkende skip blou te verf by Breyten Breytenbach. Copyright © 1972,
1976 by Meulenhoff Nederland b.v., Amsterdam. Translation by Peter Dreyer.

The poem "Luistervink" in Kouevuur by Breyten Breytenbach. Copyright © 1969 by
Breyten Breytenbach. Used by permission of the publisher, Buren-Uitgewers (Edms)
Bpk, Cape Town. Translation by Peter Dreyer.

For the Living and the Dead

CONTENTS

LIST OF MAIN ABBREVIATIONS AND ACRONYMS

FOREWORD

1
Breyten and the Price of Illusions   15

2
Cultures in Collision   62

3
Sol Plaatje and the Dream of Deliverance   103

4
Hopes and Enemies   135

5
The Shapes of the Lie   171

6
The Human Dimension   187

7
Beyond Nationalism?   203

APPENDIX: ON AZANIA   215
NOTES AND SOURCES   223
INDEX   237

List of Main Abbreviations and Acronyms

AAC   All African Convention
ANC   African National Congress (after 1923)
APO   African People's Organization
APTAC   Alexandra People's Transport Action Committee
BAWU   Black Allied Workers' Union
BOSS   Bureau of State Security (now Department of National Security)
BPC   Black People's Convention
COD   Congress of Democrats
CPSA   Communist Party of South Africa (before 1950)
ICFTU   International Confederation of Free Trade Unions
ICU   Industrial and Commercial Workers' Union of Africa
MDC   Movement for a Democracy of Content
NEUM   Non-European Unity Movement .
NUSAS   National Union of South African Students
OHSA   *The Oxford History of South Africa,* ed. Monica Wilson and Leonard Thompson (Oxford: Clarendon Press, 1969 and 1971), 2 vols.
PAC   Pan Africanist Congress
PUTCO   Public Utility Transport Company
SACP   South African Communist Party (after 1950)

SACPO	South African Coloured People's Organization
SACTU	South African Congress of Trade Unions
SAIC	South African Indian Congress
SAIRR	South African Institute of Race Relations
SANNC	South African Native National Congress (before 1923)
SASM	South African Students' Movement
SASO	South African Students' Organization
SWAPO	South West African People's Organization
UCT	University of Cape Town
VOC	Dutch East India Company

FOREWORD

THAT THERE ARE VITAL LESSONS for
us all in the continuing South African catastrophe is one of the basic
premises of this book. The struggle against the monstrous evils of
apartheid and "neo-apartheid" is, I believe, one of the most critical
single issues now facing humanity. The spiritual, philosophical, and
political choices involved have ramifications far beyond the shores
of Africa and the present time. "On the liberation of the African
depends the liberation of the whole world," said Robert Mangaliso
Sobukwe, a great South African, more than thirty years ago. This is
not hyperbole. It would be hard to find a section of humanity more
cruelly ground down, both physically and psychically, than black
South Africa. How this has come about I hope, in part, to show.
Suffice it to say here that I believe that South African liberation
remains the key to genuine freedom throughout the African continent, and is vital to the planet as a whole. We must all be judged by
this touchstone, and the issue is not only moral but also supremely
practical. The question, finally, is one of life against death.

Remarkably, too, despite the millions upon millions of words
in print purporting to explain it, the real nature and course of this
conflict have remained hidden. There is good reason for this.
Though what is going on in southern Africa strikes at all our lives,
the subject is vast, emotionally loaded, and shrouded in willful ig-
norance and hypocrisy. In attempting to fill the need for understanding, my own included, I am acutely conscious of having taken on a
task beyond the powers of a solitary individual. Yet it must be
attempted, and this is at least a beginning. Those of us who know
even a part of the truth—no matter how small or fragmentary—
have a duty to make it accessible. Silence is complicity.

It is half a century since E. H. Damce perceptively dubbed
South Africa the culture-bed of imperialism. So many of Western
society's negative and suicidal tendencies find their crudest expression here that the overall impression frequently is one of parody.
But the joke is on us all. The failure of the imagination which has
reduced "white" South Africa to a caste of exploiters—denounced
and repudiated even by the morally impoverished rulership of the
rest of the world—is closely analogous to the plunge of the human
race toward social and ecological catastrophes of potentially termi-
nal magnitude.

In both cases the hour is late. Like the blinkered South African whites preparing to defend the fortress of their privilege, we are all doomed if we continue to indulge our crasser aspirations and fears at the expense of our fellows, the biosphere, and our souls. Understandably we are reluctant to confront this, just as white South Africans fear facing their own terrible reality.

Aleksandr I. Solzhenitsyn subtitled his great *Gulag Archipelago*, "An Experiment in Literary Investigation." If a comparison may be allowed, this book is of a similar type. For reasons that form an integral part of the story, the record has been corrupted by innumerable apologists, and essential evidence is agonizingly difficult to come by. There is also the problem of compressing a great amount of necessary background detail into a limited space. Even the two volumes of the *Oxford History of South Africa*, the work of a dozen specialists, are no more than an introduction to the complexities of our past. Many crucial aspects have scarcely been studied. Any of the chapters which follow might well be expanded into a book on its own. My primary aim has therefore been to convey a sense of the situation as it impinges on me personally, and the method I have pursued shares more with biography and autobiography than with sociology and the political sciences. Rather than rehearsing facts and figures available elsewhere—though some such are unavoidable —I have tried as far as possible to reveal the human predicament in South Africa through the eyes of some of its protagonists.

Another difficulty is that of definitions. How to explain the lunatic involutions of South African "racial" categorization? Tortuous as they are, these in themselves tell a meaningful story. Thus terms designating blacks, no matter how innocuous to start with, have automatically acquired a pejorative meaning, and have had to be scrapped: examples are "Kaffir" ("infidel" in Arabic), "Native," and "Bantu." The name "Coloured" is obviously arbitrary. In South Africa, as in the United States, many of those officially regarded as white are actually of mixed race. Over the years such "play whites," as they used to be called in the Cape, forgot their origins, assimilated white consciousness, and have ended up second to none in their enthusiasm for white *baasskap* (bosshood). Obviously, too, the negative connotations of "nonwhite" and "non-European" are inherently slighting in the context of apartheid (notwithstanding that the latter was part of the title of a major "radical" group for many years). An ironical interchange between Steve Biko and Judge W. G. Boshoff at the 1976 SASO-BPC trial articulated the Black Consciousness position on the subject, and is worth quoting:

JUDGE: But now why do you refer to you people as Blacks? Why not brown people? I mean, you people are more brown than black.

BIKO: In the same way as I think White people are more pink and yellow and pale than white.

JUDGE: Quite. [Laughter.] But now, why do you not use the word brown, then?

BIKO: No, I think really, historically, we have been defined as Black people, and when we reject the term Non-White and take upon ourselves the right to call ourselves what we think we are, we have got available in front of us a whole number of alternatives—starting from natives to Africans to Kaffirs to Bantu to Non-Whites and so on—and we choose this one precisely because we feel it is most accommodating.

It is immensely important not to fall into the trap of adopting the society's definitions of race. Long ago we used to put terms like "Coloured" in quotes to stress their arbitrary nature, and from time to time I resort to this device to remind the reader that we are dealing with less than scientific concepts. But such designations are accurate when they define not skin color but racial consciousness. Thus, for example, inasmuch as South African whites virtually without exception think of themselves as "white," and allow this delusion to determine their state of mind, they are quite properly so described. The fact remains that in a book like this any attempt to impose a false consistency would be misleading, and I must trust to context to illustrate the nuances of usage over the years.

I start by trying to make sense of the strange case of Breyten Breytenbach, whose path narrowly intersected my own in the years 1959–60, and whose two political trials in 1975 and 1977 were the focuses of a *cause célèbre* that made headlines around the world. Breytenbach's story, I believe, illustrates many of the essential features of the white South African mentality, and makes a fitting introduction to the moral barbarism of apartheid society. In my second chapter I go back to the beginnings of the problem, hundreds of years in the past, in an attempt to discover how this swamp of fanaticism came to exist. Subsequent chapters endeavor to carry the story of black South Africa's long struggle for freedom up to the present time—and to show how that struggle has been sabotaged and betrayed.

Onstage pass figures—Churchill, Gandhi, Smuts, Lutuli, and others—who are known to the wider world. But my attention is mainly to the stories of little-known men and women who have had to confront the human disaster of racism. These are my witnesses —the heroes, the zealots, the victims of the South African emergency. If I have managed to convey some sense of what it is they faced, and how it relates to us, I will not have failed entirely. For it is only by such understanding that we can make a start at solutions.

What, finally, can be hoped for? Speaking to a conservative American business group, I was once asked by a questioner whether I thought a "race war" could be avoided. Seen from the black perspective, that race war, or something very similar, has been waged in South Africa for over three centuries. Certainly it is doubtful now whether large-scale bloodshed can be averted in the years to come. Worse, it is probable that the outcome of the inevitable South African revolution may be a new totalitarianism, infecting the entire subcontinent as the old infects it today. Still, over the past decades black South Africa has thrown up leaders of tremendous moral stature and courage, such as Robert Sobukwe and Steve Biko. Despite their martyrdom, there is reason to think that the spirit they represented remains alive and vigorous.

"He intended a great book—what he has produced is a great symptom," wrote a critic of Karl Popper's *The Open Society and Its Enemies*. If this is true of me, let it be so. A symptom is at any rate an indication of an attempt to resolve a crisis. It is my personal belief that the struggle for human freedom is ultimately identical with the struggle for truth, and that it is in the first place a spiritual battle which we must undertake on our own behalf as much as on behalf of all others. In this sense nothing but our own fears and thoughtlessness prevent us from participating in it.

To all those who have assisted in the making of this book, my thanks.

PETER DREYER
1980

1

BREYTEN AND THE PRICE OF ILLUSIONS

Look he is harmless, be merciful to him.
BREYTEN BREYTENBACH

To Be Hanged with a Clean Rope

SOMETIME IN THE EARLY SIXTIES an unknown young Afrikaner, a poet and painter more or less self-exiled in Paris, wrote a prayer for himself: Keep me from pain, O Lord. Let others bear it. Let it be others who are taken into custody, broken, stoned, hanged, flogged, used, tortured, crucified, interrogated, placed under house arrest,

Banished to dull islands to the end of their days
To languish in damp holes . . .
But not I

Certainly it cannot have seemed very likely at the time that any of these things would ever happen to him, increasingly familiar though they were to great numbers of South Africans. He was twenty-four, and already it was clear that he possessed unusual talents. He had acquired something of the status of a romantic emigré, and was lionized by visiting Afrikaans literati. Older South African writers then living in Paris, men who had established reputations, like Ezekiel Mphahlele and Jan Rabie, privately praised his work and gave him encouragement. Married to the woman he loved, he had a glimpse at least of "preliminary fulfillment." He was one of those who took good fortune as though by right. One of the happy few.

Why, then, this premonition of disaster?

His poems oscillate between rapture and crudity: it is a pattern in the Afrikaner mind. Vulgarity wards off many a demon. Earthiness is an effective shield against melancholy. "I eat and I sleep and my wife has orgasms," he tells us defiantly. But in his paintings and drawings, nightmares make their appearance. There are times when craziness comes on "like an armed man, all of a sudden," an insidious sense that "behind this reality pulses another," bad dreams which cannot be denied. Guilt? Conscience? He is sensitive to much that others do not even grasp. "Keep your head, Breyten Breytenbach," he warns himself.

And the fact is that all his bad dreams came true in the end. The horrors he had toyed with in Paris and banked on in Amsterdam art shows turned out to be real. The *frisson* of surrealistic fantasies was succeeded by terror. And there were horrors which he had failed to imagine. Quite apart from the violence others could do you, he discovered, there was the violence you could do yourself. And of this one could scarcely complain.

On June 20, 1977, Breyten Breytenbach was removed from the cell in the Death Row section of the Pretoria Central Prison in which he had been held in solitary confinement under maximum security conditions for more than eighteen months and transported back to the Palace of Justice, where sentence had been passed on him what seemed an eternity ago. Breytenbach was now far and away one of the most important figures in modern Afrikaans literature, the winner of a whole string of literary prizes. In Europe collectors bought his paintings. His bizarre political trial in 1975 had made his name known worldwide, though the attendant publicity evidently did little or nothing to mitigate the severity of the sentence handed down by Mr. Justice Cillié, the judge-president of the Transvaal, who heard the case.

Already a convicted "terrorist" doing a nine-year stretch in prison, Breytenbach now faced a series of fresh charges, seventeen in all. The main one was under the draconian Terrorism Act of 1967, and serious. "South Africa is asking for the death penalty," wrote Martin Garbus, an American lawyer observing the case. "Conviction is a certainty. Only world opinion may influence the authorities to impose a lesser sentence."

Garbus was wildly wrong, but his mistake was surely understandable. Even practiced Pretoria-watchers were unsure as to just what was going on. One Afrikaans newspaperman observed that the "public" (one must not forget that some 85 percent of the actual South African public are black and not usually reckoned in) scarcely knew whether it was being presented with a Greek tragedy, a James

Bond farce, or an Agatha Christie thriller: "And all the while the somber backdrop of a people in the narrows, of a South Africa under siege, of forces that sought to annihilate the white African." The sublime and the ridiculous hung in balance, and the second Breytenbach trial promised to be even more titillating than the first.

In 1975 Breytenbach had been accused of forming a secret organization known as "Atlas" or "Okhela" at the behest of the banned African National Congress (ANC) and plotting the overthrow of the South African government. His own plea of guilty had formed the basis of his conviction. What could be the state's purpose now in bringing him out of his prison cell and putting him back into the dock on a new set of charges, which as time went by began to look suspiciously prefabricated? "What he stands for constitutes a serious threat to the security of white South Africa's apartheid social system," an Okhela supporter explained melodramatically. "Breyten lives on as a symbol of the true nature of humanity inherent somewhere in every white South African." It is probably truer to say that he was the victim of mindless police spite—the Pavlovian vindictiveness of racist jacks-in-office unable to see beyond their noses. Breytenbach was neither threat nor portent for white South Africa, which his politics at root subserved. Therein lies the terrible irony, and the enduring interest, of his story.

Chief among the witnesses against the hapless poet, and kingpin of the prosecution's case, was a twenty-year-old prison warder named Pieter Groenewald, known to his friends as "Lucky." He would testify that Breytenbach had persuaded him that the whites in South Africa were fighting a losing battle, and that the only way to save his own skin was to join "the right side" in the shape of Okhela.

Groenewald, it was pathetically asserted, had also been tempted by an offer of financial reward, in addition to being encouraged by Breytenbach to look forward to a career of derring-do that appealed to his adventurous nature. One of the letters Breytenbach had smuggled out of prison was said to have supplied the descriptive details—birth dates, height, color of eyes, etc.—needed to obtain forged passports for the poet and his recruit. To heighten the drama, there was the allegation that Breytenbach had employed a code called "the Cuban code" in his illicit correspondence (Cuba having since 1975 become deeply entrenched in white South African demonology). After their projected escape, he and his former guard were to remain in South Africa "to commit sabotage and intimidation before going overseas." Thereafter, Breytenbach was supposed to have given him to understand, Groenewald would proceed to Russia for training in "terrorist warfare."

Sometime after he had been recruited to Okhela, however, Groenewald was sitting idly on his bed in his bachelor quarters when a strange man in a gray suit knocked on the door, asking for Lucky. He spoke Afrikaans with a strong accent—Groenewald could not say what sort of accent it was—and declined to identify himself. After handing over a plain brown envelope, he warned, "You know what happens to people who turn against us," and disappeared as abruptly as he had arrived. Groenewald tore open the envelope and found two green, typed documents inside, one bearing his name, the other Breytenbach's. The documents bore a coat of arms, and the words "Botswana" and "The Embassy." Also included in the package was a map of the escape route he and Breytenbach had discussed. Groenewald confessed to being frightened by all this. "I looked the documents quickly through and then destroyed them," he said. "I thought a lot about the matter and one night decided that I must go and report the whole story to my chiefs."

In cross-examining, the defense had little difficulty in picking holes in this story. "According to his evidence, Groenewald had at that stage posted only one smuggled letter for Breytenbach [to his wife]," Judge Boshoff observed. "It is therefore completely incomprehensible how it could have been possible for a person to have known about the escape route and have known that they needed documents to cross the border." Groenewald's already fragile credibility collapsed almost entirely. It was clear that Judge Boshoff was not amused.

Scared by his mysterious visitor, Groenewald said, he had made a full confession to the commandant of the prison, Brigadier Visser, and was subsequently questioned by the security police. He was given a tape recorder and instructed to continue his relationship with Breytenbach and record their conversations. The notes and letters Breytenbach gave him to smuggle out were handed over to his superiors and photocopied before being sent on. While this was going on, Breytenbach was enjoining Groenewald to be careful, and instructing him in "security tactics."

But the farce had a nightmare underside. Breytenbach did not deny that he had plotted to escape. In mitigation he argued the conditions under which he had been imprisoned. For almost two years he had been held in solitary confinement. Even the prison warders were forbidden to talk to him. When he was taken to the baths or to the exercise yard, where he took exercise alone, the windows of the cells he had to pass were covered with paper to prevent him from seeing the other prisoners, or them from seeing him. He was permitted to write one letter of five hundred words and to receive one of the same length each month. If more than one letter arrived for him, he was told but they were not given to him. Later if there was a month in which he received no mail such additional letters might be handed over. Once a month he was allowed a half-hour visit, in the presence of warders and separated from his visitor by bulletproof glass. He was allowed two library books a week. No music, no magazines or newspapers. Prison food was Spartan, and he was not allowed to buy extras, except for tobacco and toilet requirements.

Pretoria Central is the prison in which South Africa's executions take place, and the maximum-security section in which Breytenbach was held also contained the death cell and the gallows chamber. "The first thing you notice as you come into Central is the singing, the sound of the Condemneds," wrote Hugh Lewin, who also did time there as a political prisoner.

> Up behind the huge sign in the Hall saying Stilte/Silence, the Condemneds sing, chant, sing through the day and, before an execution, through the night. At times, the chant is quiet, a distant murmur of quiet humming, softly. Then it swells: you can hear a more strident, urgent note in the swell, sounding through the prison, singing the hymns that will take them through the double doors into the gallows. Fifty, sixty, sometimes seventy at a time up in the Condemneds, singing their fellows through their last nights.

Executions took place several times a month, sometimes as many as four times, and more than one prisoner was hanged at a time, sometimes as many as six, wrote Breytenbach, who had the impression that as many as two hundred people had gone to their deaths while he was in Central. ("The average execution figure for the past ten years was roughly seventy-four persons a year, so Breyten Breytenbach's impressions as regards the extent of executions are erroneous," comments the Commissioner of Prisons, in a statement which is in itself very revealing.) Prisoners were informed that they were to be hanged about a week before the execution took place, and from that time on they sang almost day and night, "wonderful voices full of grief that are simply hanged by the choir," in Breytenbach's words ("*wonderlike stemme vol hartseer wat sommer so by die koor opgehang word*"). He thought he could tell when a condemned prisoner was told "because the quality of his voice changes at once. You can hear that he sings in an entirely different way. I don't know whether you can call it a sort of ecstasy or a despair or a spiritual transport—but it's entirely another tone."

On the day of the execution you could hear the prisoners being taken to the gallows room. They sang on the way there, and perhaps it was your imagination but you could also hear the trapdoor open. Afterwards you could consult the doctor who was present at the execution about any ailments you might have. "The whole atmosphere is one of a functional place where people are killed," he said. The warders made jokes about it afterwards. "We saw a nice flick [movie] this morning," they would say. Or at lunch they might insinuate that "these people had been hanged that morning and that one was now going to eat certain parts of them." The guards took a sadistic pleasure in supplying Breytenbach with the horrible minutiae of their calling. Even on the gallows, he learned, black South Africans could not expect to receive equal treatment. When a white prisoner was hanged, a new, clean rope was provided. For blacks, however, the same rope was used again and again, though soiled with vomit and saliva from earlier executions. "Luckily," said the warders, "we don't hang many people, just Kaffirs and *meide* [black women]."

Breytenbach, it has been said, was ordered to wear the clothing of executed blacks on occasion. This the warders, who themselves washed up carefully after a hanging, must have thought a particularly exquisite torment. White South Africans are expected to feel tainted by the touch of a black skin, and as a special humiliation white political prisoners are sometimes put together with black ones. Police thinking evidently sees the psychology of whites who oppose the system as an aberration, to be cured by shock treatment. Orthodoxy is inherently incapable of grasping its own illogic.

A Choice of Victims

The police quite naturally tend to select their victims from among the dark-skinned, illiterate and voiceless (though of course the minority of educated blacks attract their attention if they are incautiously *astrant*—"cheeky" to the English speaker—an epithet which embraces most non-Bantustan politics). Conversely, the media both in and outside South Africa prefer the light-skinned, affluent and attractive. Writers, artists, poets, scientists and ballet dancers all make spectacular victims (as the Russian government knows to its cost). From a media point of view, the ideal victim is a celebrity, or at least a potential celebrity. And this is perfectly natural. But before taking up the Breytenbach case and its implications, it may be salutary to look at some others. Breytenbach is, after all, something of an exception, as becomes apparent as soon as we step outside the narrow spectrum of privilege. He has, thus far, stayed alive.

None of which detracts from Breytenbach's real suffering. Sacrifice is not competitive. It merely seems that way to us, the spectators—until we grasp that what we are surveying through the medium of a newspaper or a television set is not a sport but a reality of which we are a part.

One case we might have taken up is that of Joseph Mdluli, who within hours of his arrest by the Durban security police in March 1976 was dead in peculiar circumstances—as a result of falling over a chair, said the police witnesses during the subsequent trial of four policemen for culpable homicide. At a press conference in February 1977, Minister of Police Kruger stated that Mdluli had attempted suicide, and that the police had grappled with him. Kruger went on to suggest plaintively that as a consequence of the prosecution, other officers "might be inhibited from trying to stop security detainees from committing suicide." Photographs of Mdluli's body show obvious signs of battery.

Then there is the case of Mapetla Mohapi, said to have hanged himself with his trousers in his cell at the Kei Road police station, Kingwilliamstown, on August 5, 1976. At the inquest the magistrate found that death was due to "anoxia and suffocation as a result of hanging and was not brought about by any act of commission or omission by any living person."

Luke Mazwembe, aged thirty-two, is alleged to have hanged himself with strips of blanket on the day of his detention in Cape Town on September 2, 1976. Wounds on his body which the police were unable to explain included swelling and bruising of the right cheek bone, swelling of the scrotum, abrasions to the ankle and shoulder blades.

Dumisani Mbatha was only twenty-two when he was arrested in September 1976 and taken to Modder B prison. Ten days later "he was first approached for questioning. As his name and personal particulars were being taken down, he complained of not feeling well. He was removed to hospital where he died shortly afterwards." The postmortem report gives the cause of death as "extremely [sic] sympathetic system activity with auricular fibrillation of heart" (but extremely unsympathetic System activity may be closer to the mark).

Wellington Tshazibane, aged thirty, was found dead in his cell on December 11, 1976. "With him was found a statement in which he cleared the police of all blame and admitted suicide." Unfortunately we do not have a copy of this generous admission.

George Botha, a "Coloured" schoolteacher, aged thirty, died five days after his detention in December 1976, as a consequence of falling down a stairwell in the commercial building in which Port Elizabeth security police headquarters were located. According to the police, he jumped. They did not attempt to account for the numerous abrasions and injuries which had apparently been sustained some time before his death. The police witnesses, said the examining magistrate, had made a good impression, and the court accepted their testimony in full.

Dr. Nanaoth Ntshuntsha, a Soweto naturopathic physician, was arrested on September 14, 1976, and died in prison about a month later. The postmortem examination was inconclusive because a police constable attached to the Springs mortuary had evidently tampered with the body. There were, however, some peculiar marks in the dead man's ears which might have been caused by electrical contact, by burns, or by what the state pathologist called "impression contact," as well as other injuries. A verdict of death by hanging, probably suicide, was returned by the magistrate, who added that no living person could be held responsible.

Mathews Mabelane, aged twenty-three, fell to his death from the tenth floor of John Vorster Square on February 25, 1977, while being interrogated. The magistrate found that he had fallen accidentally.

Elmon Malele, aged fifty-one, died on January 20, 1977. At the inquest the police stated that he had fainted while being interrogated and hit his head against a desk. The magistrate declared that death was not due to any act or omission of any person, and that Mr. Malele had died of hypertension and spontaneous intracerebral hemorrhage.

Aaron Khoza, aged thirty-five, died in his cell on the night of March 26, 1977, after several months' imprisonment. According to police evidence, he was found hanging "with a jacket fastened round his neck and to a window bar with two shoelaces." The magistrate found that Mr. Khoza had committed suicide, and that his death was not due to any act or omission by anyone.

Phakamile Mabija, aged twenty-seven, was a Diocesan Youth Worker for the Anglican church at the time of his detention, with plans to get married. During his detention the police brought him home to fetch a document, his mother testified, and told him to say goodbye to his family because he would never see them again. On July 7, 1977, a few days later, he fell to his death from the sixth floor of the Kimberley police station. The magistrate found that there was no carelessness or guilt on the part of the police, and that it had been a deliberate and planned attempt to commit suicide by jumping through a louvered window.

Dr. Hoosen Hafferjee, a twenty-six-year-old dentist, was found hanged in his cell at the Brighton Beach police station, Durban, on August 3, 1977. His trousers were so tightly wound around his neck that they had to be cut away with a razor blade. There were signs of about twenty-five recent injuries, some of them far from superficial, chiefly on the ankles, knees, abdomen, back, elbows and arms.

Stephen Bantu Biko, aged thirty-one, was detained at Grahamstown on August 18, 1977. Biko, a founder of the South African Students' Organization (SASO) and of the Black Consciousness movement, was already internationally known. He had influential connections, among them a prominent white newspaper editor, Donald Woods. This did not prevent the police from murdering him. He died less than a month after his arrest of brain injuries caused by blows to the head. The examining magistrate, a Mr. Prins, found that no one was criminally responsible. Woods subsequently fled the country.

And of course there have been many others. Breyten Breytenbach compiled a similar list of names in his 1972 volume *Skryt*. All these are documented cases. We even have color photographs of some of the victims, pre- and postmortem. In life Hoosen Hafferjee looked confident, a hint sardonic, with dark glasses and fashionably thick moustache: very much the young professional man. Mapetla Mohapi, on the other hand, gazes wistfully from his snapshot, while Joseph Mdluli's eyes glint with angry fire in an otherwise rather stolid, heavy face.

All these were no doubt politicals, more or less. In some sense, they chose to risk their lives. But there are also those who do not choose to, who simply do their best to live. One was Shadrock Sello Swarathle. I collected this poem about him from a Johannesburg newspaper in 1969:

> *He*
> *died in a police van on April 2.*
> *They were taking him to Cinderella*
> *B prison, Boksburg.*
> *Constables M. Morgorise,*
> *U. Mtsime*
> *caused the van to be*
> *grossly overloaded*
> *and failed to open the doors*
> *when conditions inside became*
> *intolerable.*

How, we may ask, could a police van become so overcrowded as literally to suffocate those inside? In all probability Swarathle was arrested under one of the numerous laws and regulations relating to the influx control, or pass, system. During the year ending June 30, 1969, the average *daily* number of prosecutions under these laws and regulations was 1,732. This adds up to several hundred thousand prisoners a year, even excluding those arrested but not prosecuted. Neither was that an exceptional year. In his report for the year ended June 30, 1976, for example, the commissioner of prisons notes that 273,393 sentenced prisoners and 243,965 prisoners awaiting trial were admitted to prison, i.e., more than half a million people. Granted that these figures overlap to a great extent, they still fill a lot of police vans.

Shadrock Swarathle was nonetheless unusual. His case was reported in the papers. There are many cases which are not reported, many victims whose names are completely unknown. The minister has been known to announce the death of a detainee in almost meaningless terms: "An unknown man died on an unknown day of an unknown cause." But he—the unknown—knew who he was, knew his own name, knew the day perhaps, knew the cause.

What did Phakamile Mabija think when the police ordered him to say goodbye to his family for the last time one winter's day in Kimberley a few years ago? Did he think, as most of us might, No, they've got to be joking? Surely they can't be serious. But they were serious. They took him up to the sixth floor of the police building and threw him out of the window. David Rousset, who lived through Buchenwald, has observed that normal men do not know that everything is possible.

The Thin Man in the Green Sweater

"Ladies and gentlemen, permit me to introduce you to Breyten Breytenbach, the thin man in the green sweater," begins his earliest collection, *Die ysterkoei moet sweet* (*The Iron Cow Must Sweat*), published in 1964. Dedicated to "B. Breytenbach," this introductory poem surely, as André Brink has remarked, invites comparison with Bertolt Brecht's well known "On Poor B.B." As did the first, the second "B.B." makes elaborate protestations of innocence. There is a tradition for this—after all, Goethe himself asserted that poets sin but lightly (*"Dichter sündgen nicht schwer"*). Breytenbach returns to the theme more than once. "He was poet/painter, a needless nationalistic dreamer, but harmless," he tells us in a later, semiautobiographical book. In fact, of course, he knows very well that there is nothing harmless about those "needless nationalistic" dreams. They are the poisonous fantasies that have rotted the soul of Afrikanerdom. Awakening from them, he feels on his shoulders an enormous burden; call it apartheid:

> If one were to start unraveling all that thread you'll soon find yourself with no clothes at all; you'd have to envisage the destruction of the tribe of the Afrikaner as an Afrikaner, for discrimination is embedded in the tribe, is the *sine qua non* of its existence.

Who is Breyten Breytenbach, and how did he get from the Left Bank of the Seine to Pretoria Central?

Breytenbach was born on September 16, 1939, at Bonnievale, a small town in the Cape Province near the southern tip of Africa. His father was a market gardener there, and presently the family moved to a farm in the Riversdale district, not very far away, called Kafferskuilsrivier (Bullrush River): the name is a distant echo of the frontier fighting of the early eighteenth century (*kafferskuil* literally means Kaffir shelter). A more archetypal old-style Boer family would be hard to imagine. Father is *Oubaas* (Old Master), mother is *Ounooi* (Old Missus); his brothers have nicknames like "Blikkies" and "Stinkie." Everyone pitched in with the farm work: they raised vegetables, grain, alfalfa and sheep, and were by no means affluent. When things went badly at Kafferskuilsrivier they were forced to move yet again, this time to Wellington, where Oubaas ran a general store. Breyten did well at the Hugenoot High School, particularly in Afrikaans. He had already begun to write poetry. But he was sufficiently popular to become head boy—not a role accessible to the shy and introverted at an Afrikaans high school (if at any).

Breyten's real deviation from the norm that might have been expected of him began when, after matriculating in 1957, he chose to attend the Michaelis School of Art at the "English" University of Cape Town, rather than the Afrikaans University of Stellenbosch. Ostensibly he decided on Cape Town because he wanted to obtain a fine arts degree and a B.A. in Afrikaans simultaneously, and the combination was not available at Stellenbosch.

Now three centuries old, and lying in the wine country of the Eerste River valley about thirty miles from Cape Town, the town of Stellenbosch is picturesque and charming. The university, which evolved from a Dutch Reformed Church theological seminary founded there in the middle of the nineteenth century, is segregated, and a major center of Afrikaans *kultuur*. The two main architects of the modern apartheid state, Hendrik Frensch Verwoerd and Balthazar John Vorster, were both products of Stellenbosch. (Vorster was one of Verwoerd's students when the latter was a professor there.) The stifling certainties of the place allowed scant deviation from conformity, and it is unlikely that it would have appealed to Breyten's already rebellious sensibility.* Cape Town was by contrast a "liberal" university, doing its best to keep up at least a facade of

---

* However, it is a fact that there were Stellenbosch students prepared to give a group consisting of Victor Benjamin, Kenneth Hendrickse, Joseph Nkatlo, Hazel Ruiters, and myself a serious and sympathetic hearing when we spoke against apartheid on their campus a year or two later.

Anglo-Saxon academic freedom, and black and white students could meet there on terms of equability, if not of equality.

Breyten enrolled at the Michaelis in 1958. Cape Town, the big city, was something of a shock at first to a boy from the *Boland* (the "up-country" of sleepy Western Province rural communities that had for hundreds of years been Afrikaner heartland). But he always had a firm sense of his own significance. Some of his poems had appeared in magazines: a small taste of celebrity, since among Afrikaners, as among Russians, poets are taken very seriously. He flourished in his new surroundings. "For the first time I came into contact with and met on a base of equality, fellow countrymen of a different skin color. I also met and got to know some of the artists and writers of Cape Town, people who were advanced and had experience which I did not possess," he told the court at the conclusion of his 1975 trial. "Some of the people in the milieu inevitably exercised a strong influence on my own hesitant thinking and creative work. Like a head of cabbage in shallow earth I, too, was probably more air than leaf."

With Marius Schoon, a fellow student, he shared a flat above a seedy bar in Waterkant Street. With the walls painted black for dramatic effect and a resident ghost, it provided an appropriately exotic residence, if wanting in some of the creature comforts. Breyten was now a novice in a heady milieu that included established writers like Jan Rabie, Jack Cope, and Uys Krige. There were the foreign-born, too, like Rabie's Scottish wife, the painter Marjorie Wallace, and the Hollander Cees de Jong. One whom he may have known was the luminous young poet Ingrid Jonker, whose career, which might otherwise have rivaled his own, was brought to an end early in the morning of July 19, 1965, when she drowned herself in the icy waters of Three Anchor Bay. Ingrid renounced

the betrayers of life with the face of death and of God

and wrote despairingly that

> *My people have rotted away from me*
> *what will become of the rotten nation*
> *a hand cannot pray alone*

She made her rebellion her own way. After Sharpeville, in a poem titled "The child who was shot dead by soldiers at Nyanga" in its English version, she made an explicit political declaration, which was translated into Zulu and published in the Johannesburg magazine *Drum* for black readers:

> *this child who just wanted to play in the sun at Nyanga*
> *is everywhere*

the child grown to a man treks through all Africa
the child grown into a giant journeys through the whole
  world

Without a pass

From Waterkant Street, Breyten moved to Grassy Corners, an old house in the leafy Cape Town suburb of Newlands, which he shared with Michael Tapscott, Jobst Grapow, and Heleen Raath. "Corners," reputedly once the slave quarters of an estate from which it had long been detached, with its "crooked rooms . . . the hollows of a heart," resounding with the music of Carl Orff or Sidney Bechet, left its mark on all who lived there. Long after, in a European winter, Breyten would nostalgically remember "the lazy white house like a nut or a hollow tooth," and its colonnaded veranda and secluded, overgrown garden. But, he insisted, "I have rooted out the gods of my youth."

"It was in the course of 1959 that I took the decision to leave for abroad," Breytenbach told the court. "The point of attraction, the honey pot, was Paris." He had already dropped out of school. Now, without so much as saying goodbye to his family, or removing his paintings from the walls of his room,* he took a fourth-class passage on the *Mozambique,* a Portuguese ship bound for Lisbon. With twenty pounds in his pocket he set out for Paris.

Life in the French capital with its crowds of aspiring artists was not easy for the young expatriate Afrikaner. "My efforts at earning money, as events in later life were to bear out, cannot be described as having been particularly successful and it goes without saying that I immediately started yearning for the fleshpots of South Africa. My initial intention was to attempt staying abroad for at least one year. I was then just twenty years old and the vanity of youth does not easily admit to errors. I had to try and prove my manhood."

Shortly after he had arrived in Paris, in March 1960, came the news of the Sharpeville massacre and the declaration of a state of emergency in South Africa, and he spent his last few pounds getting to London, "because I was convinced that these events would lead to the expected explosion at home, and I had to be in England where I could at least follow the news in English." But when the news presently ran out in a welter of arrests and bannings, he returned to Paris. Breyten never felt very much at home in England, because, he said, "social usage" there "was much like that of white South Afri-

---

* As its next occupant, I temporarily inherited them.

cans, and I have discovered that I react just like a Frenchman to England." One can say with some assurance that he was too much an Afrikaner—which is to say too much of an absolutist—to be comfortable with the empiricism of Anglo-Saxon intellectual life and the chaotic laissez-faire of London.

Within the year he had staked out for himself abroad he met "a lovely woman named Ngo Thi Hoàng Liên Yolande Bubi." Born in France, she was the daughter of a Saigon lawyer who had served with the Vietnamese diplomatic mission in Paris. She had never been in Vietnam herself. Over the opposition of Yolande's widowed mother, Ngo Sach Vinh, they were married in 1962. "And the whole family lived happily, or sometimes unhappily then, in Paris." Yolande's steady job with an American legal firm provided the young couple with a necessary sheet anchor. In these early years Breyten earned little. It is impossible to say how his marriage may have influenced his politics. "Luckily," he said later, his wife's people were pro-Vietcong. "They are all against the big, ugly enemy . . ."

He had achieved his romantic dreams. Now he signed his paintings "Juan Breyten, a sophisticated name, more mysterious and with the taste of Spanish blood because the prosaic is the enemy." He "fabricates poems for his own pleasure, and in the evening plays the pinball machine at the *Malebranche,*" a cafe in the vicinity of the Palais du Luxembourg. Nearby they manage to buy a small but comfortable flat. With his "Golden Lotus" of a wife and ramshackle scarlet Citroën, he cut quite a figure.

In 1963 Breytenbach's paintings received favorable notice at a group exhibition, and the following year the visiting Afrikaans writer Chris Barnard was sufficiently impressed by his poetry to arrange for a selection to be sent to Afrikaanse Pers, a South African publisher. The following year saw the publication of both *Ysterkoei* and a prose collection under the title of *Katastrofes (Catastrophes).* The two books jointly won him the Afrikaanse Pers-Boekhandel prize, the first of five major Afrikaans literary awards he was to receive in the years to come.

It seems, extraordinarily enough, that he had thus far failed to grasp the implications of his marriage to Yolande: to realize, that is, that because of South Africa's legislation banning "mixed" marriages (and for that matter sexual relations of any kind across the color line), he would not be able to take her home.

In 1965 when his publishers invited him to South Africa to accept the A.P.B. award, his application for a visa for her was turned down. Can one really believe that this came as a surprise to him? Yes—and it is an important piece of evidence. "Perhaps one should ascribe this to naiveté or innocence," he said afterward. "Even if I did realize it, however, it would have made no difference to my love for her. . . .

"That was the beginning of my ambivalent relationship with my country. My heart had remained anchored in South Africa, and it still is, but that root which feeds my whole life—including my existence as a writer—was at times also the vehicle of bitterness and even of poison."

In a letter to the Cape Town newspaper *Die Burger* protesting the decision, he declared:

> If I could give up my Afrikanerhood today, I would. I am ashamed of my people. I am shamed by the humiliation of my wife, my family and friends and her family. . . . I hate and abhor apartheid with all its implications, and if it is representative of Afrikanerdom, if the two cannot be separated, then I see no future for the Afrikaner in our beautiful country. I hope my case makes more Afrikaners conscious of what current ideology, and specifically the Immorality Act, means in terms of the most elementary human rights: everyday life. And I don't even want to think of how the existing laws of the land rule the daily life of the non-whites in general.

In 1967, however, Breyten and Yolande traveled to Swaziland via Mozambique, and family and friends came to visit them there and make her acquaintance. When their ship rounded the Cape on the way home they were, as it chanced, able to spend a few days there too.

Thereafter Breyten was increasingly outspoken against apartheid, and politically involved with various South African exiles. Perhaps it was the dramatic events of May 1968 in Paris when, for a few short days and nights, it seemed possible that the French student-worker alliance would topple De Gaulle's regime and remake the fabric of society, that served as final catalyst. Most poets detest the status quo. It is hard to imagine that Breyten was not in the streets with the students, and the sight of the self-indulgent Fifth Republic visibly wobbling may have made him think again of another overfed state that might be made to tremble and cough up its spoils. (One can only assume in the light of later developments that he failed to notice that the African National Congress was one of a handful of foreign organizations gratuitously to endorse the reactionary stance of the French Communist party.)

"Another manifestation which was sharpened by the noise surrounding my controversial marriage, my declarations and my situation as an 'uprooted Boer' was that they attracted other expatriates and exiles towards me," Breytenbach said at his 1975 trial. "Gradually I became involved and committed to their cause and activities. Others came to look me up, perhaps not with unselfish intentions but because I could be used or misused for their political aims. However, I do not want to pretend that I was merely a victim of circumstances, a tool in the hands of others. Over the years my attitude towards my country became less clear, more complex. I became, as you know, more deeply involved with the activities which have been described to you here." In a poem (in *Kouevuur*) bylined "Paris—Easter 1968," he wrote,

> *you ask me how it is to live in exile, friend—*
> *what shall I say?*
> *that I am too young for bitter opposition*
> *and too old for wisdom or resignation*
> *to my lot?*
> *that I am but one of many,*
> *the misfits,*
> *the host of fugitives, runaways,*
> *citizens of the entrails of darkness,*
> *one of the "French with a speech impediment"*
> *or even that I feel at home here?*

He continued to write prolifically. In 1967 he had published *Die huis van die dowe* (*The House of the Deaf Man*), a collection of poems that drew its title from the famous *Quinta del Sordo* on the walls of which the aging Goya had painted his "black" pictures. The following year it went into a second edition, a remarkable achievement for any contemporary poet, and certainly for one writing in a language spoken by only a few million people. *Ysterkoei* had also been reprinted. But Breyten's publishers, Human and Rousseau, were outraged by their author's statements to the foreign press, and in November 1968 the principals in the firm, Koos Human, Leon Rousseau and Dirk Opperman, published an open letter to him in *Die Burger:*

> It was not (or not in the first place) Yolande's race which hindered you from coming to South Africa, but the fact that you have long exerted yourself in various ways for a bloody assault on your own fatherland. . . . In spite of your drastic politics you have always had a cordial reception from the Afrikaans literary community. Doesn't that mean anything to you? How many of your little friends have that much integrity?
> . . . you talk of your "freedom fighters." We would like you to know that we support South Africa's own freedom fighters and contribute to the fund against terrorists. Perhaps we should go further and contribute a rand to the anti-terrorist fund for every rand we pay you in royalties—just to keep the balance.

Breytenbach broke off his connection with Human and Rousseau, and his third collection of poems, *Kouevuur* (*Cold Fire*), which appeared in 1969, was published by Buren in Cape Town. *Oorblyfsels* [*Remnants*] appeared in 1970, as did *Lotus*, published under the pseudonym "Jan Blom." In 1971 Buren also published a prose work, *Om te vlieg* [*To Fly*], described as "an essay in five parts and an ode." This had been written some five years earlier, but Breyten had had difficulty finding a South African publisher prepared to take the risk of its being banned.

Given the direction his writing was taking, it was almost inevitable that this would happen to one of his books sooner or later. The honor fell to *Skryt: Om 'n sinkende skip blou te verf*, a collection published in Holland, which incorporated some of Breytenbach's grotesque, surrealistic drawings with the poems. It was the first piece of Afrikaans literature ever to come under South African government proscription. This was scarcely surprising since it contained the famous poem "Letter from Abroad to Butcher," with the dedication "for Balthazar,"—referring to Prime Minister Balthazar John Vorster. In part it read as the agonized testimony of a political prisoner, in part as a bitter apostrophe to the man ultimately responsible:

> *I stand on bricks before my fellow man*
> *I am the statue of emancipation*
> *with electrodes on my balls*
> *trying to scream light in the gloom*
> *I write slogans in crimson urine*
> *on my skin and on the floor*
> *I keep watch*
> *strangle on the ropes of my intestines*
> *slip on soap and break my bones*
> *murder myself with the evening paper*
> *tumble from the tenth floor of heaven*
> *to deliverance on a street among people*
>
> and you, butcher
> *you who are entrusted with the security of the state*
> *what do you think of when the night reveals her*
> *framework*
> *and the first babbling shriek is squeezed out*
> *of the prisoner*
> *as in a birth*
> *with the fluids of parturition*
> *are you humble before this bloodied thing*
> *with all its manlike tremors*
> *with the shattered breath of dying*
> *in your hands*
> *does your heart also stiffen in your throat*

when you touch the extinguished limbs
with the same hands that will fondle your wife's
mysteries?

The title of the banned collection, *Skryt*, is a word of the poet's own forming, incorporating into itself fragments of the Afrikaans words for scream (*skreeu*), cry (*kryt*), shit (*skyt*), and write (*skryf*) among others. The subtitle, *To Paint a Sinking Ship Blue*, expresses his growing discontent with the role of *letterkundige* (litterateur) to a people doomed by hubris. In the last poem of the collection, as though purged now of anger, and resigned to the inevitable, he wrote:

in front of your dwelling is a high grey mountain
so high and so grey that the sun
never touches it
and behind the mountain lies Africa

you are going to dig a tunnel through your life
so as to be able to creep back
to the sun

Breyten was readying himself to dig a tunnel through his life but it would lead not to the sunny days of his *Boland* boyhood. The purgatory of Pretoria Central, up there next to the condemneds, lay beyond. With *Skryt* he made a definitive break with Afrikanerdom and white South Africa. The sentiment was mutual. A public opinion poll would show that fully 36 percent of his Afrikaans readers thought it would be better if he wrote no more. And his publisher and former friend Daantjie Saayman declared that if Breyten "comes here with the commies, I'll shoot him."

Toward the end of 1972 Johnston Mfanakuti Makhatini, ANC leader in North Africa and Europe, proposed the formation of the organization which was initially to be christened Atlas to Breytenbach. "For security reasons," Makhatini told him not to mention it to any other ANC member. He put Breyten in touch with a French Communist organization called Solidarité, supposedly dating from the French Resistance during World War II, and active also during the Algerian War. He knew the members of Solidarité, who supplied instruction in various underground skills, only by their code names. The indications are, however, that the organization had been penetrated by agents of the French intelligence service, SDECE, which was in close contact with BOSS.

That year too, shortly after returning from a trip to Tanzania, Breyten and Yolande received news that her renewed application for a visa had been allowed on condition that the trip was to be strictly private and nonpolitical. Strings had evidently been pulled (after all, his brother Jan was a senior officer in the South African Army, and another brother, Cloete, held a post in the SABC propaganda machine). Breyten wrote to his parents to assure them that it would be purely a family visit. It was a promise he was not to keep.

In February 1973 Breyten was asked to take part in a University of Cape Town summer school program dealing with the *Sestigers,* the new group of Afrikaans writers who had come to the fore in the 1960s. He seized the opportunity of presenting the outside view to the overflow audience that came to hear him in an impassioned speech that was self-confessedly—as he said, inevitably—political. "I am convinced that the salvation of this land, if so evangelistic a word is permissible, lies almost entirely in the hands of my black and brown compatriots," he said. "And just as I honor the black man who tries to improve his people's lot, so, I believe, will the black man only respect me to the degree that I am willing to work for the transformation of my own community—and not if I try to tell him what he ought to do." He made no effort to spare Afrikaners' sensibilities or illusions:

> We are a bastard people with a bastard language. Our nature is bastardy. It is good and beautiful that it should be so. . . . Only we have fallen into the trap of the bastard who comes to power. In that part of our blood which comes from Europe was the curse of superiority[!]. We wanted to justify our power. And in order to do that we had to consolidate our supposed tribal identity. . . . We had to entrench our otherness and at the same time hold on to what we had conquered. We made our otherness the norm, the standard—and the ideal. And because the perpetuation of our otherness was *at the expense* of our fellow South Africans—and our South African-ness—we felt menaced. We built walls. . . . And like all bastards—uncertain of their identity—we began to cling to the idea of *purity*. That is apartheid. *Apartheid is the law of the bastard* [said in English].

And he prophesied dire things in store: a day when the present generation would be hated by their descendants for throwing away their birthright.

"One could almost feel the iron cow begin to sweat," wrote Schalk Pienaar, a hostile commentator, in *Die Burger.* But Pienaar conceded that Breytenbach had carried his audience, chiefly Afrikaners, with him much of the way. "The man's mastery with words is something exceptional. In addition, his emotional attack found strong echoes. Our politicians ignore at their own risk the violence with which such an audience reacts to the premise that white superiority is a thing of the past. It was 'our people' who reacted thus."

The students hoisted Breyten on their shoulders, and he was later made an honorary vice-president of NUSAS, the National Union of South African Students, an organization which Prime Minister Vorster had denounced as "a cancer in the life of the nation" ten years previously, but which had by this time been substantially outflanked by the South African Students' Organization with its call for a new Black Consciousness.

Significantly, Breytenbach was visited in Cape Town by none other than Chief Gatsha Buthelezi, subsequently leader of the Zulu Inkatha movement and Bantustan politician who, it would later appear, had his own connections with the Tambo-Makhatini wing of the ANC. Covering all bases, Breytenbach also stopped in Kimberley to pay an illicit visit to the banned Pan Africanist Congress leader, Robert Sobukwe.* The expatriate poet had definitely begun to take on the status of a celebrity, and perhaps of a political force in the land. Clandestinely he had begun to sound out possible supporters of his new revolutionary organization, and the security police were giving him a good deal of attention.

Two senior police officers approached his brother Cloete and asked him to set up a meeting with Breyten. It took place in some secrecy in a private suite in Cape Town's ultra-exclusive Mount Nelson Hotel. Breyten was plied with dinner, the finest Cape wines, and a mixture of threats and blandishments. It seems probable that General H. J. van den Bergh, head of BOSS and thus South Africa's top security man, was present. Tall and physically striking, van den Bergh had a suave manner and an evil reputation. During World War II he had, like Prime Minister Vorster, been interned for pro-Nazi activities by the Smuts government.

The idea, evidently, was to win Breytenbach back to the apartheid cause, in part by persuading him of the benevolent intentions of the state and appealing to his tribal instincts as an Afrikaner, and in part by regaling him with details of his conspiratorial activities both in South Africa and overseas in demonstration of the lengthy reach of BOSS. "The disgust and contempt with which he reacted to their overtures infuriated the security police," says a source close to Okhela—but this is not borne out by Cloete Breytenbach's account.

When Breyten and Yolande were about to leave the country, General van den Bergh made a "coincidental" appearance at the

---

* Five years afterward, Buthelezi was stoned and spat upon by young Africans at Sobukwe's funeral at Graaff-Reinet, who shouted at him "You are Vorster's man!" and "Government stooge, get away from here!" Around the same time, Makhatini, now ANC representative at the United Nations, astonished African and world diplomats by refusing to participate in a UN meeting honoring the late PAC leader.

airport, seizing the opportunity to deliver a "final appeal." It was rejected. In any case, said the security chief, he personally wished the poet well. He extended his hand, and Breyten was incautious enough to shake it. At that moment a photographer stepped forward to take their picture: later it could be used to persuade others—and in particular, of course, political prisoners whose morale the police were trying to break—that Breytenbach was in fact an informer. Such, such are the ploys.

In addition to Breytenbach, the organization formed at Makhatini's suggestion consisted of four other expatriate South Africans: Barend Schuitema, then secretary of the Dutch Anti-Apartheid Movement; Don Morton, an unfrocked priest from Pretoria; Donald Moerdijk; and Jobst Grapow. Morton and Schuitema were later identified as the authors of the Okhela manifesto, and Schuitema functioned as a channel for funds from outside the organization.* Moerdijk dropped out in 1975 in disgust at poor security precautions.

Jobst Grapow had lived in Italy since leaving South Africa, working in the film industry there, part of the diaspora that had carried all the various members of the erstwhile household at Grassy Corners to different parts of the world. When Breytenbach visited South Africa in 1973, Jobst accompanied him. While in Cape Town he was instrumental in recruiting his sister Dürten to Atlas/Okhela.

Dürten was married, perhaps none too happily, to a Pretoria nuclear scientist, Dr. Herman Rohm. She hated the injustices of apartheid, hated South Africa, she said in court. Naturally, she had not concealed her views from her elder brother when she saw him in Cape Town. "If you want to do something about it, join the group Breyten belongs to," he advised her.

In January 1973, it was arranged for her to meet Breytenbach in a Cape Town department store. A further meeting took place the following week in the Gardens, the old park in the center of the city. Breytenbach, she later recalled, told her that there were close blood ties between the whites and "Coloureds," that there was not much difference between them. Echoing his UCT speech, he said that most whites in South Africa were bastards. He allegedly said that "the Coloured people regarded him as a leader and expected him to help and secretly asked him for arms." He also asked her to help obtain details of how airports and harbors operated, because

---

* On one occasion he is said to have given Gerry Maré R3,000 in American dollar bills for purposes unspecified.

weapons would have to be brought into the country. Dürten, a gentle soul, was troubled by such talk. She noticed that Jobst changed the subject when she spoke of her fear of violence. Visualizing the importation of large consignments of arms, which she might be asked to conceal, she wondered how she was going to hide them.

According to her later evidence, Jobst instructed her in the skills taught by Solidarité: "how to split hard covers of books, use false linings in briefcases and shoe heels and shaving cream tubes to conceal messages." The organization consisted of South African exiles, she was told, and training in underground know-how and smuggling techniques was provided by ex-members of the French Resistance. "Blacks were trained in two camps in Russia, one on the Caspian sea and one near Moscow." Jobst asked her to type a letter dealing with an organization known as the Revolutionary Action Group (RAG). She was given to understand that RAG cells would be isolated, but that their leaders would maintain contact with each other. A code name, "Margo," was assigned to her (later changed to "Margaret" because someone else was evidently using "Margo"). Other members of the organization had code names too, while the South African Police were known as "Priscilla and the kids" (which would raise one of the rare laughs at Breytenbach's trial two years later).

Dürten tried ineffectually to resist being drawn into the conspiracy. On her return home from Cape Town to Pretoria she told her husband that she was afraid, and wanted to leave the country because she had been asked to join a terrorist organization. But since, in order to protect her brother, she refused to name the "terrorists" who had approached her, Rohm refused to take the story seriously—which he later had cause to regret.

In 1974, Jobst telephoned her to say that "Jack" was coming to South Africa. "Jack" (he was in fact Donald Moerdijk) passed through Jan Smuts, the international airport serving the Witwatersrand, on his way to Rhodesia. One of the projects Okhela had undertaken was exposure of sanctions-busting by the big oil companies, which continued to fuel Rhodesia despite the United Nations embargo. Moerdijk telephoned Dürten from time to time to say that he was well. As arranged, she passed these messages on. Then, in August 1975, she received a phone call from "Dick" to say that he had arrived. At first she thought she was dealing with "Jack" again, and arranged to meet him in the tearoom at Pretoria railway station. She did not immediately recognize Breytenbach, who was wearing glasses, and had shaved his beard, leaving a droopy moustache.

He was traveling on a forged passport issued in the name of "Christian Marc Galaska," bank clerk by profession. Everyone he met, he told Dürten, thought that he was simply "some Frenchman who couldn't speak Afrikaans." If he were caught, he declared, he would say he was there to arrange publication of his latest book, and that he had obtained the phony passport in the Paris underworld. He told her that they had broken into the South African embassy in Bonn and stolen documents dealing with South Africa's nuclear research program, and asked her if she could get hold of information about it through her husband.

At this point, more or less, Dürten decided that she wanted out. She was afraid for her husband's career, and for her child. And in the end, she was a white South African. "I feel I've done a very, very terrible thing," she said at the conclusion of her testimony at Breytenbach's trial in 1975. "At one stage I thought the only way for me to receive punishment was to be shot. I have many friends and I wouldn't like it but I still think I should have been shot." Her brother phoned to say how sorry he was to hear of her decision. "You are such a nice voice on the phone and you help us so much," he said.

Almost by accident, the conspirators had become involved in an area of extreme sensitivity: the alleged secret nuclear partnership between South Africa and West Germany, which is described in some detail by Barbara Rogers, late of the British Foreign Office, and Zdenek Červenka, of the Scandinavian Institute of African Affairs, in their book *The Nuclear Axis*.

German rearmament commenced shortly after the establishment of the Federal Republic, with Konrad Adenauer as first chancellor, in 1949. In exchange for French consent to West German membership in NATO, and other concessions, Adenauer pledged that "The Federal Republic of Germany undertakes not to manufacture in its territory . . . atomic, biological and chemical weapons." This did not, however, exclude the manufacture of such weapons elsewhere than on German soil (though the idea was inevitably ridiculed), and there was nothing at all to inhibit the Germans from devoting their unrivaled scientific and technological talents to the "peaceful" uses of atomic energy.

Supported by government funding, West German nuclear technology made rapid progress. By 1977 nuclear power was a key industry, employing some 100,000 skilled workers in the Federal Republic. The Frankfurt-based Kraftwerk Union, with a capacity to deliver six complete nuclear power plants a year, had orders worth DM28 billion on its books—more than any other West German company.

Among the innovative German techniques (though perhaps not entirely independent of prior American patents) was Professor

Erwin Becker's uranium-enrichment process known as the *Trenndüsenssystem*—the jet-nozzle system. "This process was given to South Africa," say Rogers and Červenka, "and it was the jet-nozzle system which became the key to South Africa's own enrichment process." Testing and development of the German system were convenient in South Africa, among other reasons because of the availability of cheap electricity, huge amounts of which are used in the enrichment process. The novelty of the South African version of this centrifugal separation system is said to be partly "a new cascade technique called the 'helikon,' in which a single axial-flow compressor can simultaneously transmit several gas streams of different enrichment without too much mixing," credited to Dr. W. L. Grant, South Africa's chief nuclear scientist.

A major supplier of uranium to Britain and the United States in the years following World War II, South Africa is not a newcomer to atomics. The South African Atomic Energy Act, passed in 1948, gave the state a monopoly on prospecting, mining, producing and disposing of uranium and thorium in South Africa, as well as the sole right to concentrate, refine or process these substances, or to produce nuclear energy. This legislation was later extended to include the mandated territory of Namibia (South West Africa), a fact of no small significance in the light of subsequent developments.

According to Rogers and Červenka, it was at the First International Conference on the Peaceful Uses of Atomic Energy, held in Geneva in 1955, that the German and South African delegations laid the basis for the subsequent collaboration between the two countries. The Germans were looking for "new partners in the promising field of atomic energy, partners who would be interested in the export of German technology and who might have something to offer in return." South Africa had both the uranium and the industrial base to make use of it.

But the Federal Republic is far from being the only nation to have collaborated with South Africa in the nuclear field. The first South African reactor, SAFARI-I, was supplied under President Eisenhower's "Atoms for Peace" program. The production of uranium hexafluoride, the final stage of processing before enrichment, which began on an industrial scale in South Africa in 1976, is probably based on British-supplied technology. France is supplying a massive nuclear power plant which will, according to the *Washington Post* (February 16, 1977), "produce as by-products every year a total of about 1,000 pounds of plutonium, enough to make 100 atomic bombs, each with a force equal to the bomb that destroyed Nagasaki."

There is reason, moreover, to believe that South Africa is operating a plutonium reprocessing plant, manufacturing the weapons-grade plutonium needed for H-bombs. The South African enrichment plant at Valindaba is totally sealed to all outsiders. "It is significant as the only plant operating outside the existing nuclear powers which is not subject to regular inspections under the international safeguards system," say Rogers and Červenka. (Pelindaba, the name given to the South African nuclear research center, is a Zulu word signifying "the story is finished"; Valindaba means "discussion closed.")

In 1975 the construction of a new South African enrichment plant with a minimum capacity of 5,000 tons of enriched uranium a year and a potential capacity of up to 10,000 tons a year was announced. This is a huge quantity, "about the same size as total American capacity prior to a recent upgrading, and more than the total Soviet enrichment capacity," according to Rogers and Červenka. Development costs were estimated at over $1 billion, some of the funding being from Iran. The minimum output of 5,000 tons of enriched uranium, Rogers and Červenka point out, would require an input of 20,000 tons of uranium oxide a year, compared with current South African production of about 3,000 tons. Even allowing for the fact that South Africa has been stockpiling against the day when its giant enrichment plant will come into production, where is this raw material to come from? The only logical answer is Namibia. The uranium deposits being mined at Rössing, northeast of Swakopmund, are thought to be among the largest in the world, and the desolate Namib desert is currently the scene of a uranium rush involving, among others, South Africa's General Mining/Federale Mynbou; Gold Fields of South Africa; the Anglo-American Corporation; Rio Tinto Zinc (U.K.); Falconbridge Nickel Mines (Canada); Union Carbide (U.S.); and the French companies Minatome and Aquitaine. Whatever happens, it seems unlikely that the enormous interests vested in Namibian uranium will be jeopardized lightly.

South Africa's nuclear strategy has been two-pronged. In the first place, Pretoria perceives in uranium a powerful card in the international energy stakes, and is already at the center of a uranium cartel along the lines of OPEC. The terrible dangers involved in nuclear reactors and the unsolved problem of safe disposal of nuclear wastes may have given pause to some, but long-term plans of the atomic energy industry are said to have aimed at expanding the number of nuclear power plants in the United States to between 500 and 1,000 in the next quarter century. The Soviet Union has a substantial investment in nuclear energy, and imports raw uranium (from East Germany, Poland, and Czechoslovakia). The projected Russian shift to plutonium breeder reactors has run into trouble, with at least one major accident, partly disabling the first Soviet breeder, at Shevchenko, on the east shore of the Caspian sea. Japan currently aims at supplying at least 10 percent of its energy needs from nuclear power plants under construction. Britain, too, is heavily committed. Third World countries also constitute a potential market for uranium. Prior to the 1979 revolution, at any rate, Iran planned on having no fewer than twenty nuclear power stations in operation by 1990, and had reportedly concluded an agreement to buy 14,000 tons of uranium oxide from South Africa.

On the other hand, once the commercial uranium-enrichment plant and reactors now under construction are in operation, South Africa will be in a position to supply weapons-grade uranium and plutonium, or even finished nuclear weapons, to threatened regimes around the world. Nonproliferation experts are said to worry about a potential "outlaw club" of nations, a "League of the Desperate," including Israel, Taiwan, South Korea, and—formerly at least—Iran, seeking nuclear armaments at any cost. Iran, South Africa's main oil supplier under the Shah, was a partner in the SASOL II coal gasification project at Secunda in the Transvaal, under cover of which uranium-enrichment technology may have been financed, according to German sources.* When the United States and the USSR combined to prevent South Africa from setting off an aboveground nuclear explosion in the Kalahari desert in 1977, some intelligence sources evidently believed that the device might be an Israeli one (Rogers and Červenka suggest that South Africa may already have conducted underground nuclear tests at sites in the northern Cape and the Namib). There is little doubt that in military matters South Africa and Israel cooperate closely. Taiwan's nuclear weapons program—evidently far advanced—is said to use South African-supplied uranium. Nations like Chile and Saudi Arabia might also conceivably be interested in South African bombs. An alternative South African strategy, Rogers and Červenka suggest, would be to follow the lead of South Korea in obliging the United States to extend its "nuclear umbrella" over the country by threatening to deploy its own atomic weapons.

Certainly the Russians are very interested in South Africa's nuclear capacity. A "Chinese source" cited by Rogers and Červenka reports that "a mysterious exchange of agents involving West Germans held by the Soviets and a single Soviet agent, Victor Loginov, was connected with their priority concern with South Africa's nuclear plans; Loginov had in fact been caught in South Africa. How

---

* Scheduled to be completed in 1982, SASOL II will process 27 million tons of coal a year to produce between 35 and 50 percent of South Africa's liquid motor fuel requirements, it is reported. Construction at Secunda is said to be the most expensive single industrial project now under way anywhere in the world, with an estimated final cost of $6.7 billion. A third SASOL plant is in the planning stages.

he came into the hands of the Germans for exchange against their own people is something of a mystery, but presumably yet another aspect of the close co-operation between the two countries over nuclear, military and other issues."

In September-October 1979, reports strongly implicated South Africa in a mysterious nuclear explosion in the South Atlantic: with the passage of time, the reality of an apartheid A-bomb becomes more and more difficult to contest.

As Rogers and Červenka tell the story, on September 24, 1975, the South African ambassador to the federal Republic of Germany, Donald Bell Sole, was the recipient of a disturbing telephone call. A reporter for the popular newsweekly *Der Stern* wanted to know whether it was true that General Gunther Rall, chief of the Luftwaffe, had paid a visit to South Africa as a guest of the South African Ministry of Defence. Since the reporter had a copy of a secret cable sent by Sole, it was difficult to deny. When he hung up, Sole asked his secretary to bring him the Rall file.

It was missing, as were eight more files dealing with the South African-West German nuclear collaboration. The tip-off had been well timed, too. The very next day a brochure entitled *The Nuclear Conspiracy* arrived on the ambassador's desk. It included photocopies of six letters from the missing files in evidence of the charge that the Federal Republic was cooperating with South Africa in the production of nuclear weapons. Copies were also sent to all Bonn embassies, ministries, members of Parliament, and West German newspapers and institutions. A week later, on October 2, *Stern* released the Rall story, accompanied by a full-page picture of the Luftwaffe general in uniform.

Rall had indeed been to South Africa, where he had conducted talks with the chiefs of defense staff and the president of the South African Atomic Energy Board; he had visited the nuclear research station at Pelindaba, the Atlas aircraft factory where South Africa's Mirages are built, and had inspected air force units, military aerodromes and academies. He had also paid a call on the "Silvermine" underground radar surveillance installation at Simonstown, where the South African Navy monitors all maritime traffic in the South Atlantic and Indian oceans, especially the 25,000 ships that round the Cape each year, using equipment provided by the West German companies Siemens and AEG-Telefunken. The *Stern* story blew up a storm, and General Rall presently expressed a wish to retire. But the fact was that he was only one of a number of German generals to have visited South Africa—and Pelindaba—in recent years.

So serious was the breach of security involved that BOSS's

chief, General van den Bergh, came to Bonn in person to investigate. It seemed likely that the files might have been taken after the embassy moved from Cologne to Bonn-Bad Godesberg in April 1975. Inasmuch as the new filing cabinets were not delivered in time, *Der Spiegel* later suggested that

> the employees of the Embassy piled up their papers in the basement garage where the entrance gate had not yet been installed: for weeks anyone interested was able to help himself free and easy and undisturbed to the contents of document boxes, waste-paper baskets and the locked safe of Ambassador Donald Bell Sole—so much so that even today the diplomats are still lacking an overview of what exactly got lost.

This was certainly uncomfortable to BOSS's pretensions. Sole himself was evidently not held to blame. He retained his post and subsequently in May 1977 went on to become South African ambassador to Washington.

What in fact transpired may never be known. The likeliest account is probably that given by Breytenbach at his 1977 trial. The theft was carried out by members of the German Anti-Apartheid movement, who handed the documents over to the Dutch Anti-Apartheid organization of which Barend Schuitema was secretary. Okhela was given credit so as to improve its credibility abroad to enable it to attract members.

A Horrible Face, But One's Own

Breyten's 1973 trip with its bold challenge had been followed by a hiatus. Perhaps General van den Bergh's revelations that night at the Mount Nelson had shaken him. In the face of the vastness of the problem, Breyten felt helpless. He had long been a member of a Zen center in Paris: how one's heart turned away from the hideous reality to the quiet of meditation, and private life! Yolande, it seems, did not approve of his political activities. She knew all too well that his besetting sin was carelessness, that he was not cut out to be a conspirator. He made an application for French citizenship: it was turned down. Atlas had by now disintegrated for want of specific goals. The South African authorities had blandly renewed his passport: he could have all the rope he wanted. "Looking into South Africa is like looking into the mirror at midnight when one has pulled a face and a train blew its whistle and one's image stayed there, fixed for all eternity. A horrible face, but one's own," he had once written.

Then there was Makhatini, to whom he felt a certain loyalty. The ANC leader proposed a new organization—or at any rate a new name: *Okhela.* The Zulu word means something like "transkindle."* Okhela was to be the spill transferring the flame from the exiled politicals in Europe to the mass of tinder that lay waiting in South Africa. For the present, Makhatini asked, all connection with the ANC should be kept secret, and the matter should not even be mentioned to other ANC members. (It would scarcely do for the ANC to be seen to be relying on whites to do its work for it, and those who set the ball rolling knew very well that the time would come—as come it did—when Okhela would have to be denied.) In prison several years later, Breyten came to the conclusion that Oliver Tambo and the leadership of Umkhonto we Sizwe ("MK"), the ANC's military wing, probably knew about it, but doubted that the movement's "Revolutionary Council" as such did.

As far as goals went, there was the project to expose Rhodesian sanctions-busting (later accomplished by the British government's Bingham Report in September 1978) and the South African–West German "nuclear axis" (though Okhela had really had nothing to do with that). Schuitema came forward with another. The ICFTU, an international trade union organization, was prepared to make available a large sum of money for black trade unions in South Africa. But it would be necessary for representatives of such unions to come to Europe and establish contact and credibility. ("In the dark, the cow that lows gets milked," as the Sechuana proverb goes; but the foreign trade unionists wanted at least nominal proof of purchase.) The South African Congress of Trade Unions (SACTU), the organization affiliated to the ANC, was in competition with the PAC-sponsored Federation of Free African Trade Unions of South Africa (FOFATUSA) and the Black Allied Workers' Union (BAWU), an organization associated with the Black Consciousness movement. FOFATUSA was perhaps moribund, but BAWU, under the leadership of Drake Koka, was a force to be reckoned with. Though placed under banning order in 1973, Koka continued to lead his organization inside South Africa until he was forced to flee the country in November 1976.

Schuitema's idea was that SACTU should open an office in Amsterdam to serve as a conduit for the ICFTU funds. When Breytenbach returned to South Africa in August 1975 in the guise of

---

* There is no exact English equivalent. C. M. Doke and B. W. Vilikazi give the meaning as "to set alight," also "to attack, provoke, slander," in their *Zulu-English Dictionary* (Johannesburg: Witwatersrand University Press, 1958), but the accuracy of these renderings has been questioned.

Christian Galaska, the French bank clerk, his "limited mission" was partly to find two suitable candidates, one black, one white, to man this office. Concealed in the covers of a book, he carried two passports forged by Solidarité for the use of these recruits if needed.

Schuitema himself had been to South Africa in August 1974, traveling on a phony Solidarité passport, and in August 1975 he returned in the same manner. The security police evidently knew that he was coming, but somehow failed to apprehend him. Just what the purpose of these trips was remains obscure.

Breytenbach, too, was expected. "I learned, as you probably also know, that we were watched and photographed even during our first meeting outside Stuttaford's—though they were looking for 'GALAZKA' at the time, of course," he later wrote to James Polley, one of his contacts. But little of what Breytenbach had been up to in fact emerged during his trial, and the police themselves treated the information as classified. "Strangely enough even the court records in the archives of the Pretoria division of the Supreme Court disappeared without trace early in 1978," wrote reporter Jack Viviers. "An enquiry by the security police apparently failed to turn anything up."

In Cape Town, Breyten evidently caught on to the fact that all was not well. Christian Galaska vanished, and he made a nerve-wracking trip back to Johannesburg under the name of E. Christie. But what he could scarcely know was that he had been under surveillance from the outset. Though they might spell it with a z rather than an s, BOSS knew even the name on his false passport. There was no escape. On August 19, 1975, as he was attempting to leave the country, he was picked up at Jan Smuts International Airport outside Johannesburg.

Trial Number One

The police swept into the net as co-conspirators those with whom Breytenbach had been in contact: Jenny Curtis, archivist of the Institute of Race Relations; Lawrence Dworkin, a trainee journalist; Horst Kleinschmidt, assistant to the director of the Christian Institute (declared an unlawful organization under the Internal Security Act by the minister of justice on October 19, 1977); Norman Lewis, a salesman who had formerly been a University of the Witwatersrand ("Wits") student; Paulus "Gerry" Maré, a member of the executive committee of the National Union of South African Students (NUSAS); Nicholas Martens, a Wits student; Glenn Moss, former president of the Wits Student Representative Council; the Reverend

James Polley, a senior lecturer at the University of Cape Town; Megan Riley, a friend of Polley's; Dürten Rohm; Karel Tip, outgoing president of NUSAS; and Robert Gordon Young, a former NUSAS vice-president. Of all these only Dürten Rohm and Dworkin (if indeed he) were actually linked with Okhela's conspiratorial activities. But the state intended to make an example of Breytenbach, and to do so to maximum effect it needed a plea of guilty. To obtain this, the other detainees—friends of his, people he had compromised—were held as hostages against his confession, a typical security police tactic. "Three of them are known to have been told that they faced a minimum of twenty years imprisonment," says one source. "Shortly before the trial they were informed that all of them, except Breyten, were to be released."

On November 10, Breytenbach appeared in the Pretoria Supreme Court, charged under the Terrorism Act and the Suppression of Communism Act with helping to set up an illegal organization to promote armed struggle in South Africa in order to overthrow the government. He was remanded until November 21. Meanwhile a campaign to discredit the Okhela conspirators was launched in the press. The Johannesburg *Sunday Times,* for example, carried an item on Barend Schuitema, alleging that "he was a cruel boy who took delight in torturing animals" and a failure socially "because of his pimply complexion." An anonymous pamphleteer [perhaps Schuitema himself?] comments: "The security police stopped at nothing in feeding the press with information to prepare the public for a show of the invincibility of white South African morals and the bankruptcy of their enemies."

Unlike some others before him, Breytenbach took the rap, pleading guilty on November 21 to the charges under the Terrorism Act on condition that the more serious ones under the Suppression of Communism Act were dropped. After a brief adjournment the prosecution, headed by Dr. Percy Yutar, agreed, also accepting a number of amendments to the charge sheet relating to times, places and incidents. The amendments included deletion of the accused's alleged aim of seeking to establish a "communistic" society, limiting the charge to wanting to establish a black government. The word "armed" was deleted before the word "struggle" on the charge sheet. Breytenbach pleaded guilty to being a supporter of the African National Congress, a banned organization, but not to being a member.

Summing up, Yutar declared that Breytenbach, far from being a leader of Okhela, was merely a pawn of "anti-South African elements abroad" that sought to seduce students into taking part in their subversive activities. "They were tempted by foreign trips and then came into contact with permissive overseas elements. These young men were then sent back to South Africa with dreams of becoming the saviors of the republic," he said. "Barend Schuitema and the other leaders hid in their skunkholes in Europe while the students were pushed into the front line."

Inasmuch as part of the evidence had been to the effect that Schuitema, heavily disguised and calling himself "Nico Waterbalk," had visited South Africa clandestinely, using a false passport, on several occasions, and had been there at the same time as Breytenbach, this was as inaccurate as it was intentionally offensive. But perhaps Yutar, Transvaal attorney-general and long the state hatchet man in political trials, lacked confidence in the stories coerced from his witnesses.

Wearing a light yellow summer suit, his familiar beard newly shaved off, Breytenbach made a final, poignant appeal to the court that again displayed his mastery with words. His *volte-face*, if not heartfelt, was certainly glib. He wanted to give the South African people an explanation for his actions, he said, and went on to outline his personal history, pulling out all stops. "I accept the responsibility for what I have done," he added.

> I know now that the manner and the methods by which I tried to work for the growth of our civilization and our future were wrong, that my behavior was foolish and that things I got mixed up in with good intentions could lead to harm to other people. . . . I am convinced that each of us, consciously or unconsciously, is in part the architect of his own life, and in that sense each of us must take responsibility for his actions. But we are neither alone or apart on earth. The beginning and the end of the individual is other people; we are a society of people. Each of us is also responsible for all the other people; we all contribute to the society, for better or for worse. As far as I am concerned, it is very clear to me now that my contribution cannot be in the field of politics and I will never poison myself again by entering it. . . . I am sorry for all the stupid, thoughtless things I did which brought me here and I ask to be forgiven for them. But I feel, I know that I still have many poems in my fingers and paintings in my eye. I hope that when one day it is given me to go out into the world again I will still be able to make my contribution to the future of our country and its people through my writing and art. It will be a privilege.

He apologized to those whom he might "unintentionally or out of thoughtlessness" have hurt or insulted, and specifically to Prime Minister Vorster "for a crass and insulting poem which I addressed to him. There was and is no justification for it. I am sorry." And with what some might have thought supererogatory zeal he extended thanks to "Colonel Broodryk of the South African

Police, the chief investigation officer in charge of my case, as also the officers who worked under him, for the correct and humane way in which they treated me from the beginning of my detention . . . their courteous conduct made these traumatic three months bearable for me." He wound up by quoting St. Paul's words to the Corinthians:

> For we know in part, and we prophesy in part. But when that which is perfect is come, then that which is in part shall be done away. When I was a child, I spake as a child, I understood as a child, I thought as a child: but when I became a man, I put away childish things. For now we see through a glass, darkly; but then face to face: now I know in part; but then shall I know even as also I am known. And now abideth faith, hope, charity, these three; but the greatest of these *is* charity.

(I Cor. 13:9–13)

Breytenbach's friends were stunned by this torrent of apology. "No poet of Breyten's caliber would ever dream of apologizing for his work," was one comment. It was argued that he must have been drugged, tortured or brainwashed—probably all three. In fact this seems improbable.

He had undoubtedly been led to believe that he would get off more lightly if he did not take advantage of his trial to launch a political attack on the government. And his treatment in prison, he had been tacitly given to understand, would depend on the extent to which he cooperated with the security police. In the last analysis, there was always the need to protect his fellow detainees, for whose plight he could scarcely but hold himself responsible.

The trial came to a conclusion with an almost exaggeratedly orchestrated bonhomie and goodwill toward the accused on behalf of police and prosecution. Colonel Kalfie ("Little Calf") Broodryk took the box to enlarge on Breytenbach's contrition. He was, after all was said and done, a poet and a romantic, Broodryk observed generously, and was bitterly sorry for his misdeeds. Attorney-General Yutar not only supported the defense's plea for imposition of the minimum sentence provided for under the Terrorism Act—five years—but waxed lyrical on the subject. He represented the accused as a mere pawn in the hands of that sinister duo "Jan Schuitema" and "the right reverend Don Morton, alias James Moeller, alias Ted." In contrast to these skulkers in alien rat holes, Breytenbach had repented his crimes and taken responsibility for them like a man, said the attorney-general, quoting the patriot poet Jan Celliers:

> *Ek hou van 'n man wat sy man kan staan;*
> [I like a man who can hold his own;]

but tactfully omitting the couplet—which almost everybody in the court must have known—to be found a little further on:

> en die bastergeslag
> in sy siel verag,
> [and the bastard breed
> in his soul despises,]

which some might have thought had relevance too. With this bemusing display of white South African solidarity (Yutar is Jewish) before him, Judge Cillié retired to consult his spleen; but he had scarcely left the courtroom when the defense dispatched an orderly to fetch him back again. It seemed that the accused wished to add to the statement he had made—an expression of thanks to the prison personnel "for their exceptionally correct treatment since I have been with them." His senior advocate, Dr. Piet Henning, seized the opportunity of responding to the attorney-general's summation. One cannot help feeling that both might have better saved their breath. Still, it seemed as though the minimum sentence was a foregone conclusion.

In delivering sentence, Judge Cillié took conspicuous care to appear correct, too. The eyes of the world were on his court. Justice must be seen to be done, the punishment to fit the crime. He conceded that it might be said that the poet's misdeeds had never gotten beyond the discussion stage. But the threat to society had been great, and the law made provision for the death penalty. Only the personal circumstances of the case and the accused's statement of remorse induced him to impose a lighter sentence.

"In the circumstances now existing, the climate now prevailing, what you have done constitutes a serious threat to the security of the state and the peaceful coexistence of the inhabitants of this country.

"In all these circumstances I have come to the conclusion that the sentence I must impose is one of nine years' imprisonment and that sentence is therefore imposed on you."

Since the Terrorism Act makes no provision for remission, Breytenbach would have to serve this sentence in full, failing some special intervention. Observers considered it a singularly savage one.

Judge Cillié's ferocity, as he himself conceded, was contingent on the times. Things were not looking well for the Republic. Scarcely a month before, on October 23, encouraged by Henry Kissinger and an array of governments including those of France and Zaire, South Africa had embarked on open intervention in the bloody Angolan civil war, backing the "pro-Western" movements Unita and FNLA against the "pro-Soviet" MPLA. At first the South African blitzkrieg went like clockwork. On October 26 the column code-named "Zulu" took Sá da Bandeira; Moçâmedes fell on October 28, followed by Lobito on November 3 and Novo Redondo on November 14. But here things bogged down as the effect of greatly stepped-up Russian and Cuban intervention began to be felt.

When the Breytenbach trial opened on November 21, the airlift of a reinforced Cuban special-forces battalion to the Angolan capital of Luanda had just been completed. "Zulu" column was still stuck at Novo Redondo. Three shiploads of Cuban troops, including an artillery regiment and a motorized battalion, were on their way, despite U. S. Navy harassment. South Africa's allies, the FNLA–Zairean force attacking Luanda, had been repulsed only a few days before. China had pragmatically withdrawn support from the FNLA in October, presumably judging it better to lose a little face than to be ranged alongside the forces of white supremacy. Kissinger (that "man of great doubts and few hopes," as the perceptive Spanish Foreign Minister José María de Areilza dubbed him) was patently failing to rally congressional support for an aggressive stance in Angola. United States Africa policy stood revealed as bankrupt. The South African expeditionary force numbered 2,000 at most, and "Zulu" column commander (code name: "Rommel") had been refused reinforcements. "If Pretoria took up the challenge presented by the Cubans she would have to commit her entire armed forces to battle several thousand miles away in unfamiliar territory against possibly superior armaments, all in the face of violent international denunciation," observes R. W. Johnson. Withdrawal was clearly only a matter of time.

That same month Kissinger and U. S. Treasury Secretary William Simon, meeting secretly with the French in the course of a monetary summit at Rambouillet, near Paris, came to an agreement whereby France abandoned her longtime championship of a raised gold price in exchange for various American concessions. For Pretoria this was disastrous, since every fall of ten dollars in the price of gold—and it was falling fast—meant a loss of more than $200 million, about 1 percent of the GNP, to the South African economy.

The grim reality of South Africa's nearly complete isolation began to sink in. It was apparent, too, that matters would presently be worse, inasmuch as Jimmy Carter's victory in the United States presidential election had been owing largely to his major share of the black vote. Kissinger, undependable ally though he might be, was undoubtedly preferable to anything to be expected from the incoming administration. To add to the Vorster regime's difficulties, France, South Africa's only remaining source of advanced weapons technology, had announced an embargo on further arms sales.

As it happened, the South African public were not told of their army's role in Angola until December 18—by which time withdrawal had already been decided on. "An official censorship was imposed on the Press which resulted in an angry controversy; so although the SA public was not told *what* was going on, they were treated to a public discussion about *why* they were not being told," Colin Legum comments.

But Judge Cillié, "one of the present Government's first and most obvious political appointments to the bench," according to one commentator, was a leading member of the powerful Afrikaans secret society known as the Broederbond, an organization sometimes difficult to distinguish from the regime itself (every National Party prime minister and most cabinet members since Malan's 1948 election victory have belonged to it). It is not at all unreasonable to suppose that he had been briefed on the Angolan debacle, and knew all too well of the collapse of South African hopes in the money and arms marts of the West. Breytenbach the *volksveraaier* (traitor to his people) made a handy scapegoat.

Many thought that the defense, put up by Breytenbach's family, had been badly managed. There was little cross-examination of prosecution witnesses, while the only defense witnesses called were Breytenbach's chief interrogator, Colonel Broodryk, and Mrs. Cecile Cilliers, a doctoral candidate in literature at the Rand Afrikaans University, who gave testimony to his standing as a man of letters. "His love poetry, erotic poetry, and poems to his parents are among the most beautiful in the Afrikaans language," she said, and recited some of them, bringing tears to the eyes of some of the spectators —but not visibly moving the judge. Present in the courtroom were a number of prominent Afrikaans writers, among them Ampie Coetzee, Chris Barnard and John Miles, who might also have testified to his merits as a poet, but were not asked to do so. "The complete understanding which existed throughout the trial between the prosecution and the defense aroused a certain feeling of unease," noted Charles-Albert Morand, representing the International Commission of Jurists, who was not allowed access to the defendant.

> The Breytenbach case constitutes a remarkable success for the government. It has helped to impress upon the white community the image of a vast subversive conspiracy. It must be expected that the government will exploit this favorable situation by intensifying the repression. The arrest of the leaders of NUSAS is the first sign. In the political context, which an impartial observer is bound to take into

account, the Breytenbach trial, like many of those which preceded it, is to be seen as a lever which enables the white government to legitimate and reinforce its dictatorial powers and to pursue its policy of apartheid.

And certainly the state perceived the outcome of the trial as a victory. In the annual report of the commissioner of police for 1975–76, "the arrest and conviction of Breyten Breytenbach" are termed "one of the major successes in the sphere of internal security."

On the afternoon of November 26, 1975, Breytenbach was taken from security police headquarters in the ill-famed Kompol building to the maximum security section of the Pretoria Central Prison, designated C-3, to begin serving his sentence. He was still in shock. The court case had been deeply humiliating. He had been manipulated into playing the part the police wanted of him, he felt, without its availing him anything. The fact that he faced nine years in prison suddenly confronted him very concretely.

During the months to come, security police and BOSS agents continued to question him frequently. Isolated and lonely, he actually began to look forward to their visits. "Any contact with the outside world was a relief to me at that stage," he later explained. In March 1976, Yolande was able to pay him a visit. It was the first time they had seen each other since his sentencing, and after she had left he was overcome by the realization that it would be a very long time before he saw her again, inasmuch as she was granted a visa to visit South Africa for only a short period. Application to the Transvaal Supreme Court for permission to take his case to the Court of Appeals in Bloemfontein had been turned down by Cillié, as judge-president. The chief justice had also rejected a petition submitted on Breytenbach's behalf. There was scant light at the end of the tunnel.

Deeply depressed, Breytenbach began to doubt his own judgment and powers of resistance. In these circumstances, on June 16 —by a terrible irony it was "Day One" of the great Soweto uprising of that year, though he could not know it—he sat down to compose a letter to General Mike Geldenhuys, head of the security police at the time, which will in all probability haunt him for the rest of his life. When confronted with it later in court, he did not deny that he had written it, but represented it as a mere fraud suggested to him by his discussions with Colonel Broodryk, who had attempted to recruit him to the security police. After all, he pointed out, BOSS had tried to recruit him as an informer as long ago as 1973, and he had rejected the suggestion out of hand.

Perhaps so. But Breyten's state of mind at the time seems to have been distinctly ambivalent: he had in fact dedicated a book of poems (*Voetskrif*) in part to Colonel Broodryk, surely almost a unique event in police annals. Perhaps Breyten simply felt as Piet Beyleveld had felt twelve years before when giving evidence against his old friend and comrade Bram Fischer. "I can think of nothing but my liberty and I am prepared to forsake my lifelong principles for it," Beyleveld had explained to the court. "I have no principle but to obtain my own liberty." And Beyleveld was, after all, a seasoned trade unionist and a member of the central committee of the CPSA, not an errant poet whose customary milieu was the Left Bank of the Seine.

"I am convinced that, in my way, I can also make a contribution, however slight, to the solution of some of the problems crowding in on South Africa," the poet wrote the general. "Up to now I have endeavored, so far as I could, to supply you with all the data that could possibly be of help. I trust you have been able to follow up on it, but I am not in a position to judge to what extent it was of use to you. It goes without saying that I will go on doing so, too, if and where it is desired of me, though I fear that what I can do under present circumstances will mean even less to you in view of my isolation from the outside world and my inactivity. In short, I believe that you can make much better use of me than is at present the case." After a brief sketch of South Africa's geopolitical predicament in terms of Cold War demonology, he pinpointed the role of the South African Communist party:

> The SACP has strengthened its grip on the ANC and the ANC is for all practical purposes now the SACP. But the influence of the SACP is not restricted to the ANC. In May 1975 I heard from Elias Mdloedebe, a PAC representative, that a PAC delegation had been invited to visit Moscow. . . . I believe that the SACP will play an even more important role than was the case with the communist parties in Frelimo and the MPLA. The SACP is the "oldest" in Africa, at present more or less intact, and certainly the most slavishly pro-Moscow party.

and he went on to propose bluntly that

> I be released and try—in collaboration with your service—to become a member of the SACP. . . . I also have a chance, I believe, to build up contact again with people—like Schuitema or [Tennyson] Makiwane or Makhatini—who for one or other reason try to stay on top of the SACP's maneuvers and plans.

"Let us take the initiative and try to keep it," he concluded. "I hope that you will accept my proposal with the sincerity in which I mean it."

No reply from General Geldenhuys is on record. The police had good reason for not believing Breytenbach. On June 22, a matter of days after he addressed his letter to General Geldenhuys, the young prison warder, Pieter Groenewald, was spilling the beans in the office of the prison commandant, Brigadier Visser.

Lucky the Pimp

Groenewald's relationship with Breytenbach began on April 17, when he first encountered the poet in the shower room early one morning. Another warder had ordered Breytenbach to hurry up; Groenewald told him that he could take his time. Breytenbach was astonished by this display of friendliness. "It seldom happens that a warder goes out of his way to give the impression that he is on your side," he said later. The next time Groenewald saw Breytenbach, he struck up a conversation, the first of many. Breytenbach showed him some of his drawings, and told him his story. "Under these circumstances one is very acutely aware of any contact that anyone tries to make, because it is literally your only field of reference," Breytenbach said.

> I was amused by his stories, which were so clearly fantasies, so clearly untrue. He told me that he had run away from his parents' home at an early age; that he had gone as far as Central Africa, where he had been a big game hunter; that he had fought a hyena with his bare hands, that he had learned to shoot lions; that he then visited the Canary Islands, where he was a deep-sea diver; that he had been arrested after returning to South Africa, and escaped from custody. I asked him what language the people spoke in Central Africa, and he said Afrikaans.

Groenewald explained that he had been called "Lucky" at school because of his "happy-go-lucky" nature. Breytenbach thought that he seemed unhappy with his work, that he got on badly with his fellow warders. In the exercise yard he overheard warders refer to Groenewald as "Lucky the Pimp," and perhaps Breyten should have taken more heed of this, since in prison slang it implied that he was an informer. But he came to depend on his conversations with the warder. He was anxious to talk to anyone. Groenewald knew a good deal about Breytenbach's trial, and he was very interested in Okhela. He gave the poet to understand that he admired him, and Breyten found himself embroidering on the facts to impress him. "Groenewald had no interest in the ideology, for him it was a matter of adventure, of people who, as he put it, had the 'guts' to defy authority," Breytenbach recalled.

I never saw him as material for a left political movement. In spite of what he knew about my attitude to blacks, he never made any attempt to change his own racist attitude to blacks. . . . When we started to talk about the possibility of escape, it sometimes assumed grotesque dimensions. At one point we talked about his not only getting me out of the prison, but the black prisoners too, the whole lot at once. He said he would get a pick-up truck and load them all into it, but when we were outside Pretoria, he would unload them, because he didn't allow Kaffirs to ride in his car.

According to Groenewald, Breytenbach told him that the white leaders of South Africa had made their plans for escape when the blacks took over, and that some of them, including Prime Minister Vorster, had already bought their houses in Switzerland. "In that case a chap like me is in the shit, because I have no money to fly to Switzerland or buy a house!" Groenewald said. Things were not as bad as all that, Breytenbach explained. In fact, it was simple: all Groenewald had to do was get on the right side. "He said I must just make up my mind, think over the business of taking out a letter for him in which he would introduce me to his organization. In exchange for this I could assure my entire future and feel safe in South Africa." He invited Groenewald to join Okhela, and when the warder agreed, concocted a swearing-in ceremony (Groenewald claimed that he had had to give the clenched fist salute and shout "Amandla!" [Power!]; this standing on the walkway above the cells with his FN rifle slung over his shoulder!) and allotted him a code name: Louis. He read the new recruit the "rules" of the organization: they consisted of nothing but safety precautions, the better to ensure that the letters and sketches Breytenbach planned to smuggle out would reach their destinations.*

The subject of escape came up early in their talk. They discussed it endlessly: possible routes, subterfuges, false passports, border crossings. Groenewald would bring a spare uniform into the prison and drop it into the cell; while Breytenbach was putting it on he would force open the louvers of the ventilation duct with a jack; Breytenbach would then climb through and they would escape together—to Botswana, to France, to Russia. Sometimes their talk veered into plain absurdity: at one stage Groenewald talked of bringing in a laser to cut the louvers. Breytenbach wondered if it would be possible to drug the other guards' tea. Groenewald thought this would be difficult, and suggested obtaining a gas pistol for the pur-

---

* One of the names Breytenbach used for Groenewald was *Gabba,* which has the implication of something hollow, such as a scoop or ladle (*skepding*), and used as an adjective also means uncultivated, primitive. The word is of Khoi origin and not in common use, and Groenewald obviously had no idea what he was being called.

pose of knocking them out. The best escape route, they decided, would be through the gallows chamber.

In fact, the real chances of escape were slight. A warder as junior as the nineteen-year-old Groenewald had scant freedom of action in the context of the maximum-security division of Pretoria Central. In August 1963, the Rivonia detainees Arthur Goldreich and Harold Wolpe had made a dramatic escape precisely by promising a bribe to a young guard (but they never paid up, reducing the chances of this working again). Precautions had inevitably been taken. The louvers in question were reinforced wolfram steel, and even assuming Breytenbach could be got out of his cell, they would still have had to pass half a dozen locked gates.

But escape remained the leitmotiv of their conversations. Breytenbach could hardly help dreaming of ways to get out, while Groenewald had seen the movie *Papillon* and clearly enjoyed fantasizing about an adventurous flight from his humdrum existence as an insignificant cog in the Department of Prisons. Once they had gotten away, he imagined, there would be press conferences, television interviews, perhaps even a film, certainly money and fame. It was all very adolescent. "Part of the tomfoolery was that we would take prison service uniforms with us and dress ourselves up in them and have our pictures taken with a couple of pretty girls and send the photos back to his colleagues," Breytenbach remembered. On one occasion Breyten's old friend and fellow political prisoner, Marius Schoon, gave the warder a piece of candy to take him along with a letter. Groenewald ate it himself, and tried to convince Breyten that it had been stolen by one of the other warders. (This was a heartless thing to do, as Breytenbach was not allowed sweets.) One of the books Groenewald smuggled in to Breyten from his brother Cloete dealt with Tai Ch'i, and from this he derived the unshakable opinion that Breytenbach must be a karate expert. It is not often that an adolescent dreamer of limited intelligence finds himself in a position of power over someone he thinks of as the equivalent of James Bond, and Groenewald was clearly enjoying it.

If his testimony is to be believed, however, there came a time when he realized that Breytenbach was seriously thinking of escaping, and expected him to help him. Since he had no intention of doing so in actuality, he arranged for himself to work in another section of the prison, where he would not have to deal with Breytenbach. It was some while after this that the mysterious stranger with the heavy accent came to his quarters to warn him and give him the green documents marked "Botswana," he said. That same night he went to the home of Colonel van Zyl, deputy head of the prison, in a funk. The next day Van Zyl took him to the office of Brigadier Visser, and he told his story again. He was given a tape recorder and told to continue his relationship with Breytenbach. Henceforth their conversations were taped, and the letters and notes Breytenbach gave him were photocopied before being forwarded to the addressees. Taken together they would form the basis of a new prosecution the following year. The trap was baited.

After watching a television interview with two recently released South African political prisoners, people who had known them before their confinement were struck especially by the degree to which they had assimilated the language and intonations of the guards who had for years been their main contact with the world; once educated English speakers, if not intellectuals, they now larded their talk with lower-class Afrikaans crudities, delivered in the thick accents of the *platteland.*

In much the same way, Breytenbach seems to have absorbed something of Groenewald. In the loneliness of his cell, which for all he knew he would occupy for the better part of a decade, surrounded by memories of failure and betrayal, and periodically assaulted by the sound of men going to execution, he came to regard Groenewald as a friend. He desperately needed to trust someone. The loony wonderment of the gangling young warder served to garnish the self-image of the poet, and at times drew forth fragments of a persona buried long ago at Wellington's Hugenoot High School. Perhaps there had always been something of a Groenewald in him, despite the great gulf of intellect and sensibility between them. In Breytenbach's more complex soul, Groenewald's adolescent daydreams underwent encoding and amplification; Okhela itself had been nothing but such a fantasy: though not, of course, on the side of Mfanakuti ("Home Boy") Makhatini.

With Groenewald to deliver them, Breytenbach now commenced to fire off a series of letters and notes of stunning indiscretion, superficially veiled in a wash of allusions, ranging from the surreal to the banal, that showed more than it hid. In correspondence that was going directly into security police files, he spelled out useless safety precautions and codes, using hoary spy-story gimmicks straight out of the pages of a Boy Scout annual: messages in invisible writing imprinted on paper smeared with candle wax and so on. What was inexcusable was that several of the people he was writing to—James Polley, André Brink, Gerry Maré—were South Africans living in South Africa. Polley and Maré had already been jailed once on his account.

He wrote to Yolande on the subject of obtaining forged passports for Groenewald and himself (though this was, of course, *after* the visit of the mysterious stranger had allegedly panicked Groene-wald into going to his chiefs). He applied to André Brink for a loan of R300, and when Brink sent the money, instructed Groenewald to buy the gas pistol they had spoken of and bury what was left over against the day of their *cavale,* as he called it.

The fact that Groenewald was able to travel to Cape Town and Grahamstown and Durban to deliver letters by hand for him—jour-neys totalling thousands of miles—triggered no warning signals. Groenewald told him that he could get leave to visit his family (who lived at Worcester, a hundred miles or so from Cape Town) and Breytenbach simply believed him. In fact Groenewald was accom-panied on all these trips by high-ranking security police officers. The police were having a field day. Breytenbach's game was, after all, their game too, and they entered into it wholeheartedly.

Around this time, Breytenbach was moved to another cell. Through Groenewald, he discovered that Marius Schoon, who had shared a flat with him in Cape Town years before, was now in his old cell. Breyten immediately sent him a welcoming note, and a correspondence began in which both hurled caution to the winds, reminiscing and naming names with great abandon. Schoon, who was due to be released in September, had been in jail for twelve years on charges of sabotage. He made no bones about his member-ship in the SACP, and Breytenbach confessed himself substantially in sympathy with the party too. "I agree with you that [Oliver] Tambo's security would have been better if he was a member of the C.P.—though one of the main reasons for the work in which I was involved was precisely the unsafety (and penetration) of the S.A.C.P.!!" he wrote to Schoon.

> My complaints are that the C.P. isn't revolutionary enough. . . . also, paradoxically, that there is something of a camouflaged dogmatism and I believe an unclear or uncertain grasp of the nature and potential of the A.N.C. (which in my opinion is at present neither a liberation front nor a party but so to speak the C.P. under another name) and that this led to the alienation of *certain usable elements* from the A.N.C. In the background, naturally, lies the ideological problematic [*sic*] of "Black Consciousness," one can almost say of "nationalism" (the old P.A.C. problem) and along with it the parallel problem of the role which black and white can and must play in the liberation strug-gle. . . . I would like to see the C.P. more strongly socialistic, more self-assured and with more confidence in the bright weapon of Marx-ism and the application of Leninist principles—and thus in a position to articulate a true liberation front (which will also include whites, *not just as individuals*—without being a front "from the bourgeoisie to the workers") from a leading position. [Italics added.]

The innate elitism and indeed racism of the circles in which Brey-tenbach and Schoon operated is apparent.

The police were presumably less entertained to find themselves dubbed "the shit" or "the Grayshit." Breytenbach's letters did not spare the feelings of his unknown readers. The Afrikaner establishment was "the Oxwagonshit," South Africa was "this country of assholes." Although he himself had warned against underestimating the security police, he was unduly contemptuous of their intelligence. "Grayshit\cannot decide whether I work for a so-called Death and Special Operations division of the CIA or for the KGB," he wrote to André Brink. No wonder that in the years to come the minister of justice would bluntly turn down appeals for his early release from organizations like PEN.

Meanwhile he continued blithely to assure his correspondents that Groenewald, though young and inexperienced, had his heart in the right place, and could be trusted. André Brink, himself a well-known Afrikaans poet and novelist, who had published an enthusiastic study of Breytenbach's writing some years back, responded loyally to his old friend's request for money for his escape attempt. But Brink soon came to see that something was terribly wrong. So did Yolande. When she came to South Africa that October to visit Breytenbach, Groenewald went to see her, though he had not been supposed to make direct contact. "Don't use the messenger too much," she wrote to Breytenbach. "You must remember that if he is trustworthy, he is risking a great deal, and if he isn't—it speaks for itself." Brink sent warning in the shape of an allegory recounting the adventures of a young pumpkin (Breytenbach) who makes the mistake of trusting a perfidious cantaloupe (Groenewald). And Breyten caught on quickly enough to respond with a pumpkin parable of his own. But it was too late. The police could read between the lines too. They realized that Groenewald's bolt was shot. It was time to move in. Probably they felt confident that they had enough evidence to nail Breytenbach for good. Toward the end of October they came into his cell and formally notified him that the game was up, and that the attorney-general was pressing seventeen fresh charges against him, including one under the Terrorism Act of 1967. The functioning of the gallows in the chamber through which he had recently plotted to escape began to take on a terrible personal significance.

It took eight months for the police to wrap up their inquiries and for the prosecution to prepare its case. Breytenbach could do no more than wait. Advocates J. C. Kriegler, S.C. (State's Counsel), and E. A. Wentzel, appointed to act for him, set to work to sort out the obvious contradictions in Groenewald's allegations.

When the case finally came to court in June 1977 a great deal had changed. The uprisings in Soweto and other black townships had shaken the apartheid state to its roots. South African vanity had taken a blow, too, from the realization that the United States secretary of the treasury to a great extent controls the price of gold. A fresh invasion of Angola, foreshadowed by a massive build-up of troops in Namibia earlier that year, had evidently been a bluff, or was written off because of international pressures. The 1976 show trial of the "SASO nine," notable for Steve Biko's eloquent testimony on behalf of the accused, emphasized the vitality of the Black Consciousness movement. The defendants, one commentator observes, "took every opportunity to symbolize their defiance of the state by singing freedom songs and raising clenched fists in the courtroom. Thus, instead of contributing to the suppression of Black Consciousness ideology, the trial, by giving the accused a continuous public platform through the press, merely disseminated that ideology even more widely." The "SASO nine" were convicted in December 1976, and sentenced to lengthy terms on Robben Island. But Biko, already a national figure, increasingly gained international status and reputation as a spokesman for black South Africa. He was talked of as a future prime minister.

Early in the decade some Afrikaner Nationalists had actually hailed Black Consciousness as a parallel to their own apartheid ideology. "To a large extent it is the product of disillusionment over the nice-sounding phrases and ideas and programs preached in the postwar years by the followers of . . . the liberal school of thought," declared *Die Burger*. Biko now spelled out what Black Consciousness meant for them. "The claim by Whites of monopoly on comfort and security has always been so exclusive that Blacks see Whites as the major obstacle in their progress towards peace, prosperity and a sane society. Through its association with all these negative aspects, whiteness has thus been soiled beyond recognition. At best therefore Blacks see whiteness as a concept that warrants being despised, hated, destroyed and replaced by an aspiration with more human content in it. At worst Blacks envy White society for the comfort it has usurped and at the center of this envy is the wish—nay, the secret determination—in the innermost minds of most Blacks who think like this, to kick Whites off those comfortable garden chairs that one sees as he rides in a bus, out of town, and to claim them for themselves." By mid-1977 the torque exerted by an altered global orthodoxy had begun to make itself felt even in Pretoria. Breytenbach's stance gradually became more comprehensible, if only to a handful of the ideologically nimble. Perhaps he had meant what he said when he told the court that everything he had done was motivated by love of his country, that for him it was a matter of "the survival of our people."

As it happened, too, Judge Cillié was busy chairing a commission into the causes and effects of the 1976 Soweto uprising, and Breytenbach's case was heard by the acting judge-president of the Transvaal, W. G. Boshoff. As the trial went on, Boshoff's fatherly sympathy for the accused and distaste for Groenewald's role as provocateur became more and more apparent. It was necessary, the judge observed, to approach Groenewald's evidence with caution. It had not been proven that Okhela existed as an organization inside the Republic of South Africa; it had simply been a device on Breytenbach's part to get Groenewald to smuggle out poems, sketches and letters in secrecy. Breytenbach's letters to Schoon had dealt with political matters, but even here there was nothing to indicate that Okhela existed as an active organization. Groenewald had enticed Breytenbach to write as many letters as possible to people who might have been involved in Okhela, and this had in fact enabled the police to establish that all his contacts had rejected the organization. The main charge and the first two alternative charges were thus found not proven. So far as alternative charges three through seventeen were concerned, the evidence showed that the letters and documents in question had indeed been smuggled contrary to prison regulations. Breytenbach was accordingly found guilty on these charges, and sentenced to a fine of R50, or three months' imprisonment. "I am so grateful," he said, before being returned to his cell to serve out the remaining seven years of his original sentence. Not long afterward, he was allowed out of solitary confinement to mix with other prisoners, and subsequently transferred from Pretoria Central to the Pollsmoor prison near Cape Town.

"To talk about poets is an uncomfortable task; poets are there to be quoted, not to be talked about," wrote Hannah Arendt, who had undertaken to try to explain how it happened that Bertolt Brecht came to end his career writing fifth-rate poems in praise of Joseph Stalin. But Brecht, the master of survival, with his Swiss bank account, Austrian passport, and Stalin Peace Prize, saw that reality is a deadly business, and that the first duty of the "bearer of knowledge" is to take care of himself. Breytenbach, by contrast, was drawn to disaster as though by a magnet. Of him it may be said that his courage was great, but not great enough. "I was misled and made misuse of, but my own illusions must take the blame," he said. And his illusions were not all innocent: primary among them was the classic self-deception of the revolutionary. "Often I feel that our people are still too 'moralistic' in attitude, too 'English,' " he wrote Marius Schoon. Ruthlessness exacts its own price. In the end it is a species of self-indulgence, for which Breytenbach has paid dearly. He may well survive prison reasonably whole of mind:

there is a hybrid toughness to the Afrikaner that can stand great punishment. It remains for him to tell his side of the story. The fact that no one will ever entirely be able to believe him is cruelly apposite.

2

CULTURES IN COLLISION

It's been mud walls against Hottentots so far,
Now we boast stone against all others too,
Thus we give fright as well to the European
As to the Asian, American, and wild African.

LINES RECITED AT THE LAYING OF THE FIRST STONE
OF CAPE TOWN CASTLE, 2 JANUARY 1666

SOUTH AFRICA'S "MAIN PROBLEM," a liberal historian asserts, "is still what it has always been: the relations between the different groups that live in the country." Looked at superficially, this seems undeniably true. Closer examination shows it to be mere wishful thinking, the sort of hopeful piety which stands between the whites and a solution to the predicament in which they find themselves trapped. For they themselves are the main problem.

Certainly it is valid to say, as do the editors of the *Oxford History of South Africa*, that "modern apotheosis of liberal history," that "the central theme of South African history is interaction between peoples of diverse origins, languages, technologies, ideologies, and social systems, meeting on South African soil." Even before the arrival of Europeans and Asians in southern Africa, there were at least two distinct sets of inhabitants sharing the country—three if the Khoikhoi ("Hottentots") and San ("Bushmen") are regarded as separate peoples, and not as branches of one Khoisan race. There were also numerous tribal and clan distinctions, both among the Khoisan and among the Sutu-nguni ("Bantu") peoples,* which made for cattle-raids, conflict, even outright warfare. Interaction there was aplenty, both fighting and trading. Preconquest South Africa, was not a never-never land of primeval stasis, and contact

---

* In using the term "Sutu-nguni" instead of "Bantu" I follow the lead of Jordan Ngubane in his *An African Explains Apartheid* (New York: Praeger, 1963), p. 76.

with whites further stimulated change in both the political and economic structures of African societies. These developments were aborted when racist ideology relegated blacks to political limbo and economic helotry.

The whites did not come on the scene as a tribe among other tribes. They represented a fundamentally different order of things, a world system which gave them access to power, resources and information which those they colonized could not hope to rival. Frontier heroics notwithstanding, the victory of the newcomers was a foregone conclusion. This had nothing to do with race, but at the time it seemed as though it did to almost everybody.

Within half a century of their arrival, a few hundred Europeans at the Cape were lording it over once-powerful Khoi tribes numbering tens of thousands, and the disintegration of Khoi society was far advanced. When the great smallpox epidemic of 1713 wiped out the majority of them, Richard Elphick notes, the Khoikhoi of the Western Cape had not only ceased to constitute an obstacle to the advance of white settlement, but had been incorporated into the labor force. Far from seeking their destruction, the colonists regretted their virtual disappearance as a "very great inconvenience" (*zeer groot ongemak*).

Experience with the Khoikhoi encouraged white Afrikaners— some of them were already calling themselves that by the first decade of the eighteenth century—to look down on the aborigines. The next stage in the evolution of white racism involved the San, or "Bushmen," who could not, for the most part, be integrated into the colonial economy except as child slaves. San depredations against livestock outraged the highly developed European sense of property, while their use of arrows tipped with mysterious and deadly poisons inspired both fear and hatred. Few stopped to think that white hunters and stock farmers were depriving the San of the game on which they depended, and that they were simply defending their right to territory which they had long inhabited. "The race is to be entirely subdued or destroyed," read the instructions of the colonial governor, Baron Joachim van Plettenberg, to Field-Commandant Gottfried Opperman in 1774. Opperman did his brutal best, as did those who came after him. It was on genocidal expeditions such as these that the commando system characteristic of Boer military power was developed—and Boer racial attitudes along with it.

The third stage brought the Afrikaners face to face with the Sutu-nguni tribes, the most formidable foes they had yet had to confront. But the Boers had the technological edge, and behind them lay the might of the British empire, which after 1806 never ceased to regard them as its subjects, their recalcitrance notwithstanding.

Thus when the commandos of the bankrupt Transvaal Republic and their Swazi allies failed to defeat the Pedi chief Sekhukhune in the 1870s, and it seemed likely that the still intact Zulu armies of Cetshwayo might seize the opportunity of attacking, it was British regulars who broke the power of Pedi and Zulu alike. One might argue that the Boer republics (which could probably have fielded at least 20,000 men at that point) would ultimately have been able to cope with both Sekhukhune and Cetshwayo if they had come to constitute a real threat to survival. But this was never put to the test, and in consequence of its weakness the Transvaal found itself annexed, albeit temporarily, to Britain's expanding African holdings. With the "imperial factor" serving as catalyst, the mix of fear, contempt and hatred was now complete. The next century would merely serve to confirm it.

But though Afrikaner racism, as the core of white racism in South Africa, is the element which has in the final analysis made it impossible to achieve a South African consensus, it is also true that Afrikaners see themselves as persecuted and misunderstood victims of forces beyond their control, hemmed in throughout their history by implacable enemies (blacks, British, Communists).

The common assumption is that Afrikaners are Dutch South Africans, but this is inaccurate. Certainly the original Cape settlement was founded, in 1652, as an outpost and provisioning station of the Dutch East India Company. The company's charter stipulated that as few foreigners as possible were to be recruited into its service; nonetheless "in 1691 one-third of its army and civil service were foreigners, of whom half were German, while in 1778 two thirds were foreign, almost all German." The distinction between Dutch and German was far less sharply drawn. "You are to employ Dutch and Germans only, that we may be safe from the malice of traitorous strangers," Commissioner Ryklof van Goens instructed Van Riebeeck in 1657. The minutes of the Cape Court of Justice for December 1671 make telling reference to "our, or other German people" (onse, ofte andere Duytse natien).

Germans frequently held top positions in the early colonial hierarchy. The second commander of the Cape station was a Dresdener, Zacharias Wagenaar (Wagner); the ancestry of the Breytenbachs may go back to the German commander of the garrison in the 1670s, Conrad von Brietenbach. Throughout the 1700s the majority of the immigrants entering the colony were German, not Hollanders, and by the year 1800, according to one writer, the nationalities making up the Afrikaner people can be estimated as being 45 percent German, 27 percent French, 22 percent Dutch, and 6 percent others.

When, a few years after the founding of the Cape station, it was decided by the company's directorate, known as the *Here XVII*, or Lords Seventeen, to establish a population of free colonists at the Cape—free, that is, in the sense of not being company employees —Dutch or German Protestants were those specified. But it was not always easy to find suitable candidates willing to emigrate to the remote tip of Africa. In 1687, following the revocation two years previously of the Edict of Nantes, which had provided religious toleration in France, the Lords Seventeen notified Commander Simon van der Stel that they were sending him "among other freemen, some French and Piedmontaise fugitives, all of the reformed religion." When these arrived, they expanded the smaller settler population substantially, contributing both to its skills and to the psychology of persecution. Names of Huguenot origin—de Villiers, du Toit, du Plessis, Marais, Roux, Joubert—are still among the commonest Afrikaans surnames. Others have been Afrikanerized almost out of recognition: thus Mesnard became Minnaar; Retif, Retief; La Grange, Lagransie; Villon or Villion, Viljoen; Therond, Theron; and Bouchaud, Boshoff. The Huguenots came in search of the civil rights and liberty of conscience and worship which they were denied in France. It is ironic, but nothing exceptional in human history, that they and their descendants were to engage so extensively in restricting the liberties of others. In any event, they came to stay, regarding the Cape as a permanent refuge.

These transplanted fragments of European society took root amazingly quickly. "By the end of the seventeenth century the crystallization of a distinction between 'Afrikaners,' burghers who regarded the Cape as a permanent home, and 'Europeans,' largely Company servants who were only temporary residents, was already under way," says M. F. Katzen. And a century or so later, a traveler noted of the Cape burgher, "He is proud of the name Afrikander; Citizen of the Cape seems to him a great title." It was around this time that the first stirrings of republican activity were heard from the country districts of Swellendam and Graaff-Reinet. In 1795, even as a British fleet under Admiral Sir George Elphinstone moved in to take possession of the colony, a gathering of adventurers and rustic Jacobins constituted themselves into a "National Assembly" at Swellendam, articulating *inter alia* the following resolve:

> Bushmen, Bushwomen and Hottentots captured by commandos in the past and future shall henceforth remain from generation to generation the property of the burghers to whose lot they fall, and all Hottentots who run away shall be returned to their owners to be punished according to their deserts.

Transplanted to South Africa, the dreams of the French revolutionaries had undergone a sea change indeed: the Cape Jacobins saw the right to enslave their fellows as an important element in their own liberty. Bolshevism, a century and a quarter later, would suffer almost equally odd transformations here.

Afrikanerdom was molded in intimate coexistence with Khoikhoi, with Asian and African slaves, and with folk of mixed blood who separately evolved into the so-called Cape Coloured, the brown Afrikaners whose rejection and subordination was the paradigm of apartheid. This was true from the earliest period of its existence. But there are also important prenatal influences, so to speak, to be taken into account.

The Europeans who came to the Cape were men who had been forged in a world at war. Holland herself had been at war for longer than anyone living could remember, since the 1560s. Dutch records refer unambiguously to "our public enemies, the Spaniards and Portuguese."* Between 1618 and 1648 Germany and much of Central Europe were ravaged by the mercenary armies of the Thirty Years' War, "murdering and being murdered, slaying and being slain, torturing and being tortured, hunting and being hunted." Year after year, decade after decade, hordes of hired killers fattened on a peasantry grown ever more destitute and helpless. "The sword to till the land, and plunder for their harvest, such was the burden of their outspoken songs, and they practiced what they sang," says C. V. Wedgewood of the mercenaries.

Out of the long years of struggle came "a new generation of soldiers and statesmen. War-bred, they carried the mark of their training in a caution, cynicism and contempt for spiritual ideals foreign to their fathers." Perhaps most terrible of all, in the end no one was even sure what the war was really about. "Morally subversive, economically destructive, socially degrading, confused in its causes, devious in its course, futile in its result, it is the outstanding example in European history of meaningless conflict," Wedgewood concludes. Not even the world wars of the twentieth century took a proportionate toll of Europe. The twenty-one million inhabitants of the German Empire in 1618 had been reduced to thirteen and a half million by 1648. Across the Channel in England these were years of strife too, of the Puritan Revolution and Civil War, culminating in the beheading of King Charles I in January 1649.

Against this backdrop of chaos and violence, the Netherlands

---

* Portugal was part of Philip II's Spanish empire between 1580 and 1640; after regaining her independence, she lapsed into the role of an ally of England, with whom the Dutch found themselves at war in the very year of the founding of the Cape station.

achieved not only stability but power and great wealth. The revolt of the United Provinces of Guelderland, Holland, Sealand, Utrecht, Friesland, Overyssel, and Groningen against Philip II's Spanish Empire in 1581 was the original bourgeois revolution: England's followed only in the next century. "Holland, the first country to develop the colonial system to the full, had attained the climax of its commercial greatness as early as the year 1648," Karl Marx noted in *Capital*. Marx cited the historian Gustav von Gülich to the effect that the Dutch Republic was then "in almost exclusive possession of the East India trade and the commerce between the south-east and the north-west of Europe. Its fisheries, its mercantile marine, and its manufactures, surpassed those of any other country. The total capital of the republic probably exceeded that of all the rest of Europe put together." And he added, "Gülich forgets to add that by 1648 the common folk of Holland were more overworked, more impoverished, and more brutally oppressed than those of all the rest of Europe put together."

Nearly half the shipping tonnage of Europe was Dutch, and any contemporary "*Fortune* 500" list of top corporations would have led off with the name of the Generale Vereenighde Nederlantsche Geoctroyeerde Oostindische Compagnie, the General United Netherlands Chartered East India Company (VOC for short). The company was virtually a sovereign state, with powers that make those of today's transnational corporations seem modest. It levied taxes, made treaties, waged war, issued letters of marque authorizing freebooting against its enemies, inflicted punishment up to and including capital punishment, fixed the prices of commodities, appointed governing officials, and bestowed military and naval ranks on its employees. Eventually it even came to issue its own currency. It was the largest and most profitable trading company in the contemporary world, and for two centuries paid an annual dividend averaging 18 percent to its happy stockholders.

In addition to the massive concentration of finance capital in the Netherlands, there was also the explosive psychic capital of the Reformed Religion. "Calvinism undoubtedly ranked among the principal cultural forces in the North," says Pieter Geyl. "With its conception of a 'chosen people,' of the Netherlands as a second Israel, whose history embodied the profoundest sense of the grace of God, it gave style to a larger body of opinion than that of its professed adherents." This exclusivist psychology Afrikanerdom would inherit in full measure and cultivate to the point of obsession.

When Jan van Riebeeck came out to the Cape with his little expedition in 1652 to found a way station for the ships of the VOC, his men were very far from being the first Europeans the indigenes had encountered. Conventional wisdom to the contrary, the pattern of European relations with the Khoikhoi had long been established —and more, it might be argued, by Portuguese and English seafarers than by Dutch.

Van Riebeeck met a race who had already taken the measure of the sea peoples, who must have seemed as much of a piece to the Khoikhoi: in either case, arrogant, dangerous, and for the most part thievish. For all Van Riebeeck's tact and diplomacy, learned in his dealings with the punctilious authorities of Nagasaki, Taiwan, and Tonkin, he would be unable to halt or reverse the process of polarization which, as we shall see, had begun almost on first contact a century and a half before.

Rounding the tip of Africa in 1488, the Portuguese mariner Bartholomeu Dias saw herdsmen with numerous cattle near a bay he named Angra dos Vaqueiros; whether or not contact was made is uncertain: one later account says that he killed one of them with a crossbow. In 1497, another Portuguese seaman, Vasco da Gama, made landfall in the vicinity of what is now Saint Helena Bay, about a hundred and twenty miles north of the Cape of Good Hope, to obtain water, firewood and meat. On shore Da Gama's men saw "two savages who appeared to be gathering herbs and honey at the foot of a hill, as each had a firebrand with him. Surrounding them quietly and stealthily, one was captured, who appeared greatly terrified on being made prisoner by such strange beings as Europeans must have been to him."

Da Gama treated his South African prisoner well enough, however, and after wining and dining him, sent him off with a few trinkets. Though it must have been an experience not unlike being taken prisoner on a flying saucer, the man soon returned with about fifteen or twenty of his clanspeople. From the fact that they carried assegais—spears of fire-hardened wood—Theal concludes that they were "Hottentots of the beachranger class" rather than Bushmen, but the distinction may well be academic. "They were small in stature, ill favoured in countenance and darkish in colour," he says. "Their dress was a kaross of skin. When speaking they used so many gestures that they appeared to be rolling or staggering about. Their food consisted of wild roots, seals, whales that washed up on the coast, seabirds, and every kind of land animal or bird that they could capture." Initially relations between the sailors and the beachcombers were friendly, but after a few days trouble broke out, evidently caused by a soldier described as "the most arrant braggart of his exploits and his bravery in the whole fleet." In the ensuing skirmish, some sailors were slightly wounded, as apparently was Da

Gama himself. For their part the Portuguese came away with the opinion that they had "caused some execution" among the shore people with their crossbows.

Some weeks later, Da Gama made another landing, this time on the southeast coast (having rounded the Cape without touching there). At what is now Mossel Bay—it was Dias' Angra dos Vaqueiros—he encountered both men and women, some riding oxen. Going ashore, he distributed the customary baubles and bartered for a few sheep. "The Portuguese listened with pleasure to the tunes which these Hottentots played with reeds, their usual way of entertaining strangers. Treachery, however, was suspected, and quarrels arose, so after a while Da Gama moved from his first anchorage to another to get away from the wild people, but they followed him along the shore, upon which he fired at them to frighten them, when they fled inland." Before departing from this place, Da Gama caused a pillar to be set up bearing a cross and the arms of Portugal. Exhibiting a remarkable degree of understanding, the Khoikhoi pulled it down even before he had sailed away.

Idealized in Camões' saga *The Lusiad* as the discoverer of the sea route to India, Da Gama was not, Theal observes, a lovable man. Returning from his pioneering expedition in 1498, he wantonly bombarded the Somali city of Mogadishu. A few years later on another voyage he terrorized Arab and Egyptian shipping in the Indian Ocean, and to compel the banishing of Moslems from the city of Calicut on the southwest coast of India, seized thirty-two harmless fishermen and hanged them from his masts. The next day he had their heads, hands and feet cut off and sent to shore with a contemptuous letter addressed to the local ruler, and concluded by firing a cannonade that caused much loss of life.

In 1503 Antonio de Saldanha sailed into what is now Table Bay, and climbed Table Mountain. He, too, encountered Khoikhoi; he, too, had a skirmish with them. The bay was to be known as the Agoada de Saldanha, Saldanha's watering place, for the next century or so. By involuntary association, the inhabitants came to be known as Saldanhars, or Saldanians, to the Dutch and English, who at this stage got most of their information about Africa south of the Sahara from Iberian sources. Later the name Saldanha Bay would, however, become attached to another bay somewhat to the north, apparently in connection with the tribe of "proper Saldanhars" who were found living there, a people the Hollanders thought different, "much bolder and livelier men than the *Strandlopers*," or beachwalkers, whom they first encountered.

Late in the year 1509, Dom Francisco de Almeida, the retiring Portuguese viceroy of India, sailed from Cochin on the Malabar coast with a small squadron homeward bound. After a stopover at Mozambique, he doubled the Cape in February 1510 and put into Table Bay for water. Khoikhoi were met with on the beach, and cattle were bartered for some bits of calico and iron. A party of twelve or thirteen Portuguese accompanied the South Africans back to their kraal, or village, a few miles away (evidently in the vicinity of the present Cape Town suburb of Mowbray). There was the inevitable misunderstanding. It is significant that some of their own officers thought that the sailors were to blame. Perhaps in reflection of their own uncertain consciences, the Portuguese were always quick to suspect treachery. They had, moreover, come to think themselves invincible against Asians and Africans, a belief which "contributed greatly to their daring, while it also made them arrogant in their dealings with those they came in contact with, so that strife was often needlessly provoked." The Khoikhoi were not to be slighted or bullied with impunity, and blows were struck. De Almeida, said to have been a humane man by comparison with some of his contemporaries, was persuaded against his will that it was necessary to teach these savages a lesson. Accordingly, before dawn on the morning of March 1, 1510, he landed with a hundred and fifty men to administer it.

In this first battle between Europeans and Africans on South African soil, the aliens came off much the worse. Armed mainly with swords and lances, though a few of them probably had crossbows, the Portuguese marched to the Khoikhoi kraal and took possession of the cattle and seized the children they found there as hostages. They came under attack by about a hundred and seventy natives, who flung their assegais from behind oxen, which they controlled by whistling. ("The whistle was full of discord, as if five men had whistled together, and not by us to be counterfeited," wrote a seventeenth-century English visitor of this unique ability.) The Portuguese retreated to the beach, but by the time their boats were able to take them off, sixty-five had died, among them De Almeida himself and eleven others of high rank. It was a mighty victory for the little tribe—the greatest, as it happened, that Khoikhoi were ever to achieve over whites.

Undoubtedly the epic battle with the Portuguese passed into their oral tradition, was told around campfires in the years to come, and gradually became encrusted in the legendary past. "Small societies have a short time depth, all history being squeezed into ten or twelve generations," says Monica Wilson. A hundred years later the fight with De Almeida's men probably assumed the character of saga. But it would be a century and a half before a Brunswicker, George Frederick Wreede, made the first systematic study of Khoikhoi language, and more centuries before Europeans gained any conception of the beliefs of what was, by then, a moribund culture. If in Khoikhoi tradition the people from the sea went down as enemies against whom ancestral heroes had fought and triumphed, the whites did not know it. But the Portuguese needed no ethnographic confirmation. Henceforth, though the brother of one of the captains who had perished with De Almeida stopped there briefly in 1512 to set up a cross on the mound where the bodies were buried, they avoided this "Cabo de Boa Esperança."

The next ships to stop at the Cape appear to have been English. In 1580 Francis Drake passed by, noting it to be "a most stately thing, and the fairest cape we saw in the whole circumference of the earth." In 1591 three ships out of Plymouth under the command of Admiral George Raymond put in to gather shellfish and shoot wild fowl. "One day some hunters caught a Hottentot, whom they treated kindly, making him many presents and endeavouring to show him by signs that they were in want of cattle," Theal says. Eight days later the man returned with thirty or forty of his people, bringing oxen and sheep. The English paid two knives apiece for an ox, one knife for a sheep. They do not appear to have had any trouble, but in 1598 thirteen men off the Dutch vessel *Leeuw* were set upon while attempting to barter Khoikhoi cattle in Table Valley, and killed. Much evidently depended on the stance of the aliens, and it is a fact that the English generally did much better than the Dutch. Only three years later, in 1601, a fleet under Sir James Lancaster bought no fewer than 1,000 sheep and 42 cattle; in this case the admiral negotiated personally, taking care to keep his men away from the natives, whom he addressed "in Cattels Language (which was never changed at the confusion of Babell) which was *Moath* for Oxen and Kine, and *Baa* for Sheepe."

But the bargains to be obtained at the Cape were so great that the Lords Seventeen soon established it as policy that outward-bound VOC fleets should always put in to Table Bay for supplies. In the early stages of contact the Khoikhoi hunger for iron, Elphick observes, "allowed whole fleets to be fed in return for miscellaneous junk readily available on any ship." Thus in 1608 Cornelis Matelief bartered thirty-four oxen, five calves, and a hundred and seventy-three sheep from the Khoikhoi for almost worthless scrap iron. The same year the crews of the English East India Company's ships *Ascension* and *Union*, who spent about two months at the Cape and built a temporary fort there, bought livestock at the rate of a yard of iron hoop from their empty water casks for an ox and half a yard for a sheep.

Doubtless the Europeans congratulated themselves on the

hard-headedness of their trading, and for the most part thought the natives fools to sell their cattle for such trash. Their opinion of the Khoikhoi was not high. Sir Edward Michelbourne, a visitor in 1605, declared them "the most savage and beastly people as ever I thinke God created." The Reverend Edward Terry, who was there ten years later on his way to the court of the Great Moghul in India as chaplain to the English ambassador, thought them "beasts in the skins of men, rather than men in the skins of beasts." Khoikhoi speech, he said, "seemed to us inarticulate noise, rather than language, like the clucking of hens, or gabling of turkeys." But it was their eating habits that really repelled Terry: "they would eat any refuse thing, as rotten and mouldy biskets, which we have given them, fit indeed for nothing but to be cast away; yea, they will eat that which a ravenous dog in England will refuse." When the Europeans slaughtered the cattle they had purchased, the Khoikhoi draped the guts around their necks to carry them off, "and when they were hungry, they would sit down upon some hillock, first shaking out some of that filthy pudding out of the guts they wore about their necks, then bowing and bringing their mouths to their hands, almost as low as their knees, like hungry dogs would gnaw and eat the raw guts; when you may conceive their mouths full of sweet green sauce."

Though seventeenth-century Englishmen were not a notably squeamish breed, this was certainly cultural difference with a vengeance, and Terry's words still resound with the revulsion he felt. Europeans always regarded the Khoikhoi custom of wearing innards around their necks with bemused horror; evidently it was connected with rites of passage and the ritual slaughter of animals which were their chief source of wealth and prestige. And as one commentator observes, the Khoikhoi "in regarding the entrails of a freshly-killed grass-eating animal as a nutritious delicacy, were no different from the giant species of lions that prowled the Cape Peninsula." That "sweet green sauce" was full of nutrients, especially Vitamin C, that the scurvy-plagued seafarers so badly needed, the lack of which brought them thither, in Terry's own apt phrase, "with very crazy bodies."

Communication was on the most rudimentary level, usually by making signs, or by onomatopoeia ("there are good store of cattle . . . called by the barbarous inhabitants, Boos; and sheep, which they call Baas," wrote Terry ingenuously). "The sharpest wit among us could not learn one word of their language," wrote Captain John Middleton. "Their speech is wholly uttered through the throat, and they cloke with their tongues." Not only the English and Dutch found the click speech of the Khoikhoi impossibly difficult. "When they speak they fart with their tongues in their mouths, yet, although their speech is without separation of word from word, they understand each other readily," observed Jean-Baptiste Tavernier, a Frenchman who was at the Cape in 1649 (and following the general pattern judged the indigenes "horrible and beastly").

The term "Hottentot" itself has frequently been assumed to be a derogatory reference to Khoikhoi click-speech, and postulated to derive from a Dutch word meaning "stutterer" or "stammerer": in fact, it seems probable that it was the other way around. Its earliest recorded appearance was in 1620, when another French voyager, Augustin de Beaulieu, who was at the Cape almost a month, noted of the people there that "They speak from the throat, and in speaking, appear to be sobbing and sighing. Their usual greeting in meeting us is to dance and sing, and the beginning, middle and end of their song is 'Hautitou.'" A similar observation was made three years later by Jón Ólaffson, an Icelander sailing on board a Danish ship. "Their dance was after this fashion—on uttering the word 'Hottentot!' they snapped two of their fingers and clicked with their tongue and feet, all in time," he wrote. One interpretation, based on Namaqua usage, was that the word—actually a phrase—meant "I will have you," with the implication "I will get the better of you," the dances being competitive. The natives' own name for themselves was Khoikhoi or Kwekwena, both signifying "men of men," but by mid-seventeenth century, it seems, Europeans had on the strength of this frequently heard refrain from their dances begun to call them "Hottentots."

In return they called the whites "Honquecqua," meaning "smooth-haired people," or perhaps simply "hairy people," "bearded ones." Beguilingly enough the singular form is "onkey." The word still survives in Nama (a Khoikhoi language spoken by perhaps 50,000 people in Namibia) in the shape of /hon-khoib, used to signify "master" or "work-boss," while in recent times the descendants of the Griquas are known to have sometimes called whites "smooth-hairs" or "needlenoses."

The need to communicate grew from year to year. There was increasing difficulty in obtaining cattle for ships on their way to the Indies, which was blamed on "pirates," who landed to steal livestock and shot the Khoikhoi herders. Moreover, the Europeans were particularly interested in questioning the natives about gold and precious stones rumored to exist in the African hinterland. As the Dutch would in years to come, the English decided that it would be far better if the natives could be taught their language (it seemed impossible to master Khoikhoi click-speech, though children brought up at the Cape later acquired it easily enough). The best way to achieve this seemed to be to bring some of them back to

England, where they would be able to learn English by what later generations of language instructors would call "the direct method."

Accordingly, in May 1613 Captain Gabriel Towerson, master of the English East India Company's ship the *Hector*, which was returning from the Indies laden with cargo, took aboard a Khoikhoi captain named Xhoré or Cory, along with an unnamed companion. They may have been enticed on board and made drunk, or simply kidnapped by force. In any case, says the Reverend Terry,

> being thus brought away, very much against both their minds, one of them (merely out of extreme sullenness, though he was very well used) died shortly after they put to sea; the other, who call'd himself Cooree, (whom I mentioned before) lived, and was brought to London, and there kept, for the space of six months, in Sir Thomas Smith's house, (then governor of the East-India company) where he had good diet, good cloaths, good lodging, with all other fitting accommodations. Now one would think that this wretch might have conceived his present, compared with his former condition, an Heaven upon Earth; but he did not so, though he had to his good entertainment made for him a chain of bright brass, an armour, breast, back, and head-piece, with a buckler, all of brass, his beloved metal; yet all this contented him not, for never any seemed to be more weary of ill usage, than he was of courtesies; none ever more desirous to return home to his country, than he; for when he had learned a little of our language, he would daily lie upon the ground, and cry very often thus in broken English, "Coree home go, Souldania go, home go;" and not long after, when he had his desire, and was returned home, he had no sooner set footing on his own shore, but presently he threw away his cloaths, his linen, with all other covering, and got his sheeps skins upon his back, guts about his neck, and such a perfum'd cap, as before we named, upon his head; by whom that proverb mentioned, 2 Pet. 2, v. 22, was literally fulfill'd, *Canis ad vomitum;* "the dog is return'd to his vomit, and the swine to his wallowing in the mire."

It was in June 1614, after some four months at sea, that the English redeposited Xhoré at the Cape. He obtained a few cattle for them to buy, presented the captain of the ship which had carried him with a young steer, and the next day "departed from us, carrying with him his copper armour and javelin, with all things belonging to him, promising to come againe to us the third day after; but he never came againe." This Khoikhoi chieftain was no fool. Terry remarks that "it had been well if he had not seen England; for as he discovered nothing to us, so certainly when he came home, he told his country-men (having doubtless observed so much here) that brass was but a base and cheap commodity in England; and happily we had so well stored them with that metal before, that we had never after such a free exchange of our brass and iron for their cattle." The English almost immediately noticed a rise in the prices of cattle and sheep. In his journal the purser of the *Hector* wrote sourly, "The Saldanians brought us down some few cattle, which formerly we bought for brass, but now they altogether desired copper, of which mettle we supposed that Quore, who returned with us, had given them knowledge of; which was all the kindness he requited us with for being got ashore with his tinckerlie treasure." Here we have the archetypal cry of the exploiter: they don't appreciate what we've done for them!

Few imaginable forms of colonization could be more destructive of amity than the dumping of condemned criminals in newly discovered lands, yet the English did this not only in America and Australia, but also in South Africa. About a year after Xhoré's return home, a group of convicts reprieved from the Tyburn gallows for the purpose were landed at the Cape. They acknowledged the leadership of a picaresque rogue who called himself Captain Cross,

> formerly a yeoman of the guard unto King James, but having had his hand in blood twice or thrice, by men slain by him in several duels, and now being condemned to die with the rest, upon very great suit made for him he was hither banished with them; whither the justice of almighty God was dispatched after him, as it were in a whirlwind, and followed him close at the very heels, and overtook him, and left him not 'till he had paid dear for that blood he had formerly spilt.

Xhoré and his people met the ships bringing the convicts and traded cattle for brass, copper, pots, pans, and knives. The trip to England had evidently prompted him to set up a European-style "town," of about a hundred habitations. Most of the tribe could repeat "Sir Tho: Smithe English Shipps," it was reported, and some wanted to go to England too, "seeing Corey had sped so well, and returned so rich with his copper suit, which he yet keepeth in his house very charily. Corey also determined to return and to carry one of his sonnes when our ships are thence bound homewards." As it chanced, another English ship, the *Merchant's Hope*, entered the bay before the fleet sailed on to India, and remained there after the rest had departed while her men recuperated from the inevitable scurvy. On board was Edward Dodsworth, formerly of the *Hector*, and he left an account of what happened.

Trouble soon broke out between the Khoikhoi and the "Newgate men," of whom there were about eight or ten. One of the convicts was killed, and two others were injured. Cross asked Dodsworth for guns "with which he doubted not in safety to go and bring down Quore." For his part Xhoré came down to consult with Dodsworth, whom he had known on board the *Hector*, as an old friend, bringing his family with him as a mark of trust. He did not accept responsibility for the attack on the Newgate men, and asked what they were doing there, but "understanding theie were thither sent by Sir Thomas Smith, seemed very glad." He asked that a house be built for him "after the manner of England," and proposed an alliance against the tribes from over the mountains, suggesting in fact that Cross and his men might be given muskets for the purpose.

Departing, Dodsworth thoughtfully left Cross a longboat in which to escape to Robben Island, which proved necessary. Later, according to Terry, in consequence of his "quarrelling with and abusing the natives, and engaging himself far amongst them," Cross was killed by Khoikhoi with "darts thrown, and arrows shot at him . . . making him look like the figure of the man in the almanack, that seems to be wounded in every part; or like that man described by Lucan, *totum pro vulnere corpus*, who was all wound, where blood touched blood."

However, Martin Pring, master of the *New Year's Gift*, which anchored in Table Bay on March 1, 1616, asserted in his logbook that Cross had actually been drowned while trying to get off Robben Island on a makeshift raft. Pring took three of the surviving Newgate men back to England with him. Within a few hours of landing, they stole a purse near Sandwich, in Kent, and were taken before the Lord Chief Justice, who ordered them summarily hanged in execution of their former sentences, since they had never been pardoned but banished on condition of not returning. The remaining convicts at the Cape may have been taken off by a Portuguese ship; their fate is unknown.

Among the Khoikhoi the comings and goings of the strangers had considerable impact; along with iron weapons they purveyed European notions and a Eurocentric view of the world. "I asked Coree who was their God," Terry wrote, "he lifting up his hands answered thus, in his bad English—'England God, great God, Souldania no God.' " Traditionally the Khoikhoi had lived in a magical community governed by the spirits of their ancestors, the hero Heitsi Eibib and Tsuni-//Goam, "the first Khoikhóib from whom all the Khoikhoi tribes took their origin." Now they were confronted by that most destabilizing of all ideas, monotheism. And the one God, it was to be constantly drummed home in the centuries to come, was the deity of the whites.

European ships were now putting in at the Cape in such numbers that more than one nation was giving serious consideration to the establishment of a permanent base there. In June 1620 an English fleet commanded by Andrew Shillinge and Humphrey Fitzherbert found nine Dutch ships at anchor when they arrived in

Table Bay. The Hollanders let it be known that they had plans to establish a settlement the following year, and after they had left, Shillinge and Fitzherbert hoisted the flag of St. George on the hill called Lion's Rump and proclaimed the sovereignty of James I over the whole country. This ceremony was observed by the captain and officers of another Dutch vessel, the *Schiedam*, which had since arrived, but the latter neither raised objections nor troubled to explain to the English that the letters VOC carved on a "post office stone" in the valley, under which dispatches were buried, denoted a prior Dutch claim. Possession, it was clear, would be most parts of the law. The English hopefully presented the Khoikhoi (who must have watched these proceedings with some wonderment) with a small flag, "to preserve and exhibit to visitors, which it was believed they would do most carefully." Quite clearly it was supposed that they would jump at the opportunity of becoming subjects of King James, but as it happened the Khoikhoi were to be spared European overlordship for some decades more.

In August 1627 an unnamed Welshman, who kept a journal in his own tongue, visited Table Bay and noted of the indigenes that "They hate the dutchmen since they hanged on [one] of the blackes called Cary who was in England & upon refusal of fresh victuals they put him to death." Thus perished Xhoré, who was probably the first South African ever to visit Europe.

The Dutch Move In

Shillinge and Fitzherbert's preemptive proclamation had the backing neither of the directorate of the English East India Company nor of the British government, and it came to nothing. The British, Theal points out, were too busy colonizing North America to bother with the Cape. Not long after Xhoré's murder, moreover, they found a new, more satisfactory agent in the shape of Autshumao, the leader of a small band of Strandlopers, or beachrangers, whom they mockingly dubbed "King Harry."

Harry (also known to history as Hadda, Adda, or Haddot) was taken to Bantam, in Java, in 1629 by John Pynn, and brought back to the Cape the following year. Early in the 1630s he got the English to transport his followers and himself to Robben Island, which the Khoikhoi had not been able to reach before. Here he reigned secure in the enjoyment of the great numbers of penguins and seals there for the taking, and ran an entrepôt for both the English and the Dutch. Incoming ships could easily be signaled from the island, and Harry would go down to greet the landing parties coming ashore, ceremoniously clad "in English habitt from head to foote." In his capacity as postmaster and interpreter, he spoke something of several European languages. In 1632 we find him informing some French seafarers that he was "au service de messejieurs Holandois et de messjeurs les Anglois." Toward the end of the decade, most of the seals and penguins on the island had been eaten, and he and his people had themselves transferred back to the mainland by their foreign patrons, and continued their brokerage there.

Neither were the Dutch quick to establish a permanent settlement. They, too, were able to employ Harry's services, and they made enemies among the more powerful peninsular clans. In 1632 twenty-three men off a Dutch ship lost their lives at the Cape in what must have been a serious fray. "The cause of these quarrels is not known with certainty, but at the time it was believed they were brought on by Europeans attempting to rob the Hottentots of cattle," Theal says.

Fifteen years after this, however, in March 1647, the Dutch East Indiaman *Nieuw-Haerlem* went aground in Table Bay with a valuable cargo of pepper, cinnamon, sandalwood, dyes, furniture, porcelain, and linens. Part of her crew found passage to St. Helena on two English ships, but the remainder were obliged to camp on shore in a makeshift fort until the arrival of the return fleet from Batavia in mid-March 1648. Efforts to reship what could be saved of the *Nieuw-Haerlem*'s cargo went on for several weeks. "At the Cape there were now 12 ships and 1,500 people—what activity it must have been after the long solitude," writes E. C. Godée Molsbergen. Among those assisting in salvage operations was a young factor called Jan van Riebeeck, who had recently been removed from his post at Tonkin, in Indochina, for private trading, an activity the VOC strictly forbade its servants. While at the Cape he managed to find time to do a good deal of exploring.

On their return to Holland, two of the castaways submitted a remonstrance to the company recommending the establishment of a fort and a garden at the Cape for the resupply of ships traveling between Europe and the Indies. They squarely laid the blame for past conflict with the Khoikhoi on "our people who give them cause, always concealed; for we firmly believe, that the farmers of this country, were we to shoot their cattle or take them away without payment, if they had no justice to fear, would be not one hair better than these natives." Not the savagery of the indigenes, "but the rude unthankfulness of our own people," was responsible for the friction. Thus, they noted, the Dutch fleet that put into Table Bay in 1648 "instead of making to the natives any recompense for their good treatment of those of the *Haerlem*, they shot seven or eight of their cattle, and took them away without payment, which may likely cost some of our people their lives if opportunity offers, and whether they have not cause, your Honors will be pleased to consider."

This memorial had its effect, and in 1651 Van Riebeeck followed it up with one of his own. Notwithstanding what the castaways had said about the Khoikhoi, he expressed the opinion that the latter were "a savage set, living without conscience . . . we should, therefore, act cautiously with them, and not put much trust in them; and the same in regard of the English, French, Danes, and particularly the Portuguese, who are always envious of the increase and extension of the Company's power." The potential use of a base at the Cape was obvious, and as Van Riebeeck took occasion to remind them, his credentials to head it were excellent. He was young, in good health, an experienced trader who had traveled in India, China, Japan, Thailand, Greenland, and the West Indies, and a licensed surgeon into the bargain. The Lords Seventeen gave him the job he wanted, engaging him for five years at the extremely modest salary of seventy-five guilders a month, and his expedition sailed from Texel on Christmas Eve, 1651. After a voyage of over three months, he landed at Table Bay in April 1652 to claim possession for the VOC. The bay was empty of ships, and there was no one other than the Khoikhoi, who had not the slightest idea of the fateful step being taken, to contest the occupation.

It is of some significance that one of Van Riebeeck's first acts was to issue a proclamation to the effect that "whoever ill uses, beats, or pushes, any of the natives, be he in the right or in the wrong, shall in their presence be punished with 50 lashes, that they may thus see that such is against our will." The whole purpose of the planned Cape station was to barter cattle from the Khoikhoi, and Van Riebeeck had few illusions about the men he commanded. Poorly fed, brutally disciplined for the slightest infraction of orders, many of them had been pressed into service in the first place, or obtained by so-called *"ziel-verkoopers"* ("soul-sellers"), who made them drunk and then got them to sign binding contracts. "Mostly they were individuals who had come to grief elsewhere and for whom no other way out was left," says E. C. Godée Molsbergen. They made up a motley collection of nationalities, including Poles, Flemings, Scots, French and Portuguese, as well as Germans and Dutch.

The first desertions took place in September, four men setting out to make their way overland to Mozambique—a project so wild as to leave little doubt as to the desperation they felt. One of the deserters, Jan Blank, kept a pathetic journal in red chalk, recording their brief adventure. Armed with four swords and a couple of pistols, with a dog for company, they managed to last less than a week before resolving to return to the Fort "in hopes of mercy and grace in God's name." Blank, as ringleader, was keelhauled—pulled under the keel of a ship at the end of a rope—and given 150 lashes; he and his companions were then set to work as slaves in irons for two years. They were probably lucky not to be executed.

On landing, Van Riebeeck and his men almost immediately encountered Harry and his Strandloper followers, who came to perform their customary services, setting up camp near the Dutch tents. At about noon the next day, however, nine or ten members of another clan appeared, and Harry's people at once "placed themselves in an attitude of defence, running towards them with such courage and fury with *hassagaayes* [spears] and bows and arrows, that we had enough to do to stop them, their wives having run away to the mountain." The newcomers, who also knew many broken Dutch and English words, "were very handsome active men, of particularly good stature, dressed however in a cow (or ox) hide tolerably prepared, which they carried gracefully upon one arm, with an air as courageous as any bravo in Holland can carry his cloak on arm or shoulder."

Aside from the Strandlopers, a subtribal group who owned no livestock and consisted of impoverished refugees and outcasts from other clans, two Khoikhoi tribes occupied the peninsula. The Goringhaiqua numbered "about 300 men capable of bearing arms," and were led by a corpulent captain called Gogosoa, locally the senior chief. More formidable numerically were the Gorachouqua, with perhaps twice that number, whose chief, one Choro, may perhaps have been Xhoré's heir. The Dutch loosely called all of these "Capemen," but in after years the Gorachouqua came to be known as the Tabackteckemans ("Tobacco-Takers" in Khoikhoi pidgin incorporating both English and Dutch words) after they had expropriated about 100 pounds of standing tobacco from a field planted by Dutch free burghers.

All Khoikhoi spoke a mutually intelligible language, and were related in a complex hierarchy of clans, ascending in seniority as one moved east. The Strandlopers, or Goringhaicona ("children of the Goringhaiqua"), were the low men on the totem pole, and probably owed their very cohesion as a group to their ability—strictly speaking, it was Harry's ability—to act as brokers to the whites: in a sense, they had been incorporated into the European economic order even before the founding of the settlement. As Elphick observes, they were important despite their numerical weakness, "since from their members came the first subordinate native group in colonial society." Naturally they resented attempts by other clans to horn in on their pitch.

To the north of the Cape peninsula dwelt the Cochoqua, a people whom the Hollanders came to identify as the "true Saldanhars," able to muster several thousand men. Beyond them lay the Guriqua and the Namaqua, a people rich in cattle. Eastward of the peninsula were yet other tribes: Chainouqua, Hessequa, Gouriqua, Attaqua, Damasqua, Hamcumqua, or Inqua, and Gonaqua. All were nomadic pastoralists, but in the east they cultivated *dagga* (*Cannabis sativa*), an important item of trade, "which stupifies the brain like opium, ginger, strong tobacco, brandy, or the like; and of which these tribes are consequently very fond." As has been mentioned, the line of seniority ran east, and all Khoikhoi owed a nominal allegiance to Khoebaha, senior chief of the Hamcumqua.

But the Dutch also heard of another people, called the Choboqua, or Chobona, said to be rich in gold and gemstones, whom the Europeans excitedly conjectured might be the inhabitants of the mysterious kingdom of Monomotapa. According to some informants, the Khoikhoi recognized these Chobona as their suzerains, but Harry, who had encountered them among the Chainouqua, denied that they were rulers of the Khoikhoi, asserting that they were "black Caffres, like the Guinea and Angola slaves." On one occasion when the Hollanders questioned visiting Chainouqua about the Chobona, he "appeared to rage as if he was mad, saying that the Chobona, and not he, must *soubat* [entreat, beg, implore]," spitting on the floor and saying "that, and thus for Chobona!" These Chobona were in fact the Xhosa, who intermingled with the Khoikhoi in the Eastern Cape, and the suggestion of their paramountcy raises some interesting questions. The vehemence of Harry's objections seems of itself to suggest that there was something in the claim. Elphick observes that

> The rule of the Chobona was, of course, purely honorary, and seems not to have been recognized by all Cape Khoikhoi. Yet it seems strange that any Khoikhoi would give any honor at all to a non-Khoikhoi people who could not have been their ancestors. Of course, it is possible that there had been real or imputed marital links between some Xhosa royal line and the ancestors of the chiefly Khoikhoi lineages. An alternative solution to this puzzle may be found in the vague racial connotation of the word *Chobona*. Evidence given by the Attaqua strongly suggests that the Khoikhoi also denoted as "Chobona" other Khoikhoi—specifically the Gonaqua—who as a result of intermixture with negroes were darker than normal.*

---

* In "The Cabonas," *African Studies* 27, no. 1 (1968): 41–43, M. D. W. Jeffreys traces the name "Chobona" to the Nguni greeting *sakubona*, which has the meaning of "We saw you from afar," or, figuratively, "We have already recognized you." The

But whether or not the Khoikhoi owed the Xhosa some sort of allegiance, there was also a degree of antagonism, as Harry's attitude makes clear. According to Hahn, the Khoikhoi sometimes referred to the blacks as *Xun* (things) or *arin* (dogs), and distinguished themselves from them as *IAva-khoin* (i.e., red men). But here we may perhaps see the influence of white racial ideology.

The Cape Khoikhoi at the time of the Dutch settlement numbered between 100,000 and 200,000 individuals, divided into numerous tribes but all recognizably of the same cultural, linguistic and political origins. They had trading connections with the Tswana to the north, whom they knew as the Bricqua (goat people) and with the Xhosa, or Chobona, to the east, to whom they also had some sort of political tie. But the ethnic picture with which the Hollanders were confronted was more complex yet. In addition to the Khoikhoi and the distant Sutu-nguni, there were also the San, or "Bushmen," umber-skinned hunters of small stature whom the Europeans learned to call Soaqua or Sonqua. Among the Khoikhoi they had the status of either enemies or clients. Van der Stel reported from Namaqualand in 1685 that "the Sonquas are like our poor in Europe, every tribe of Hottentots has some of them, and they are employed to give warning when they discover any strange tribe. They do not plunder anything whatever from the kraals in whose service they are, but from others." Elsewhere, in their own range grounds, however, the San were a fiercely independent people, subsisting by hunting, raiding, and gathering wild *veldkos* (roots and berries). "Soanqua are banditti, subject to none except the power of the arrow and assagay, upon which they chiefly depend," Van Riebeeck himself noted.

The name "San" means, speculatively, either "aborigine" or "gatherer." The latter interpretation receives some support from the fact that a tribe of herders and fishers, also called the "Vischman," were initially identified to the Dutch as "Soaqua." Harry endeavored to explain to Van Riebeeck in his broken English that the "Watermans" and "Saldanhamans" were constantly at war with these "Vischmans" (the whites were unclear as to whether these names were to be construed as belonging to peoples, their chiefs, or both). The Vischmans, said Harry, possessed no sheep, only cows, and fished from the rocks with lines. He proposed more than once

---

Nguni are said to have known the Khoikhoi as *Ungibonabonephi*, literally rendered as "You saw me—and you saw me where?" Perhaps this was the salutation, appropriate to a feudatory people seeking acknowledgment of recognition, which originally elicited *sakubona* in response?

to the Dutch that "if we desired to do him and the Saldaniers a friendship, we must kill them and take their cattle for ourselves, which was easy to be done, because, according to his statement, they were weak in people."

If "San" does mean "native," however, implying that the Khoikhoi recognized them as the original inhabitants of the country, the word may conceivably have acquired derogatory overtones even before Europeans arrived in the ethnic cul-de-sac of southern Africa. "The Khoi-khoi often speak of *!Uri-San* (white Bushmen) and mean the low white vagabonds and runaway sailors," Hahn noted in the 1880s.

The chief physical difference between San and Khoikhoi was the smaller stature of the former. This was an advantage to a hunter, and attractive to San women, hence a criterion of sexual selection. When hunters took up a pastoral or agricultural way of life, they tended to have children taller than themselves. While the Khoikhoi all spoke a language that was recognizably the same, the San languages were as different from each other as they were from the Khoikhoi, with which they had "only the clicks and some harsh sounding faucals and a few roots of words in common." The San, Hahn observed, "lead the life of a Pariah . . . having to suffer most . . . from the hands of their own nearest kith and kin, the Khoikhoi, whom I have, on more than one occasion, seen manifesting more charity for a dog than for a starving Bushman." This was, of course, after several hundred years of interaction with whites had structured existing antagonisms and created new ones.

The cupidity of the Europeans seems to have rubbed off. Perhaps it merely confirmed similar tendencies among the Khoikhoi, to whom cattle-pilfering and the fighting likely to ensue were somewhere between sport and ritual. (Their pugnacity could be judged "from the frightful scars and wounds of which the naked bodies of almost all of them are filled.") Familiarity bred contempt on either hand. It is hard for people who plan to bilk each other to retain mutual respect. The Dutch were still getting their livestock cheap: paying an average of one and a quarter pounds of tobacco and three and three-quarters pounds of copper per head of cattle during the period 1652–67, and reselling at a markup of between 200 and 400 percent. For their part the Khoikhoi, unless coerced, brought chiefly inferior stock for sale—animals that were old, sick, or lame, few of which were healthy enough to be used as breeding stock.

Appropriately it was while the Dutch sat at sermon one Sunday in October 1653 that Harry and his troop made off with their cattle—or at any rate they disappeared simultaneously. A Dutch herdboy was murdered to prevent word being carried back prematurely. Relations with the other peninsular Khoikhoi now deteriorated rapidly, the indigenes "stealing and carrying off all they could, and even on finding our people unarmed close to the Fort, taking all their things from them by force, aye even laying hold of children and boys for the brass buttons on their clothes, in spite of all our good treatment and kindness within and without the Fort, with a view to entice them."

Following their instructions, the Hollanders, at least at command level, did their best to turn the other cheek, making no effort to seek revenge after the initial pursuit had failed, and showing the Khoikhoi even "more kindness than before." But Van Riebeeck (whose communications to the management in Holland were always remarkably frank) wrote that they did this only

> to make them less shy, so as to find hereafter a better opportunity to seize them with all their cattle, 1100 or 1200 in number, and about 600 sheep, the best in the whole country. . . . with which live stock the Company would be at once, and by breeding almost for ever, supplied with cattle enough, and could derive good service from the people in chains, in killing seals, or in labouring in the silver mines, which we trust will be found here . . . this, considering the execrable murder of the boy, and the robbery of the cattle, they have well deserved; and we can perceive that other tribes will not sympathize with them, as we have often remarked that on seeing these rogues about the Fort they retire again with their cattle, apprehending annoyance from these audacious rogues; for we observe that whenever the natives of the other tribes get any tobacco or brass, these allies of Herry always help themselves to a share, to the great displeasure of the others.

But the Lords Seventeen presently replied instructing him that if he were able to get hold of the murderer, he should be executed as example, but that if it could not be proved that Harry was responsible for the herdboy's death, he should be banished to Batavia "to be there employed in chains on the public works. If you cannot recover the cattle taken from you, you will, on falling in with their cattle, take in return as many as have been stolen from us by them, and not more."

The Khoikhoi continued to raid, and the Hollanders continued to plot the retaliation their orders did not allow them. In May 1655 Van Riebeeck was scheming (or at least daydreaming) about seizing the cattle of "Herry's allies," and at the same time getting hold of "all their persons, with their wives and children . . . to banish them, which may be as easily effected as seizing their cattle, as we can at all times get them, with wives and children, within the Fort, and make them as drunk as pigs." The Khoikhoi in the western Cape had acquired the fatal taste for spirits which was in the long run to prove so disastrous for their descendants. To slake their cravings the Dutch now imported arrack—rice or palm brandy—in large quantities from the East, and doled it out at every opportunity. For hundreds of years afterwards labourers on the white farms of the Cape would receive part of their pay in *vaaljaapie,* cheap, sour wine served at the end of the workday.*

The fact was, however, that Harry needed the Dutch as much as they needed him, if not more. Two years after the robbery and murder, he had once again managed to work himself into the good graces of the Europeans, insisting that it was really his so-called allies, the "Capemen," who had committed the crime, and even seeking to stipulate that "we should always support him as the chief of these Cape hordes, and that none other than him might be with the Dutch Commander, or be acknowledged as master of this land."

For their part, the Capemen informed Van Riebeeck that "if we would only take away Herry alone, and kill him, it would be to them the greatest kindness in the world, that they would take care that we should get from the Saldanhars as many cattle as we desired, for that they also would be much obliged by our killing Herry." Before the coming of the whites, they observed, he had been an impoverished nobody who slept in the bush without even a hut of his own, "and now he would fain play the master over the Caepmans."

But there may have been more than a little white wishful thinking in the accounts of apparent dissension, spurred on perhaps by the smooth tongues of Harry and his compatriots. Soon enough, "Herry, Caepman, and associates" were once again allied, with no very benevolent intentions toward the Europeans, whom they went to some trouble to injure. For instance, noted Van Riebeeck, "seeing that whenever they have decamped, we have fetched away with wagons the dung left in their craels, to manure our land, have thus perceived that it is of great use to us; they have, on decamping on the present occasion, set fire to their craels and burnt all the dung . . . causing us thereby great inconvenience."

Desirous as they were of the foreign luxuries the whites supplied, especially spirits and tobacco, it seems clear that the Khoikhoi strongly resented their presence as permanent settlers. Willing to ally themselves with the sea people in internecine quarrels, the natives were, nevertheless, capable of uniting temporarily when an

---

* As a boy I myself assisted on occasion in dishing out the evening *sopie* of wine to the *volk* on a Karoo farm.

occasion to harass the whites offered itself. In February 1655, not three years after the first landing of the settlers, the Khoikhoi intimated to the Dutch that, "we were living upon their land, that they perceived that we were building with activity, in order never to go away, and therefore they would not barter to us any more cattle, for we took the best pasture for our cattle." At a later occasion, Harry and the fat Goringhaiqua chief, Gogosoa, hearing the Dutch talk of building houses here and there (some of them now understood Dutch so well that an interpreter was scarcely needed), asked them "if we built houses, and broke up the ground there, which they observed to be our intention, where should they live?" The whites answered that they "might live under our protection, and that there was room enough every where for them to graze their cattle; that we were going to employ this land to grow bread and tobacco, when we would, like good friends, give them a share, &c. on which they expressed themselves satisfied, but it might be easily seen that it was not quite to their mind."

In actuality, the Hollanders were considering how they might fortify the peninsula and turn it into their sole preserve, excluding the natives. They even thought of cutting a canal which would separate it from the African continent and turn it into an island, which it had been in prehistoric times. When this proved impractical, they fell back on more conventional defenses—blockhouses and cavalry. Twenty mounted men, Van Riebeeck thought, would eliminate the need for fortifications, and so it proved.

There was little sign of any lasting Khoikhoi solidarity in the face of the intruders. On occasion Harry proposed, for example, that when the inland tribespeople came to the Fort with their cattle, the Dutch "should seize them all, and kill or banish them, taking their cattle for the Company and for him." And, in March 1658, he and the Goringhaiqua spokesman called Dominie suggested that the Dutch unite with the Goringhaiqua and Goringhaicona to attack the Gorachouqua and another clan led by Ngonomoa, the so-called *Swarte Kaptein* (Black Captain). Since they hoped to open up the cattle trade with the more northerly tribes, the Hollanders were of no mind to cooperate in these schemes.

March 1658 also saw the importation of the first significant group of slaves. Before that there had been some Madagascar slaves in various households, some of them having been sent as a present to Van Riebeeck's wife, Maria de la Quellerie, by the Madagascan king. In years to come the great island would be the main source of slaves at the Cape. Of mixed African-Indonesian origins, the slaves spoke Malagasy, a Malayo-Polynesian language, and would leave their linguistic and genetic stamp on the Cape "Coloured" people. "Malgas" is still sometimes used as a sobriquet in Cape Town.

Those who arrived in 1658 were, however, Angolans, taken from a captured Portuguese slave ship. A hundred and seventy were landed alive, "many grievously sick; moreover they were mostly girls and small boys, from whom in the next 4 or 5 years little service is to be expected." The captives were clothed, fed, and had their names registered or were given names. Classes were set up to instruct them in High Dutch and Christian prayer. At the end of each lesson they were rewarded with a quid of tobacco and a nip of brandy. The strongest were put to work. Van Riebeeck's age, like every recorded age before it, saw nothing much wrong in owning human beings as property. Color was not the determining factor. Numerous Europeans were enslaved in North Africa and the Ottoman domains, some of them sold to the Turks by other whites, as Africans sold their fellows to Arabs and Europeans.

The Dutch preferred the tractable Madagascans, but West African slaves were cheaper and they imported them from Guinea and from various Portuguese settlements on the Gold, Ivory and Slave Coasts of which they had possessed themselves. In Angola one could buy a slave for a handful of beads. Down the Benguela slave route through the "Hungry Country" traveled "the ancestors of half the negroes in the United States and of nearly all in Cuba and Brazil," supposed Nevinson, who found slaves still coming down it when he was there in 1904.

In the 1640s, the Dutch had made a bid to seize the Angolan slave marts from the Portuguese, in collaboration with local potentates. "The Calvinist invaders established surprisingly cordial relations with the Roman Catholic King of the Congo, and with the cannibal Queen 'Nzinga of the Jagas," says Boxer. "In August 1648, these strangely assorted allies were on the point of annihilating the surviving Portuguese defenders of Angola . . . when a Luso-Brazilian expedition from Rio de Janeiro recaptured Luanda and reversed the situation at the last minute of the eleventh hour." In this forgotten saga we may perhaps seek the explanation for the presence of the "American" in the list of enemies in the poem quoted as epigraph to this chapter. Conceivably some of the Hollanders present at the inaugural ceremonies for Cape Town Castle in 1666 had fought Brazilians, whether in Angola or in Pernambuco.

Naturally, the slaves ran away at the slightest opportunity, and the Khoikhoi, especially the women, seem to have had some sympathy for them. In July 1658 Van Riebeeck noted that "the female Hottentoos were from the first too familiar with the slaves," giving them "broiled tortoises and other food" and indicating to them by signs that they should escape to the mountains. On the other hand, some Khoikhoi males could be persuaded to track down and return runaways. They were, it was said, "very jealous of them, cannot endure them, and . . . always quarrelling with them." In any case, escaped slaves had so difficult a time of it in the wild and unfamiliar interior that some returned of their own accord.

By mid-1658 word had reached the settlement that the peninsular Khoikhoi were planning "a general union of the natives to fall upon us altogether," and the following year what has been called the First Khoikhoi-Dutch War broke out. Far from having achieved a general union, only the Gorachouqua and Goringhaiqua were involved in the hostilities against the whites. The former, at least, were on the face of it a formidable enemy, numbering, Van Riebeeck thought, "about 1,000 active fencible men," but at no point does the Fort seem to have been seriously threatened. Nonetheless, the Hollanders were worried, and they went so far as to arm the slaves with half-pikes against the Khoikhoi—the slaves being "much excited against them, and would gladly eat them," as Van Riebeeck put it in a fanciful moment.

Though Harry does not seem to have played any significant part in the war, it is noteworthy that the Dutch did not trust him in the least. In October 1659 he was secretly banished to Robben Island, "without his people being told any thing about him, and they asked about him no more than if he had never existed." Two months later, however, he and another Khoikhoi prisoner managed to escape in a small boat, which they successfully beached on the mainland, in spite of the fact that it was so leaky that the Dutch were certain they must have drowned.

Leading the resistance among the Goringhaiqua was the former interpreter called Damon or Doman, which the Dutch wiseacres rendered as "Dominie" ("Parson") "because he was such a very simpleminded man." (The name may in fact have had reference to his function as a spokesman and translator, and is possibly cognate with the Khoikhoi word for tongue, *tamma*.) After Doman had lived at the settlement for some time, the Hollanders came to believe that he was attached to them, and faithful to their interests—an impression he took care to cultivate. In April 1657 he was taken to Batavia (Djakarta) in the Netherlands Indies by the overweening Commissioner van Goens, and returned the following year with the adopted Christian name Anthony.

It is unclear whether he had been covertly working against the intruders all along, or whether his trip to Java, where the Dutch were busy putting down a Bantamese rebellion, gave him a fresh perspective on the danger they represented to the life of his people. In any case, Doman now emerged as chief tactician against the whites. Van Riebeeck had earlier noted that "it were much to be desired that he had never been at Batavia, or that he could be induced, by fair words, to return thither, more particularly because he has learned the perfect use of firearms, and we have enough to do to keep such out of his hands." Now he taught the Khoikhoi to attack in rainy weather, when the firelocks of the Dutch would not discharge, and along with another warrior called Carabinga (or "Flat-Nose" by the Dutch) took the lead in the fighting.

Finally, in July, after the unequal struggle had gone on for several months, Doman and four other Khoikhoi were ridden down by a squadron of Dutch cavalry. Wounded in the head by a shot, Doman managed to escape by jumping over a stream, as did one of his companions. Two of the remaining Khoikhoi were killed and the fifth, a man named Eykamma, was taken back to the Fort on horseback "with his neck pierced, his leg shattered, and a severe wound in the head." He was asked why his people had made war on the Dutch and, though almost overcome by pain, he countered by asking why the whites had plowed over his people's land and sought to take the bread out of their mouths by sowing corn on their best pasture. The Khoikhoi had attacked for no other reason, he said,

than to revenge themselves for the harm and injustice done to them: since they were not only commanded to keep away from certain of their grazing grounds, which they had always possessed undisturbed and only allowed us at first to use as a refreshment station, but they also saw their lands divided out amongst us without their knowledge by the heads of the settlement, and boundaries put up within which they might not pasture. He asked finally what we would have done had the same thing happened to us. Moreover, he added, they observed how we were strengthening ourselves daily with fortifications and bulwarks, which according to their way of thinking could have no other object than to bring them and all that was theirs under our authority and domination. To this our men replied: "your people have now once for all lost the land around the Cape through war, and you must accordingly never dwell on the idea of getting it back again through peace or through war."

Three weeks later, on August 12, Eykamma died of his wounds. His statement makes it perfectly clear what the Khoikhoi felt about the alienation of their ancestral territory, and the reply of the Dutch soldiers equally effectively sums up the founding principle of the apartheid state: might makes right.

The Khoikhoi never resorted to total war against the Europeans. Elphick points out that they did not make use of poisoned arrows, which they had available. Had the struggle been more vigorously prosecuted and had things gone worse for the settlers, the Dutch might have been persuaded to abandon the Cape station, if only to cut costs. Thus, in December 1659, the governor general and council in India informed Van Riebeeck with customary petulance that they had "never entertained any high idea of the Cape scheme; there was far too much said at the commencement, of what we must now see turning out most unfortunately; however, what is done cannot be undone."

To complicate the defense, a projected rebellion was discovered that month, involving "4 English, 4 *Schotten,* 3 Dutch Company's servants, a black convict, and 15 slaves." The conspirators were said to have planned "to scale the walls of the Fort and murder all in it, down to the youngest child," and then to seize and make off with the *Erasmus,* a ship which had arrived from the Indies sometime before. This "great treachery" was uncovered by the chief surgeon, "Mr. Wiljam Robberson, of Dondey," and among the conspirators, who were sent to Batavia for trial, were "Pieter Barber, of Hamstede; Jacob Born, of Glasco; Patricq t'Jock, of Glasco," names which emphasize how multinational the company's service and the Cape station were at this early date.

The bloodthirsty intentions imputed to the conspirators seem to imply either an uncommon degree of hysteria on Van Riebeeck's part or a genuine fear of the men under his command. He would probably have sympathized with the Duke of Wellington's legendary exclamation about his men, "I don't know whether they frighten the enemy, but by God they terrify me!"

Punishment for insubordination, let alone mutiny, was ferocious. During Van Riebeeck's time a volunteer named Gerrit Dirk was given a hundred blows with the butt of a musket for calling the skipper of the vessel *Goede Hoop* "Captain Fishhead"; another man got the same for "expressing among the men discontent with the provisions issued, and wishing the devil to take the purser for serving out penguins instead of beef and pork." Sentences of a hundred lashes were commonplace. Offenders were frequently keelhauled, branded, condemned to work in chains for long terms, or were pitched from a ship's yardarm into the sea. Thus, for "mutinous words and threats on board of his ship, (N. B. said, he had command in his prison in England, and would have the same here also)" one "Harman Willems, of Edenburgh, soldier" was sentenced to "fall thrice from the yard, and to receive on his posteriors, while still wet, 100 lashes." It is certain, too, that he was not the only jailbird among the company's troops. It was with such men, rather than with the elegant Van Riebeeck, that the ordinary Khoikhoi had to deal daily.

"Any sufficiently advanced technology is indistinguishable from magic," Arthur C. Clarke has observed. Despite relative familiarity, the cannons, muskets, and tall ships of the Europeans must have seemed akin to wizardry to most of the Khoikhoi, and aside from militants like Doman the struggle against them lacked heart. "The Khoikhoi wanted to drive the Dutch out of South Africa by depriving them of their cattle and destroying their crops; they did not want to goad them into massive retaliation," Elphick suggests. "As a consequence, they killed Europeans only when it was necessary to achieve their limited ends." More important, probably, was the fact that to the rear of the Capemen lay their traditional enemies, the powerful Cochoqua chiefs, Ngonomoa (the "Black Captain") and Oedasoa. Not only did the Cochoqua refuse to help the Capemen, they threw their support to the Dutch. Oedasoa sent word to Van Riebeeck that, after the Capemen had been defeated, the Cochoqua would occupy the Table Bay hinterland, and he and the Dutch commander would live like "two brothers whose hearts beat as one."

Peace was concluded early in 1660. The war had been little more than a series of skirmishes. Only two Europeans lost their lives, and the number of Khoikhoi killed was relatively small. The Dutch were told that Doman was in disgrace for having instigated the fighting; he, too, came to treat for peace, and his influence dwindled. Harry, who had been supplanted as leader of the Goringhaiconas, was treated to a small roll of tobacco and informed that he might come and live at the Fort again, provided he undertook to ensure a good supply of cattle. The following year, the Cochoqua made good on their promise to occupy the Capemen's pastures, and the latter were reduced to begging aid from the Dutch. The reduction of the Khoikhoi in the immediate vicinity of the settlement was now complete; it had taken less than ten years.

Doman and Harry both died in 1663. They were, noted the Dutch second-in-command, Abraham Gabbema, "always considered as very mischievous and malicious men, and as the greatest opponents of the hon. Company."

Eva: "A Dutch Heart"

In the woman they christened Eva (her Khoikhoi name was Krotoa), the Hollanders found a more reliable instrument than either Harry or Doman. Only ten or eleven in 1652, when the Cape station was founded, she was taken into Van Riebeeck's own household, and learned to speak Dutch "almost as well as a Dutch girl." She also picked up some of the Malayo-Portuguese lingua franca of the Indies trade from Indonesian house slaves.

At first Eva was thought to be one of Harry's daughters; later, however, it was determined that she was more likely his niece. After her sister married the Cochoqua captain Oedasoa, she assumed considerable importance to the Dutch. The cattle of the Cochoqua were said to be "as numerous as the grass in the field," and she traversed the hinterland to persuade the clans of the interior to come to the Fort to trade. "The everywhere-traveling-Eva does the Company the greatest service," Van Riebeeck wrote. Doman patently thought her a traitor, and accused her outright of toadying to the Dutch. "I am Hottentoosman, and not Dutchman, but you Eva *soubat* the Commander," he told her. When the Hollanders took Schacher, the son of the Gorachouqua chief, as hostage, she warned that if he were not released, they would kill her in retaliation. She had, she asserted, "a Dutch heart in her breast."

But there was an innocent, almost conditional quality to these squabbles. Though her mother lived among the Capemen, Eva on occasion took Harry's part against the latter, pleading for him at the Fort "like Esther for her uncle Mordecai." Sometime after this, she and Doman "asked leave to pay a visit to their friends, requesting, in return for their services in interpreting, some brass, iron, beads, tobacco, bread, and brandy." Normally Eva wore European clothing or the Indonesian sarong and *kabaja* (a loose gown); now, taking leave and thanking the Hollanders for her reward in good Dutch, "on getting outside and into Doman's mat huts, she immediately put on her skins, and sent her clothes home, so that she might put them on when she should again come into the presence of the Commander's wife." Doman returned a day or two later, but Eva went on to the camp of the Cochoquas (where Elphick supposes she may have undergone the "ritual isolation and reentry ceremonies" associated with puberty). When she came back about a month later, she told the Dutch that she had been plundered of her baggage by the Capemen on leaving the protection of the Fort.

Doman, Van Riebeeck thought, was Eva's worst enemy. For her part, she declared that Doman was a good-for-nothing liar, "trying only to incite the Dutch against the Cochoquas, the latter against the Dutch, and therefore Oedasoa dared not come, for otherwise he could easily have driven them [Capemen] out of the way, but that they threatened him with our power, for which all the natives are so afraid, that when they hear us spoken of, or see the houses, and in particular the Fort, from a distance, they shake and tremble with fear."

At Eva's suggestion, Van Riebeeck sent Oedasoa presents, consisting of "15lbs. of brass, 2 bunches beads of various colors, red, lavender, violet, milk-white, &c. ½ gross tobacco pipes, 7lbs. tobacco, a case with 4 tin flasks of Spanish brandy, 1 do. with beer,

100lbs. of bread, some cinnamon, cloves, nutmegs, mace, pepper, and ginger, also some white and black sugar, all which articles and others Eva had mentioned." Oedasoa returned the compliment with gifts of three cows, two calves, and nineteen sheep. At the time when these negotiations were going on, leading to the de facto alliance between the Cochoqua and the Hollanders which did so much to save the settlement, she was a girl in her mid-teens. Her savoir faire can only be called remarkable.

No one did more than Eva to bridge the gulf between the Netherlanders and the Khoikhoi. Though she evidently trusted the Dutch and identified with them, Eva could live in either world, and she seems to have enjoyed switching back and forth between the freedom of the veld and the confined sophistication of the Fort. Tragically, she failed to comprehend the degree to which even the amiable Van Riebeeck was ruled by the harsh practicalities of trade and promotion. He did not conceal this from his diary (though since he kept it chiefly for the benefit of the Seventeen, he may have exaggerated somewhat), writing in December 1660:

> The interpreter Eva is again living in the Commander's house, laying aside her skins, and dressing herself in her clothes in the Indian manner, that she may resume the exercise of her functions as interpreter; she seems now again to be somewhat tired of her own people, and we allow her to indulge this changeable disposition, according to her own fancy, so as to have the better service from her; but she seems so much habituated to Dutch customs and Dutch food, that she will never be able entirely to relinquish them.

In 1664 Eva married Pieter van Meerhoff, the surgeon's assistant, who had come to the Cape as a soldier in the company's service five years before. She was then twenty-one; Meerhoff, a Dane from Copenhagen, was twenty-seven. When the banns were published she had already borne two children, whether to him or to other whites is not clear. On the face of it, this "first marriage, according to christian custom, which has ever taken place here, with any of the natives of this country," had official approval. Commander Wagenaar, who had replaced Van Riebeeck, noted,

> Eva has now served the Company for many years as interpreter, without ever having received any thing, except food and clothing in return, it is resolved . . . to give her as a marriage gift, according to the usual custom with Company's children, a sum of Fifty Rix-dollars; and as soon as the marriage is performed, a merry bridal feast; and further, that in order to encourage the bridegroom, who has served out his time here as surgeon's assistant, that he shall be, in compliance with his request, promoted to the rank of surgeon.

Eva's own people seem to have been less well pleased, if one is
to judge by the fact that Oedasoa, according to her account, withheld the dowry of 100 cattle and more than 500 sheep due her;
"otherwise she would have gladly sold and delivered them to the
Company," Wagenaar wrote. "As this, however, is a matter which
does not particularly concern us, we shall allow it to take its own
course and have nothing to do with it."

That Meerhoff was presently appointed superintendent of the
desolate Robben Island penal station was probably scant compensa-
tion. With her taste for the refinements of life, Eva can scarcely have
been glad to move there. And there may have been another element
to the appointment. "Was it purely coincidental that Jan Wouterssen, married to a Bengali slave, and Jan Sacharias, also married to
one, should both have served as Superintendants on the island?"
asks its historian, Simon de Villiers. Molsbergen thought that Wagenaar had insisted that Meerhoff make an honest woman of Eva; but
that line having once been drawn, the surgeon perhaps had to pay
the penalty for his indulgence.

A third child was born to her on the island. Eva now more and
more dulled her sensibilities with drink. On one occasion, while
under its influence, she fell and hurt herself so badly that her husband had to send to the mainland for medical supplies to treat her.
Bad luck seemed to pursue her. While he was still the *onder Barbier,*
or surgeon's assistant, Meerhoff had participated in a number of
pioneering expeditions into the Cape interior, and had acquired a
reputation as an explorer. On the strength of this, he was sent on an
expedition to Madagascar in 1667, and lost his life in a fight with
some of the islanders.

After his death Eva moved back to the settlement. But the Van
Riebeecks, her friends, almost her foster family, were gone. Communication was no longer a significant problem for the colonists, as
more and more Khoikhoi spoke Dutch. Without a meaningful role
to fill, she lapsed deeper into drink. (In this, it seems, she was not
alone at the Cape: "If the farmers in the Netherlands drank like
those here, neither cow, nor plough, nor harrow would remain on
the land," wrote Commander Quaelbergen to the Seventeen in
1668.) One night Eva's children came into the hall at the Fort virtually naked, their mother having gone off to her tribespeople drunk
as a fish, taking with her their clothes and bedding. The fiscal, or
treasurer, and two of his men went in search of her, and found her
sitting on a sand dune, smoking her pipe and hawking the children's
things to some Khoikhoi. She laughed in their faces and admitted
she had sold her bedding for tobacco and spent all her money on
drink.

The churchwardens took the children in charge, and Eva was again banished to the island where her husband had once been commander. There she apparently bore several illegitimate children, the last of which she brought over to the mainland for baptism on July 28, 1673. The following year, aged thirty-one, she died, and was buried as a Christian within the walls of the recently completed Castle.

Her surviving children by Van Meerhoff, Pieternell (Petronella) and Salamon, were taken to Mauritius in 1677 by a friend of their father's to be educated. Pieternell married a Dutch farmer, Daniel Zaijman, there. In 1709, she and her husband returned to South Africa, and settled in the vicinity of Stellenbosch to raise a family of eight children. Psychoculturally the ur-mother of the "Coloureds" of the Cape, Eva is also among the ancestresses of Afrikanerdom.

The Company's Stave

By 1670 the integration of the peninsular Khoikhoi into colonial society was already far advanced, while the Cochoqua clearly regarded themselves as allies of the Dutch. When a French flotilla on its way to the Indies made a halfhearted bid to annex Saldanha Bay that year, a large Khoikhoi war party, presumably Cochoqua, are reported as offering assistance in repelling any invasion. But as the VOC extended its hegemony, and white hunting parties moved into the interior in search of game and treasure, relations inevitably deteriorated. The Capemen, now thoroughly subordinated, served where necessary to legitimize the company's sway. In 1673, for example, five Cochoqua convicted of murdering white hunters were handed over to the local Khoikhoi, who beat them to death with shouts of "Kill the dogs!" (In fact, it seems probable that the hunters had been killed either by San or by Ubiqua—a mixed Khoikhoi-San people—on whose range they had intruded.) In the so-called Second Khoikhoi-Dutch War (1673–77) the whites also had the benefit of numerous allies among the tribes of the hinterland, especially the Chainouqua, traditionally the enemies of the Cochoqua. The war in effect consisted of a series of stock raids disguised as punitive expeditions. It concluded with the acceptance of company suzerainty by the "Black Captain" of the Cochoqua, Ngonomoa, who was at his own request confirmed in his position by the award of the brassbound stave of office stamped with the arms of the VOC with which feudatory chiefs were recognized. Before long the Chainouqua and the Hessequa, too, found themselves living under company

law, and by the end of the century the captains of all the Western
Cape tribes held their office at the pleasure of the Dutch governor,
and carried the VOC's *rottang* (from the Malay for "cane") as a mark
of authority.

In 1671 Commissioner Isbrand Goske, subsequently appointed
the first governor of the Cape colony, gave orders that male and
female slaves were to be united as man and wife in order to prevent
"communication between Europeans and female slaves." The prog-
eny of couplings between whites and slave women, twelve of whom
were then at school, "might in due time enjoy the freedom to which,
in right of the father, they were born." Instructions to Commander
Simon van der Stel, dated July 16, 1685, note that "Marriage shall
not be permitted between our Netherlanders and emancipated female slaves, but this restriction shall not apply to the children of
female slaves by Dutch fathers." The development of a mixed population could be impeded, but given the high ratio of white males to
white females, it could not be prevented.

Slaves came from Indonesia as well as from Madagascar ("Mal-
gasse"), Mozambique ("Masbiekers"), and West Africa. The first
Malays came as early as 1667, according to Theal. Slaves had been
imported from Asia before this, but they were not Moslems. One
such was the Catherine of Bengal who married the Hollander Jan
Wouters in 1656, the first "mixed" marriage at the Cape. The names
of individuals banished to the Cape from Java and Ceylon (in Dutch
possession from 1658 to 1796) are on record. "In 1725, 1737 and
1749 further groups of political exiles of high standing were brought
to the Cape from Java," writes I. D. du Plessis. After 1767, however,
Asians ceased to be imported, and the majority of slaves came to be
of African origin.

In 1754, a century after Van Riebeeck, there were according to
the census returns, "between 5,000 and 6,000 colonists (including
half-castes and manumitted slaves *between whom and the Whites
no official distinction was drawn*) and 6,200 slaves." [Italics added.]
The majority of these slaves were in service within fifty miles of
Cape Town; further afield colonists depended on Khoikhoi for labor
even in such relatively skilled tasks as pruning and wine-making.
The ratio of slaves to colonists remained relatively stable through
the rest of the eighteenth century, and at the time of the first British
occupation in 1795, there were just under 16,000 "whites" to 18,000
slaves. Since the British government frowned on the slave trade and
encouraged immigration, the number of colonists henceforth pulled
steadily ahead. At the emancipation in 1834 there were fewer than
40,000 slaves in the whole colony. Even so, they by this time almost
certainly outnumbered the Cape Khoikhoi, whose numbers had
been terribly depleted by disease.

Unlike the Sutu-nguni peoples, the Khoikhoi seem to have had little genetic resistance to the common Eurasian childhood diseases, and they died like flies. As early as 1658, Van Riebeeck noted that "they say that all the inhabitants have been suddenly seized with a great sickness." In 1663 it was reported that there was "among all the Saldanhaise Hottentoos, an infectious or contagious disease, which had for some time back carried off many people." Commander Wagenaar's memorandum for the information of his successor Quaelbergen in 1666 noted that the Cochoqua were "very much diminished and melted away by a sickness which prevailed among them." And in 1673 Governor Isbrand Goske notified the Seventeen of epidemic among the Chainouqua too:

> Captain Claas and some of his grandees came to state, that for a few days back there had been an infectious disease among his people, of whom 9 or 10 males or females had already died very suddenly; this they regard as a bad ömen, for no particularly severe sicknesses are known among them, and Death usually contents himself with old worn out people.

So it continues. The year 1678 is on record as a "particularly unhealthy" one, "47 Dutch and 125 Company's slaves, male or female, having died . . . sickness and mortality have been very prevalent among the Hottentots also." In 1687 "a very severe and deadly sickness among the Hottentots, who do not know what to do for it; and although they decamp and move from place to place, the sickness still pursues them," was recorded by Commander Simon van der Stel. "The burning fever drags many, both old and young, to their graves," he adds.

What these diseases were can only be guessed at: dysentery, measles, mumps, influenza and syphilis all played their part. But the greatest killer, smallpox, did not arrive until 1713, when it was accidentally introduced into the settlement from a passing ship. Whole tribes were engulfed by the disease, so that even their names were forgotten. Cursing the whites for bewitching them, the Khoikhoi fled into the interior to escape. New smallpox epidemics struck in 1755 and 1767, and henceforth the Khoikhoi were reduced to "a landless proletariat—labourers or vagrants on the lands of their ancestors."

The Extermination of the San

But on the frontier the Khoikhoi and their Baster half-brethren continued to provide both the great part of the farm labor force and soldiery against the San and the Xhosa. The San, whose way of life was utterly at variance with settled farming, came to be perceived as a kind of vermin fit only for extermination, and the Khoikhoi and the Basters were pressed into the dirty work. "The great commando of 1774 against the Bushmen . . . consisted of 150 Bastards and Hottentots as against 100 Europeans," notes Marais. "In 1778 the Field Sergeant Adriaan van Zyl reported that 'all the Hottentots and Bastards fit for commandos are going away to the Namaqua country to evade serving." In this struggle against the San, the dual morality characteristic of Afrikanerdom makes its first appearance. Thus a certain Commandant Nel informed the traveler Thompson, who roamed South Africa widely in the period 1821–24 that

> within the last thirty years he had been upon thirty-two commandos against the Bushmen in which great numbers had been shot and their children carried into the Colony. On one of these expeditions not less than two hundred Bushmen were massacred. . . . this Veld-Commandant, in many other points a meritorious, benevolent and clear-sighted man, seemed to be perfectly unconscious that any part of his own proceedings, or those of his countrymen, in their wars with the Bushmen, could awaken my abhorrence. . . . The hereditary sentiments of animosity and the deep-rooted contemptuous prejudices, that had blinded Nel's judgement and seared his better feelings on this point did not, however, operate to prevent him judging properly enough in a neutral case: as, for example, where two of the native tribes were opposed to each other.

In 1862 Governor Sir Philip Wodehouse sent the civil commissioner for the newly created division of Namaqualand, L. Anthing, on a mission of inquiry into what was called Bushmanland. In the pages of his report—which Marais calls "a terrible document"—the last stages of the extermination of the Cape San are documented. Hunted from shelter to shelter, the little people fought back tenaciously. But like the Tasmanians and California Indians who were also being wiped out in this era, they were doomed. As in California, the brutal business of kidnapping women and children nurtured a breed of professional desperado, operating under the aegis of the commando system. The following quotation, drawn from the report of the Indian agent in Yuba City, California, in 1861, almost exactly parallels what was happening in the Cape interior. "In the frontier portions of Humboldt and Mendocino Counties a band of desperate men have carried on a system of kidnapping for two years past," wrote Agent W. P. Dole.

> Indian children were seized and carried into the lower counties and sold into virtual slavery. These crimes against humanity so excited the Indians that they began to retaliate by killing the cattle of the whites. At once an order was issued to chastise the guilty. Under this

indefinite order a company of United States troops, attended by a considerable volunteer force, has been pursuing the poor creatures from one retreat to another. The kidnappers follow at the heels of the soldiers to seize the children, when their parents are murdered, and sell them to the best advantage.

Fortified by hymns and brandy, and reinforced by Khoikhoi and half-breed auxiliaries, the Boer commandos hardened their hearts and gunned down the San as subhuman predators. Neither they nor their descendants would easily escape the shadow of these crimes. It was perhaps especially in this period that the foundations of the apartheid morality of modern South Africa were laid.

For a century the central Cape was a killing ground. The "whites" were not the only killers: the extermination of the San by the Sutu-nguni may be largely myth, but there is no doubt that Bastard captains like the infamous Jager Afrikander, whose bandit followers slaughtered several hundred San in the Zak River country in the 1790s, joined eagerly in the work. If only in part racially European, they were creatures of the colonial spirit.

Though their bloodlines run into the Cape "Coloured" gene pool, the South African San are all but extinct as a race. Perhaps 50,000 more or less closely related "Bushmen" survive in Namibia and Botswana.

Afrikaners, Light and Dark

Apartheid is historically as well as socially founded in hypocrisy. In 1799 Khoikhoi troops were sent to help put down a new insurrection among the Jacobin-inspired Boers of Graaff-Reinet. The use of these Pandours, as the men of the "Hottentot Regiment" were called, was the subject of much noisy resentment, both then and in years to come. Yet almost in the same breath with which they fulminated against the deployment of Pandours against whites, the rebels threatened to enlist Xhosa aid on a massive scale against the British. Coenraad de Buys, one of the leaders of the frontier Jacobins, had emigrated to Xhosa territory, where he became first the lover, then the husband of the young Chief Ngqika's mother, who as a widow had the privilege of living with whomever she chose. De Buys gathered a group of renegade whites around him at Ngqika's court, and there was reason to think that his influence with his "step-son" was considerable. It at any rate seriously worried the British military when rumors were put about that the Xhosa planned to invade under the leadership of this enigmatic outlaw.

For a quarter of a century warfare on the eastern frontier had been a hopeless tangle. Far from the fighting taking racial lines, all sides enlisted whatever help they could get. The so-called "First Kaffir War" around 1780–81 amounted to a series of bloody cattle raids, after which the Boers shared the spoils they took from the Xhosa with their Khoikhoi companions; on the evidence the Xhosa, too, had Khoisan allies. The "Second Kaffir War" in the early 1790s was largely an interference of whites and their Khoikhoi auxiliaries on either side of a Xhosa intratribal conflict that pitted Ngqika (Gaika) against his uncle Ndlambe. When the "Third Kaffir War" erupted in 1799, hundreds of armed and mounted Khoikhoi fought on the Xhosa side, and Coenraad de Buys and his followers were still thick as thieves with Ngqika.

The Pandours remained in the pay of the Cape government until 1870, and were thought some of the best frontier troops. "It is no exaggeration to say that in the Xosa wars of 1846–7 and 1850–3 the Coloured People played a greater part in the defence of their country than the European burghers, who responded badly to calls for service," says Marais.

Two kinds of Afrikaner were steadily developing, the light and the dark, and the gulf between them rarely narrowed. In Cape Town around 1800, writes Freund, the atmosphere prevailing was one of "intense racial prejudice and snobbery not yet given legal expression." Whites lorded it over slaves, Khoikhoi, "free" blacks, and Bastards. The Khoikhoi, being recognized in law as a "free people" both under the VOC administration and its British successors, could not be made slaves. Yet they mingled with slaves, and to European eyes they seemed in some ways even more degraded. For a pittance in the way of drink or tobacco they would dance for the amusement of sailors to the chant of "ho-tani-du." Word of the ritual excision of one testicle, and of the elongated labia minora of the Khoikhoi women had spread, and visitors often bribed them to show their genitals.

The youngest of the Indo-European languages, Afrikaans grew up among speakers of many ancestries. In the slave cabins and among "free" blacks and Khoikhoi as much as among the racially exclusive burghers of Cape Town and the Boland, the language spoken was the *taal*, increasingly diverging from the seventeenth-century dialect of Amsterdam seamen and High Dutch alike. In the speech of the Cape the intonations of forgotten Khoikhoi tongues lent a lilt to gutturals from the shores of the North Sea. Words were added from Malay and Portuguese. Vowels altered shape, and among the dark-skinned, *j* tended to become *tch*.

Bloodlines, too, constantly diverged. Lighter-hued slaves, with the marks of European descent, were more valuable than dark-skinned ones, and slave-masters frequently encouraged miscegenation even where they did not personally practice it. One case is on record of a slave-owner who hired an Irishman solely for the purpose of "improving" his stock. The reduction of human beings to the status of property had the familiar moral consequences. "Sir," said a young Afrikaner condemned to death for killing a slave in 1822 to the clergyman attending him on the scaffold, "slavery is a bad system. It is even worse for the masters than it is for the slaves." Testimony of this sort is usually self-serving, but may perhaps be admitted when it precedes hanging.

The notion that there was something wrong with being a bastard was far from universal, as it later became. The Griqua, a people half Khoikhoi, half *trekboer*, "in varying degrees hunters and gatherers, pastoralists, hoe-cultivators and gun-carrying predators," who set up their own state along the lines of the Cape Colony, called themselves "Basters" as a matter of pride, until in 1813 the missionary John Campbell "represented to the principal persons the offensiveness of the word to an English or Dutch ear." But for that matter there are people in Namibia who unashamedly call themselves Basters to this day.

Griqualand was an open polity, one of the few truly nonracial societies that postconquest South Africa has known. Among the Griqua leadership were men like Jan July, by birth a Sotho; Donald Strachan, a first-generation immigrant from Britain; and Mosi Lipheana, an African chief: all received the title *Veld Kornet* (fieldcornet) from the Griqua captaincy. But the independence of the Griqua could not last. Caught between the Voortrekker republics and the advancing claims of the British empire, they were destined to be obliterated.

Afrikaans-speaking Christians, born like the Boers to the use of guns and horses, living under a European-style code of laws, the Griqua were still too African to win acceptance from a world founded on the dual code of race and property. They renounced race as a social criterion. Being who they were, they could scarcely do otherwise. And, at least in Griqualand West, they long continued to hold the earth in common. The captains administered the land on behalf of the people, and individuals and families had a right only to what they produced on it. Whites found this system of tenure as flimsy as they did in America. ("They have got as far as they can go, because they own their land in common," said United States Senator Dawes of the Five Civilized Tribes. "There is no selfishness, which is at the bottom of civilization.") And it is a fact, of course, that whenever Africans lost their political independence, they soon enough lost their land.

"The Griquas as a tribe," wrote the Civil Commissioner in 1903, "are practically extinct, and the few that are met with no longer possess any land: the old people who are alive are paupers, and their children are common labourers. All this has been due to drink." In Barkly West alone, the whites complained, there were thirty-five canteens supplying liquor to the Griqua trade in the year 1897. It was not asked why the once proud Griqua now stupefied themselves at every opportunity, but it seems reasonable enough to suppose that it was for the same reason that Eva had done so almost two and a half centuries before—from a sense of contumely, helplessness, and in general what is summed up in Afrikaans by *minderwaardigheid* ("lessworthfulness"). Reinforced by Social Darwinism and other pseudoscience, racist morality and ideology were in the process of becoming nearly universal. To be classed as "Coloured" was a stigma that blotted out humanity. As the melancholy refrain of the Rehoboth Basters of South West Africa had it, *"Dis treurig om 'n Baster te wees!"* ("It's sad to be a Baster!") Skin color, not character, was to be fate in South Africa.

3

SOL PLAATJE AND
THE DREAM OF DELIVERANCE

The voice of Mgijima reechoed
In the land, sobbing as it began.
He said: Here are the whites,
He said: Here is the gun,
He said: Here is overweening power,
He said: Today we die.
ZULU SONG.

A Kaffir's Life

"AFTER PARTAKING OF HOT CROSS buns at the family table of a dear old English family," wrote Solomon Tshekisho Plaatje, first secretary-general of the South African Native National Congress, one Easter Sunday in the depths of World War I, "I went to Walthamstow, and there heard a moving discourse . . . on the sufferings and death of Christ for the redemption of mankind."

Plaatje (pronounced Plai-key) had accompanied the Reverend John Dube, president of the SANNC, to England to protest the imposition by the all-white Parliament of the Union of South Africa of the Natives' Land Act of 1913. Of four and a half million black South Africans at that time, almost a million were tenant squatters on farms owned by whites. Reduced to this during the final phases of white conquest in the late nineteenth century, they were, to some extent, among the lucky ones. Many tribespeople in the Transvaal had, after their military defeat, been distributed as "apprentices" to white farmers by the republican authorities. Others were forced into servitude in the mines and towns by laws patterned after the Cape Colony's Glen Grey Act of 1894, which taxed all landless African males who did not work three months out of the year.

With time, many of the black tenant farmers had come to enjoy a moderate prosperity, though they might have to hand over

---

as much as 50 percent of their crop to the landlord. African peasantries were showing that they could adapt to the new economic order. Relations between farmer and tenant were frequently harmonious, so much so, thought Plaatje, as perhaps to cause an outside observer arriving on a South African farm to "wonder as to the meaning of the fabled bugbear anent the alleged struggle between white and black, which in reality appears to exist only in the fertile brain of the politician."

But the Natives' Land Act, which made it illegal for blacks to occupy farmland throughout the greatest part of the country, except as wage laborers, put an end to these "happy relations." The terms of employment offered to the former sharecroppers seemed a cruel joke: a few pounds a month for the labor of an entire family, with their livestock to be handed over to the white *baas* into the bargain. "Awakening on Friday morning, June 20, 1913, the South African Native found himself, not actually a slave, but a pariah in the land of his birth," Plaatje wrote bitterly.

Plaatje's view of the bucolic tranquillities disrupted by the new law may be extravagant, but he was correct in identifying political opportunism as the prime catalyst of conflict. Like much other South African legislation before and after, the act pandered to the inarticulate prejudice of the poor white electors who had, ironically, been given a controlling interest in the state in the name of liberty. Many farmers were undoubtedly opposed to it. Landowners had profited by leasing land to their black tenants, and were now conscious that they were being denied the right as a matter of crude political expediency. "How dare any number of men, wearing tall hats and frock coats, living in Capetown hotels at the expense of other men, order me to evict my Natives?" demanded one "Free" State Boer hotly. Even the minister who had introduced the law into Parliament, J. W. Sauer, long regarded as a liberal, "subsequently declared himself against it, adding that he forced it through only in order to stave off something worse."

In the circumstances it is hard to imagine what that might have been. Under the terms of the Natives' Land Act, blacks were to be prohibited even from renting pasturage for their livestock outside "Native Locations" which formed about one-eighteenth of the land area of the Union. Any landowner who allowed the stock belonging to a black tenant to remain on his property became liable to a fine of five pounds a day, while the penalty for accommodating a landless African squatter was a hundred pounds or six months in prison.

Scarcely comprehending that it had been made a crime for them to cultivate the land on their own account in their own country, tens of thousands of blacks took to the road to seek better terms, kinder masters. But though there were a handful willing to defy the law, landlords were not given the option of being kind within its bounds. There was nowhere for the people to go. Animals, children, the old and sick perished from exposure in the wintry weather. The Native National Congress sent out observers to monitor this "sickening procedure of extermination." John Dube visited Natal and the northern Transvaal; Saul Msane, Congress organizer, went into the eastern Transvaal; Richard Msimang, a Johannesburg attorney, traveled through other Transvaal districts; Plaatje himself visited various parts of the Transvaal, the Orange "Free" State and the Cape Province. Mostly they traveled on their own funds, or on what local sympathizers could provide. Plaatje rode a bicycle. On the road he fell in with a Boer mounted policeman, who amiably refrained from demanding the "pass" which all blacks were required by law to carry. (Since he did not have one, Plaatje was risking a fine and imprisonment.) The constable was companionable, even prepared to discuss the Land Act and its effect on the squatters:

> "The poor devils must be sorry now," he said, "that they ever sang 'God save the Queen' when the British troops came into the Transvaal, for I have seen, in the course of my duties, that a Kafir's life nowadays was not worth a ———, and I believe that no man regretted the change of flags now more than the Kafirs of Transvaal." This information was superfluous, for personal contact with the Natives of Transvaal had convinced us of the fact. They say it is only the criminal who has any reason to rejoice over the presence of the Union Jack, because in his case the cat-o'-nine-tails, except for very serious crimes, has been abolished.

Notwithstanding, Plaatje's personal advice to the wretched black refugees he met while cycling along through the *platteland,* was that they should try to escape from the "quasi-British Republic" that South Africa had become, and seek asylum in Bechuanaland (Botswana), a territory still "entirely British," for which "as a Bechuana we could not help thanking God."

Having sampled the rule of a democratically enfranchised minority, and with few illusions about the topsy-turvy scheme of things, Plaatje cast his vote for the lesser evil. He would have sympathized with the dedication of his Indian contemporary Nirad Chaudhuri's autobiography to the empire "which conferred subjecthood on us but withheld citizenship; to which yet every one of us threw out the challenge 'Civis Britannicus Sum.' "

It was a challenge voiced by subjects as disparate as Jan Smuts and Mahatma Gandhi. Like Gandhi, Plaatje believed "that British rule was for the benefit of the ruled, and that racial discrimination was a local un-British perversion, which could be cured." For him, as for Gandhi at this period, there was no avenue of emancipation visible save that opened up by the empire. If this was compromise with the realities of power, it was also sheer idealism. *Realpolitik* was balanced by the dream of empire—"a circle whose center is everywhere and which has no circumference."

Sol Plaatje was born in 1877 in the Orange "Free" State district of Boshof, a few dozen miles from Kimberley, where only a few years previously the greatest diamond mine in the world had been opened. His people, the Barolong, were a Tswana clan who earlier in the century had been allied with the Boers.

In 1836 Voortrekker pioneers, moving into the interior, had come into conflict with the warriors of the Ndebele (Matabele) warlord, Mzilikazi. The Ndebele, who numbered perhaps 80,000 at this time, had previously forced the Barolong from their homes on the other side of the Vaal river. Now they carried off all the Boers' horses and livestock, though unable to break into the ox-wagon laager, or encampment protected by a ring of the wagons. After the attack had been beaten off, the Voortrekker leader, Andries Hendrik Potgieter, sent to the Barolong Chief Moroka for help, which was promptly given in the shape of milch cows, sheep, goats, and draught oxen, without which the trekkers were effectively immobilized in their progress upcountry. Barolong warriors were sent to bring the Boers to safety at Moroka's stronghold of Thaba Nchu (Black Mountain). Here they licked their wounds and were presently reinforced by another Voortrekker party under Gert Maritz. Potgieter now assembled an alliance against the hated Ndebele. ("In our wars men killed other warriors, and captured the unarmed and non-resisting," says a character in Plaatje's historical novel, *Mhudi* [1930], which drew on the surviving oral tradition of the Barolong in describing these events. "They took the women and children home. But the Matabele, oh, the Matabele!")

In addition to the Boers and the Barolong, there was a contingent of Tlokwa sent by Sekonyela, the son of the famous warrior queen, MaNthatisi; there were the followers of a Griqua captain named Pieter Dout; and as it moved north the commando was joined by various Korana, chiefly of the Taaibosch clan, and a group of Bergenaars "composed of Christian men, so called, Bastards, Griquas, Namacquas, etc." These Bergenaars (Mountain Men) were bandits and cattle rustlers, led now by the notorious Jan Bloem the younger, son of a German fugitive from justice of the same name and a Springbok Korana mother, who preyed impartially on blacks, whites, and Griquas.* A few years earlier the West Griqua captain Andries Waterboer had executed six of them for banditry, and the Tlokwa (Mantatees, as they were called after MaNthatisi) had no reason to love them either. But all allies were acceptable in the struggle against the Ndebele.

This motley crew, totaling not many more than two hundred fighting men, of whom perhaps half were whites, carried the day. Mzilikazi's people sustained their most serious defeat at the battle of eGabeni in November 1837. In fact, the Ndebele were already on their way north, and the fighting with Potgieter's commando and its allies was more in the nature of rearguard cattle-raiding than war. Mzilikazi's great fear was the Zulu kingdom of Dingane to the east, from which he had originally broken away in 1822, followed by only a few hundred warriors. Since then he had built up a mighty fighting force, largely by assimilating those whom he defeated, but the primal fear of the Zulu survived. It would subside only after 1879, when the Zulu King Cetshwayo went down to defeat at the hands of a British army, and the Zulu nation was split into thirteen segments, each ruled by a British-appointed kinglet. It seems, too, that Mzilikazi had been warned to avoid conflict with the Boers by the famous missionary Robert Moffat, whom the Ndebele knew as the "King of Kuruman," and regarded with great respect. For all these reasons, they now vacated the Transvaal and crossed the Limpopo river into what became known as Matabeleland in the territory subsequently christened Rhodesia, now Zimbabwe. The Voortrekkers and their allies shared out the lands to the south.

With the Ndebele out of the way, Moroka's people took the field alongside the Boers against the southern Sotho kingdom of Moshweshwe, which has been described as "the core of African resistance to white expansion in south-eastern Africa throughout the 1850s and most of the 1860s." There were commonly more blacks than whites in the commandos of what came to be called the Orange Free State, among them Sotho defectors, Mfengu and Tlokwa as well as the Barolong. The Boers had so many native servants and spies that they knew all the paths into the Sotho mountain fortresses, Moshweshwe wrote bitterly to Theophilus Shepstone, the Natal secretary for native affairs, in 1868. The overriding power of the whites rested with technological superiority: rifles and cannons, which the Boers did not make themselves but bought through the Cape and Natal. Primitive pastoralists though the Afrikaners might be, they were nonetheless linked to the Euro-

* It is ironic that Jan Bloem's name was to be perpetuated in that of Bloemfontein, South Africa's judicial capital.

pean world order more closely than the Basotho. "Whites never fall
out, only blacks do," said the Tswana. One thing almost all whites
agreed on as a matter of principle—it was embodied in the Sand
River Convention between the British and the Boers—was not to
supply arms and ammunition to Africans. The Sotho fought
doggedly and bravely, but their defeat was inevitable.

And it was inevitable, too, of course, that the alliance between
Boer and Barolong would break down. After Moroka's death, the
"Free" Staters found a pretext to annex Thaba Nchu. Meanwhile
those Barolong who had elected to return to their ancestral homes
in the northwest found themselves in conflict with the Transvaal
Republic. Seeking to block the British advance northward into the
vast territories of Zambesia, the Transvaalers called into being two
unsubstantial satellite states, the republics of Goshen and Stellaland. If Britain failed to act against these trial balloons, the territory
was patently destined for incorporation into the Transvaal. Worse,
Bismarck's Germany had declared a protectorate over Angra Pequena in August 1884. "Bechuanaland . . . described as worthless a
year before, suddenly attained high and urgent importance as the
territorial wedge between the German hinterland and the Transvaal
Republic." Fighting broke out between the Goshenites and the people of the Barolong chief Montshiwa, and on the familiar pretext of
"restoring order," the imperial government sent in a force of 5,000
men—an enormous number in the circumstances—and annexed
the whole area under the title of the Crown Colony of British Bechuanaland in January 1885.

As both sides grasped, the essence of British strategy—we
might better call it Cape strategy—in the century-long chess game
played out over the South African veld, was to isolate the Boers
from the sea and from independent links with the European powers,
gradually to swamp them with English-speaking settlers, and ultimately to incorporate them once more into the polity they had tried
to flee in the 1830s. Their right to independence was never really
recognized. Even after the Boer victory of Majuba Hill (1881), only
"complete self-government, subject to the Suzerainty of Her Majesty," was conceded. In the context of southern Africa, the empire
was superpower without rival. The German threat was indirect,
since the Royal Navy could always block Bismarckian intervention.

The Boers, playing the hopelessly weaker hand, but always
refusing to concede the right of Downing Street (or Cape Town) to
rule them, watched themselves boxed in with mounting fury and
frustration. The irony of their historical experience was that in their
search for space they gradually found themselves further and further
hemmed in. It was appropriate that their national symbol should be

the ox-wagon laager, the mobile fortress of the Nguni wars. In the century to come they would make the whole of South Africa into a laager. But even now the world could not be shut out. Boer power —guns and information—and simple pleasures—coffee, tea, sugar, and spices—had always lain in contact with the world. For all their nomadic independence, they were a branch of Europe.

By the 1880s there were only two significant military powers left in South Africa: Boers and British. The independence of the Sutu-nguni peoples had been lost. In the Cape a century of struggle against the Xhosa terminated in triumph for the whites. But much of the actual fighting had been done by Khoikhoi/"Coloureds" and by the so-called Mfengu, or Fingoes, Nguni refugees originally displaced during the Mfecane, or "time of troubles," that accompanied the rise of Shaka's Zulu empire in Natal in the 1820s. Their name is said to derive from the word *siyamfenguza,* implying peaceful intentions even though spoken by armed men. Though driven from their homes, these Mfengu remained formidable fighters. From the 1830s onward they were the whites' greatest allies against the Xhosa, functioning as spies, guides, and shock troops. Having been through the terrible experience of the Mfecane, they were ruthless soldiers, who fought to the death and gave no quarter. Even in the war of 1850– 53, when numerous Khoikhoi/"Coloureds" made common cause with the Xhosas, including members of the Cape Mounted Rifles regiment, the Mfengu remained loyal. They considered themselves British subjects, but when the last war on the eastern frontier drew to a close in 1879, they were disarmed along with all other Cape Africans.

After their defeat by the Voortrekkers at Blood River on December 9, 1838, and the subsequent death of Dingane, the Zulus retrenched north of the Tugela. The new Zulu king, Mpande, took appointment at the hands of the Boer leader Andries Pretorius, and until the time of the British annexation a few years later, was a Voortrekker vassal. "In many ways Shaka's political revolution prepared Africans for the colonial take-over," says Shula Marks. "This was not only because after a long period of warfare the Africans of Natal were thankful for the milder conditions of British rule after 1843. It was also because colonial administrators were able to assume the centralized powers which the Zulu king had initiated without undue stress." African sentiments concerning the imposition of the Pax Britannica are debatable, but initially the imperial authorities interfered little in Zulu life, aside from abolishing the Shakan regimental system. As white settlement expanded, however, the inevitable encroachments began. "First comes the trader, then the missionary, then the red soldier," said the last Zulu king, Cetshwayo, who made a final bid for independence in 1879. Though ultimately defeated, the Zulu impis killed almost one thousand British veterans in the single battle of Isandhlwana, where more officers died than had fallen at Waterloo. The defeat at Isandhlwana sent reverberations through the empire. In faraway Burma, King Theebaw is said to have drunkenly ordered an attack on Rangoon when he heard the news.

At the Place of the Rocks

The Barolong tribal capital of Mafikeng, the Place of the Rocks, which the whites called Mafeking, came to have symbolic signifi-cance out of all proportion to its strategic value. For the Boers, the Union Jack that waved over Mafeking was a mark of their contain-ment; to the Cape imperialists, led by Cecil Rhodes, the town was a bastion on the march northward to Zambesia and beyond. Its psychic importance was grasped by Robert Stephenson Smyth Baden-Powell, who as commander-in-chief of the so-called "Rhode-sian Frontier Force" moved his troops into Mafeking with the assur-ance of a sleepwalker. (It was contrary to his orders and made no strictly military sense.) Baden-Powell was one of those who dreamed of coloring the map British pink from Cape to Cairo. During the second Ndebele War of 1896, he had played a leading part in crushing resistance to the operations of Rhodes's British South Africa Company; at one point Sir Hercules Robinson, the British high commissioner for South Africa and governor of the Cape Colony, a Rhodes ally, was sufficiently outraged to order Baden-Powell's arrest for the summary execution of the Ndebele leader Uwini by firing-squad. ("I felt sorry for him; he was a fine old blackguard," was "B-P" 's comment on this atrocity.) A court of inquiry found Baden-Powell not guilty; Uwini, it was asserted, had been a "notorious instigator of crime and rebellion" and shooting him "exercised a very wholesome influence on the surrounding dis-trict and undoubtedly expedited its final pacification." Now Baden-Powell was enthusiastically preparing for a war that would finally bring the Boers to heel.

The trouble was that British public opinion by no means wanted a South African war, and neither did the British cabinet, with the vital exception of the ex-radical from Birmingham who was now colonial secretary, Joseph ("Pushful Jo") Chamberlain. From the backwaters of the Board of Inland Revenue, Chamberlain plucked a suitable instrument in the shape of Sir Alfred Milner, whom he sent to Cape Town in 1897 to replace Sir Hercules. Between them the "Man from Birmingham" and the German-trained Milner introduced a whiff of Prussian steel into England's late-Victorian *fin de siècle*. If anyone could locate *casus belli* in South Africa, Milner surely would.

From Mafeking, Baden-Powell's chief staff officer, Major Lord Edward Cecil, fourth son of the British prime minister, Lord Salisbury, went to Cape Town to obtain supplies for the siege which was anticipated once hostilities had been provoked. He had no proper authority to do so, but after consulting with Milner, he raised the necessary cash himself, signing a personal "note of hand" for half a million pounds. The contractors "banked on Lord Edward's personality and his father's position, and the deal saved Mafeking," wrote his wife. (After Ned Cecil's death she married Milner and became his viscountess.) Sir William Butler, British commander-in-chief in the Cape Colony, presently resigned in protest against what he believed to be "a plot to force war on the Transvaal."

With only a truncated mission-school education behind him, the young Sol Plaatje had found his first job at the Kimberley Post Office as a letter carrier. He was just sixteen.* In his spare time he studied typing, shorthand, Dutch, and African languages. Taking the Cape Civil Service examinations, then conducted on a nonracial basis, he came first in every subject, and in 1898 he was appointed official interpreter at the Kimberley Magistrate's Court. Transfer to the Resident Magistrate's Court at Mafeking in the same capacity followed not long afterward. When the long-anticipated war broke out in October 1899, and the Boers showed their susceptibility to the symbolic by investing Mafeking with a large force which they could ill afford to spare, Plaatje found himself interpreter to the Court of Summary Jurisdiction, over which Lord Edward Cecil presided. In addition, he functioned as confidential clerk to C. G. H. Bell, the resident magistrate in charge of "native affairs," a sad-eyed, dyspeptic-looking man with a striking resemblance to Cecil Rhodes.

Black South Africans were relegated to the role of bystanders as Boer and Briton fought over the subcontinent. Those like Sol Plaatje, who played a part, did so under the delusion that a victorious England would champion their rights. They thought of themselves as black Englishmen. ("I am inclined to believe that the Boers have fully justified their bragging, for we are citizens of a town of subjects of the richest and strongest empire on earth and the Burghers of a small state have successfully besieged us for three months,"

* Coincidentally, more than half a century later I also worked for the Kimberley Post Office at sixteen.

we find Plaatje writing in January 1900.) It must have seemed inconceivable that when the war ended the British would prefer their white enemies to the loyal blacks.

In beleaguered Mafeking, as the editor of Plaatje's siege diary has pointed out, the biggest single population group was neither Boer nor British, but black—specifically, Barolong boo Ratshidi. As Bell's liaison officer and interpreter, Plaatje produced weekly reports on everything that had to do with the Barolong, which were greatly valued by the military command. He later asserted with customary wit that "this arrangement was so satisfactory that Mr. Bell was created a C.M.G. [Companion of the Order of St. Michael and St. George] at the end of the siege."

Notwithstanding the determination of both sides that it should be a "white man's war," Barolong frequently went through the lines to raid Boer cattle to supply the garrison with beef. There was also a so-called "Cape Boy Contingent," described by Plaatje as "a company of mixed classes in varying degrees of complexions." (Black males were "boys" no matter what their age.) These heirs to the Pandour military tradition turned out to be crack snipers. Afrikaans-speaking for the most part, they bantered during lulls in the shooting with their Boer opponents, with whom they had far more in common than they did with the British for whom they were risking their lives. There is reason to think that it was not the first time they had seen action: Baden-Powell had led two corps of "Cape Boys" against the Ndebele in 1896. At Mafeking they were commanded by Sergeant-Major Taylor—said to have been a bricklayer in civilian life—who was killed by a shell fragment in the fourth month of the siege. "His funeral was attended by General Baden-Powell [sic: B-P was still only a colonel; his promotion to major-general would come only after the relief of Mafeking had made his name a household word in England] and other staff officers, and was probably the only funeral of a coloured person in the South African war that was accorded such distinguished military attendance," Plaatje wrote.

Other blacks who fought at Mafeking included a unit of Mfengu, heirs like the "Cape Boys" to a long alliance with the English, and a so-called "Black Watch," comprised in Plaatje's words of "Mozambique and Zambesi boys, Shangaans and others from among the blackest races of South Africa," i.e., largely of what South Africans term "foreign natives." The latter unit sustained disaster when thirty-three of them out on a cattle raid were surrounded by a Boer commando, who slaughtered them to a man. The Mfengu and the Black Watch had been promised a farm as their reward when the war was over. They were never to receive it.

The use of black troops against them outraged the Boers. Their righteous indignation was articulated by General "Honest Piet" Cronje's senior medical officer, Dr. John E. Dyer, in a stiff note of protest:

> It is understood that you have armed bastards, Fingoes and Barolongs against us. In this you have committed an enormous act, the wickedness of which is certain, and the end of which no man can forsee. . . . I would ask you to pause and even now, at the eleventh hour, reconsider the matter, and even if it caused you the loss of Mafeking to disarm your blacks and thereby act the part of a white man in a white man's war.

This expression of the quintessential white South African attitude on the subject is lent irony by the fact that Surgeon-General Dyer was an American volunteer.

B-P's staff, his biographer observes, read like a page out of *Burke's Peerage, Baronetage and Knightage,* the who's who of the British aristocracy. In addition to Cecil there were his intelligence officer, Lieutenant the Honourable Algernon Hanbury-Tracy, son of Lord Sudeley; aide-de-camp Captain Gordon Wilson, son-in-law of the Duke of Marlborough; Captain Charles Fitzclarence, a descendant of William IV; Captain the Hon. Douglas Marsham, son of the Earl of Romney; and Lieutenant Lord Charles Cavendish-Bentinck, half-brother of the Duke of Portland. They roughed it in style, feasting come Christmas 1899 on turkey, plum pudding, wine, and brandy. Plentiful stores still included delicacies such as tinned salmon, duck, preserved fruit, and champagne. The Boers sportingly allowed a truce for the festivities.

For the blacks in besieged Mafeking things were different. For threepence a pint—a cruel imposition on a penniless people—they were supplied with a gruel made of horsemeat and oat husks. The soup kitchens realized over three thousand pounds during the course of the investment. Bell, the magistrate, more sensitive than most, noted,

> I am considerably worried during all hours of the day by hungry Natives, who lean against the garden wall and stare at me, exclaiming at invervals—*Baaije hongore Baas* [sic; the Afrikaans for "Very hungry, Boss," transcribed phonetically]; at the same time the fact is demonstrated by the supplicant smiting with his hand the black empty leather bag which represents his stomach.

Most people, *Times* correspondent Angus Hamilton wrote, were quite indifferent to the sufferings of the natives who, since they possessed no adequate bomb shelters, were killed and injured in far greater numbers than the whites. Hamilton himself was deeply impressed by the fortitude with which the blacks bore their injuries: "When the gaze of the curious is turned upon his mangled and wounded form, he attempts to laugh, makes every effort to assist himself, and even if he knows that his injuries be fatal, he makes no sign."

While Baden-Powell and his men celebrated Christmas night with concert parties and enjoyed a "screamingly jolly entertainment" in a makeshift theater, complete with amateur Christy Minstrels, one Jim Mbala, found guilty of rumor-mongering and of being outside the lines without a pass, was executed by firing squad in the native village. He was only one of a number of Africans shot by the British for alleged spying; others were sentenced to death by Cecil's Court of Summary Jurisdiction for minor crimes, such as the theft of a goat or a horse. As for Sol Plaatje, the only African drawing European rations in Mafeking, he spent the festive season ill in bed with flu, thinking nostalgic thoughts about his distant wife and baby son. "Surely," he confided to his diary, "Providence has seldom been so hard on me."

Captain Fitzclarence made a surprise attack on a Boer shelter one night and butchered the dozing defenders with sword and bayonet. "The work was largely held by boys who, of course, had to take their chance with the men in the massacre," wrote Emerson Neilly, correspondent for the *Pall Mall Gazette*. "It is not too much to the taste of your soldier to bayonet a lad of thirteen or fourteen; but if any shame attaches to the killing of youngsters, it must rest on the shoulders of those fathers who brought them there." Outnumbered in all their wars, and more so than ever in this one, the Boers did not exclude boys from the battle line. On this occasion Fitzclarence personally dispatched three or four of them with his sword. He later received the Victoria Cross. To be fair, the British leadership viewed the deaths of its own men with almost equal impassivity. An attack on a Boer fort on Boxing Day resulted in heavy losses for the British. In this debacle Baden-Powell professed to perceive only "a brilliant example" which must certainly, he thought, have caused the enemy to take note of "the fatal results of storming a position." And presently he was back to his famous practical jokes and amateur dramatics. For B-P it was a lovely war.

In retrospect, Mafeking has been seen as a high-water mark of empire, which thenceforth ebbed steadily. In South Africa, British vanity sustained something of the shock that America would suffer in Vietnam seventy years later. Though England won the war, she learned that she was not invincible. "We must face the facts," Winston Churchill had written after his sensational escape from Pretoria. "The individual Boer, mounted in suitable country, is worth

.from three to five regular soldiers. . . . The only way of treating the
problem is either to get men equal in character and intelligence as
riflemen or, failing the individual, huge masses of troops." In the
end it was the mass army which Britain was obliged to opt for,
pouring almost 450,000 men under arms into South Africa to defeat
largely irregular Boer forces of perhaps 50,000. The war lasted three
years, and cost the British taxpayer the then stupendous sum of a
quarter of a billion pounds.

The Boers saw their struggle as a fight for freedom. "It is or-
dained that we, insignificant as we are, should be the first among
the peoples to begin the struggle against the new world of tyranny
of capitalism," wrote Smuts, who exhorted his people to answer
England as the Greeks had answered Xerxes, and as their own ancestors had resisted Richelieu, Alva, and Louis XIV. A storm of anti-
British feeling went round the world—sometimes taking odd forms,
as in Haiti, where the Boers were widely believed to be rebel blacks.
The European press was filled with anti-British cartoons. As Victoria's reign drew to a close, British pink still colored a quarter of the
globe. But two great powers, Germany and the United States, were
pulling ahead in the vital areas of technology and industrial production. Britain had almost been at war with France in 1898 over the
Fashoda incident, and the fifth power, Russia, displayed a voracious
imperial appetite and sometimes seemed the greatest threat of all.
The jingoes were whistling in the dark. The "Age of Imperialism"
sought more for security than for empire.

The war also served to mobilize radical opinion in England.
The role of bully was not one Englishmen could accept with equa-
nimity, though there were only a handful—among them men like
Lloyd George and G. K. Chesterton—who had the courage to be
openly pro-Boer. Opposition was voiced in pamphlets such as W. T.
Stead's *Shall I Slay My Brother Boer?*; organizations such as the
Stop the War Committee were formed. But most people draw together under pressure, and this instinctive solidarity lay behind the
war fever which engulfed Britain. It reached its peak in May 1900
when the long-awaited relief column made its way into besieged
Mafeking. Wild scenes of jingoist hysteria swept England and the
loyal Dominions, a new verb, "to maffick," temporarily making its
appearance to describe the goings-on.

Something of a sea change may be seen in England after the
orgy of Mafeking Night. The myths of the aristocratic kindergarten
were being supplied with mass underpinnings. The urbane rulers of
the past were giving way to a new breed of party politician, as Lord
Salisbury had been obliged to give way to Pushful Jo over South
Africa. A new and nastier spirit was finding its way into public life,

and new means had to be found to discipline the middle class patriotism which was henceforth to be the strong arm of the nation. Into this breach stepped the Hero of Mafeking. Beginning in 1907, Baden-Powell's Boy Scouts (whose motto "*Be Prepared*" he characteristically derived from his own initials) took on the task of "making the rising generation, of whatever class or creed, into good citizens or useful colonists." Support came from Yellow Press tycoon Cyril Arthur Pearson, owner of the London *Daily Express* and *Tit-Bits*, and when the war with Germany which he had long been predicting broke out, Baden-Powell was able to inform War Secretary Lord Kitchener that "The Boy Scouts are now ready in all counties and are already at work in several, in numbers of not less than a thousand in each county, in assisting the local defence, civil and municipal authorities."

Baden-Powell kept up a steady stream of books with titles like *My Adventures as a Spy* (1915), *Life's Snags and How to Meet Them* (1927), and *Lessons from the 'Varsity of Life* (1933). He and his real and fictional avatars (Lawrence of Arabia, Biggles, Monty, James Bond) supplied millions of middle class boys with food for fantasy. In the Anglo-Saxon world the generation which grew up after World War I found its spiritual nourishment in the boys' weeklies which George Orwell described in a famous essay as "sodden in the worst illusions of 1910." But why 1910? What were they, after all, but the illusions of Mafeking?

B-P's influence knew no frontiers. In Fascist Italy, Mussolini created the counterpart of the Boy Scouts in the Balilla and Avanguardisti movements; in Germany there was the Hitler-Jugend; in Russia the Komsomol. We will not go so far as to trace all these to the Cadet Corps organized in Mafeking by Cecil and Baden-Powell. South Africa, "the culture-bed of British Imperialism," merely served as a focus for forces already abroad.

Discovered hidden inside the cover of an old scrapbook, almost seventy years after it had been written, Sol Plaatje's Mafeking diary is unique in giving an African perspective on the events of the siege. Nothwithstanding his literary and other abilities, the dandified interpreter of the Court of Summary Jurisdiction was only twenty-two. His studied urbanity expressed unthinking allegiance to what he clearly saw as the Top Culture. He had many painful lessons yet to learn.

Firmness in the Truth

When the Anglo-Boer war ended—even the Pretoria *News* conceded —Sol Plaatje would have been able to claim a prominent position in the administration but for the color bar. Instead he became a news-paper editor, first of the Mafeking weekly *Koranta ea Batswana* (*Botswana Courant*), then of *Tsala ea Batho* (*The People's Friend*), a trilingual weekly published in Kimberley. In the short time since their exposure to it, South African blacks had grasped the printed word as a weapon. John Tengo Jabavu had begun publishing his famous paper *Imvo Zabantsundu* (*The Brown People's Opinion*) at Kingwilliamstown in the 1880s. Another prominent paper was John Dube's *Ilanga lase Natal* (*The Sun of Natal*). In Johannesburg, Ku-nene and Soga brought out *Abantu-Batho*, the national organ of the SANNC. But it rapidly became apparent that if blacks were not to be utterly dispossessed in the land of their birth, they would need to move from polemics and pleas to political action. Since they were almost entirely excluded from the electoral process, what form could such action take? They had before them an impressive model in Mohandas K. Gandhi, later called the Mahatma, who in the fate-ful year 1906 launched the Satyagraha movement in the Empire Theatre, Johannesburg.

Indentured Indian laborers, chiefly low-caste Hindus from Madras, Calcutta, and Bombay, had been imported to work sugar plantations in Natal from as early as 1860. A percentage of Indian women came with them. On completing their five-year contracts, many of the Indians decided to stay on in the new country, and another population group rapidly sprang up. A fresh element was added to the Indian community by Muslim merchants attracted to South Africa by prospects of trade. When Gandhi first stepped ashore at Durban in 1893, there were about seventy-six thousand Indians in South Africa as a whole. In Natal itself, where they were most numerous, they slightly outnumbered the whites. (Within the boundaries of the future Union there were then between six and seven hundred thousand whites, between two and three million Sutu-nguni, and several hundred thousand "Coloureds"; despite great increases in all these population groups, the ratios remain roughly the same today.)

Even by the rough-and-ready standards of the Cape Colony, white Natalians, mostly first- and second-generation English and Scottish immigrants, presented a picture of deep-seated racial big-otry. So-called "responsible government" had been granted the whites by the imperial administration in the year of Gandhi's ar-rival. By the frank admission of one of their representatives in the Natal Legislative Assembly, its main object had been "to get control of the natives into the hands of the colonists." The settlers lived in close proximity to the Zulus, traditionally the most warlike of black South African peoples, who as recently as 1879 had all but annihi-lated a British regiment that had been sent against them. Fear aside, many whites were given to the curious notion that blacks had a bounden duty to work for them—something for which the Zulus had little taste. By contrast the Indians were meek and pacific, lived frugally and worked hard. As everywhere in Africa, they prospered at trade. There was little doubt that, unhampered, they would eventually present the whites with serious competition. As Milner's protégé Lionel Curtis told Gandhi, it was not the vices of the Indians that the whites feared, but their virtues. Knowing little or nothing about them, most South African whites entertained extravagant biases against Orientals in general. The Indians were said to be "squalid coolies," devoid of any sense of decency, and with profligate sexual appetites, who were likely to suffer from "loathsome diseases." In the Transvaal, segregation was imposed on them for "sanitary" reasons. Both in Natal and in the Transvaal, legislation aimed at further restricting their rights was in the offing.

Into this morass of neurosis came the shy, puritanical young Gandhi, bound for Pretoria on legal business on behalf of a Gujarati firm with interests in the Transvaal. In one of history's great demonstrations of the force of the individual will, he rapidly mobilized hitherto passive Indian opinion behind him, and in 1894 launched the Natal Indian Congress. Though partly modeled on the National Congress of India, an elitist organization established under English patronage less than ten years previously, the NIC was far more revolutionary in its aims. Within a few years the young lawyer—he was not yet thirty—had become the outstanding spokesman of Indians in South Africa.

The outbreak of the Anglo-Boer war in 1899 posed Gandhi with a dilemma. His sympathies, like those of many other Indians, were contradictory. As Nirad Chaudhuri, a small boy in distant Bengal at the time, later expressed it:

> We thought of the Boers as a heroic people and of their leaders, particularly of Cronjé and Botha, as men of superhuman valour. Our reaction to the Boer War, as to every war in which England was involved, was curiously mixed. One-half of us automatically shared in the English triumph, while the other and the patriotic half wanted the enemies of England to win.

Gandhi was, moreover, a romantic, who instinctively sided with the Boer David's stand against the British Goliath.

On the other hand, he had personally been booted off the sidewalk outside President Kruger's Pretoria residence by a ZARP (Zuid-Afrikaansche Republiek cop), and subjected to various other indignities. And he saw himself as a citizen of the empire, which for all its flaws was a structure capable of development, with a demonstrated sense of responsibility for its Indian subjects. "Hardly ever have I known anybody to cherish such loyalty as I did to the British Constitution," he wrote in his autobiographical book *The Story of My Experiments with Truth*. The Mahatma-to-be had a deeper grasp of potential than most men (perhaps because things were possible for him which were not so for others). In any case, he could not remain uninvolved. He set about raising an ambulance corps, which ultimately numbered some 1,100 Indians in its ranks. Though the high command accepted this contribution to the war effort by the despised coolies with some reluctance, the Indians got on well with the ordinary soldiers.

Like many Africans, Indians tended to believe that British victory would open the way to a fresh dispensation in South Africa; consistent with his commitment to the empire, Gandhi loyally commemorated the death of Queen Victoria by placing a wreath at her statue in Durban on behalf of the Indian community. The new day was slow in dawning. Real power increasingly passed to the reconciled Boers personified by Smuts and Botha, and their English South African counterparts.

The clarity of Gandhi's convictions overcame any hesitations he may have felt about the path of right action. In 1903 he established *Indian Opinion*, a cooperatively produced newspaper which was to prove crucial in mobilizing for the coming struggle. A Transvaal Indian Congress was formed to complement the Natal organization. Also important for the struggle were the nonracial agrarian communities he set up under the influence of Tolstoy and Ruskin both in Natal and in the Transvaal. Tolstoy Farm, about twenty miles from Johannesburg, was to prove a haven for weary *satyagrahis*. Tolstoy himself, in correspondence with Gandhi in the years before his death, endorsed the Mahatma's work in South Africa as "the most important now being done in the world."

As early as 1900 a Natal Native-Congress had been formed by a group including Mark Radebe, Saul Msane, John Dube, Josiah Gumede, and Martin Lutuli (uncle of the future Nobel Prize winner). Its aim was to articulate mounting African grievances against the white oligarchy. In so doing, it proceeded cautiously. The leadership of the congress were many of them ministers of religion, and as such represented the vanguard of the Kolwa, or "Believers," as Christian Africans were called in Natal. They saw armed resistance to white power as futile, not to say suicidal. The way to freedom, they believed, lay through education and political organization. It was to further these ends that Dube founded his famous newspaper *Ilanga lase Natal* (which still exists) and established the Ohlange Institute, a school for Africans inspired in part by the work of

Booker T. Washington, whom Dube had met on a visit to the United States, at Tuskegee, Alabama. But though Cetshwayo himself was long dead, the spirit of Isandhlwana survived, and a new "pan-Zulu feeling" coalesced around his son Dinuzulu. "Even peoples who had previously seen themselves as refugees from the Zulu kingdom and regarded its king as their enemy were now prepared to look towards the Zulu Royal family for their inspiration," writes Shula Marks. The morbid fantasies of the settlers were exacerbated when Africans began slaughtering the white animals among their stock, which was seen as precursory to an uprising against white rule. Resistance began with widespread refusal to pay the harsh poll tax, which escalated into full-scale rebellion in 1906.

There was never any serious threat to white rule, but the events of 1906, which will always be associated with the name of Bambata, the deposed Zondi chief who was the main African leader, illustrated the colonial mentality at its most brutal. Military operations were entrusted to Colonel Duncan McKenzie of the Natal Carbineers, a fanatical "nigger walloper," whose progress was marked by drumhead courts-martial and firing squads. Bambata and his men retreated into the Nkandhla forest, where they were tracked by a settler expeditionary force and cut down by machine-gun fire. In the years to come the Zulu would sing:

> You black man who know not come and see;
> Here are white bones.
> Don't bring tears to my eyes,
> The bones are white at Nkandhla.

Overall, some thirty whites and between three and four thousand blacks died. Accompanying the Natal forces in the later stages was a contingent of twenty-five Indian stretcher-bearers under the command of Sergeant-Major M. K. Gandhi. Most of their patients consisted of "suspects" who had been flogged at McKenzie's orders. There was nothing to justify the name of "rebellion," Gandhi wrote, no visible resistance. What he saw in Zululand had a profound effect on him, and he determined to devote his life to the service of humanity.

Dinuzulu, who had never openly associated himself with the rebellion, was tried for high treason, imprisoned, and finally exiled permanently from Zululand. He died in the Transvaal in 1913. In many ways, the Bambata rebellion can be seen as a turning-point in the history of black South Africa. The period of tribal resistance, long futile in the face of superior organization and technology, now came to an end. The struggle for national liberation and democratic rights began. This was also perhaps the last occasion on which Downing Street made a serious bid to exert imperial authority in

South Africa. Twelve men sentenced to death by one of McKenzie's courts-martial were ordered reprieved by London, but the Colonial Office backed down in the face of the resignation *en bloc* of the Natal government, and a wave of protest from white South Africa. The twelve were shot in front of their assembled countrymen.

While Gandhi was leading his stretcher-bearers in Natal, news came of a new assault on Indian rights in the Transvaal, where Lionel Curtis was pushing a permit system for all Asians, including women and children, equivalent to the pass system which regulated the movements and domicile of Africans. Gandhi's philosophy of passive resistance, the famous *satyagraha* (the Gujarati translates as "firmness in the truth") is viewed historically as having evolved in response to this challenge. But there is much evidence that his experiences in Zululand were even more decisive to it. "The term denotes the method of securing rights by personal suffering; it is the reverse of resistance by arms," Gandhi wrote.

The effects of *satyagraha* were to spread far beyond the borders of South Africa: in India to the horrors of Amritsar and finally to independence; in the United States to Martin Luther King's civil rights struggle, Selma and Little Rock; and to a worldwide revulsion against colonialism. "South Africa's white leaders provoked it, thus lighting a fire which was to spread across the Indian Ocean in a setpiece of Imperial suicide," says Gandhi's biographer Geoffrey Ashe. In all this the doomed uprising of Bambata and his people played a part.

In South Africa, too, Bambata had his influence. "I thank Bambata," said a member of the audience at one of the first meetings of the South African Native National Congress addressed by John Dube in 1912. "I thank Bambata very much. Would this spirit might continue! I do not mean the Bambata of the bush who perished at Nkandhla, but I mean this new spirit which we have just heard explained."

Gandhi's success in mobilizing South African Indians to act against racism remains unique: at one stage 2,500 of the 13,000 Indians in the Transvaal were simultaneously in jail. Initially double-crossed by the wily Smuts, Gandhi in the end saw all his demands met. He spent several terms in South African prisons. While there he made a pair of sandals which he presented to his arch-enemy Smuts on departing the country. Though Smuts is reported to have worn them, he was clearly glad to see the last of Gandhi. "The saint has left our shores," he wrote. "I sincerely hope forever."

In 1902, the Natal Native Congress was joined by another African organization, the South African Native Congress, founded in the Eastern Cape. Early in the new century, too, the redoubtable Dr. Abdul Abdurahman (1872–1940) had established the African People's Organization in Cape Town. The paradoxes of South African political life have always been abundant, however, and the APO did not seriously attempt to address the Sutu-nguni mass of the African people, but aimed rather at organizing "Coloured" and "Malay" opinion. Still, Sol Plaatje became a member.

The modern South African state came into being with the passage at Westminster of the South Africa Act of 1909. A few years later, on January 8, 1912, the South African Native National Congress (later the African National Congress of South Africa) was formed. John Dube was president, Sol Plaatje was general corresponding secretary, and P. Ka I. Seme, a Columbia University graduate and Middle Temple lawyer, who had been the chief inspirer of the new organization, became treasurer. The formidable real obstacles in the path of the SANNC may be judged from one of the resolves it presently came to:

> This Congress hereby decides to appoint a committee to investigate all cases of shooting of natives by Europeans in each province, and to place the result before the Government.

The government, alas, had been responsible for shooting more Africans than even the energetic *plattelanders* could independently accomplish.

A 1921 report to the Comintern by D. I. Jones for the International Socialist League of South Africa, precursor of the Communist party, dismissed the SANNC as a "small coterie of educated natives" who were "satisfied with agitation for civil equality and political rights." This illustrates the patronizing mentality of the white South African radicals, and their inability to see further than their Marxist-Leninist noses. Nonetheless, the educated minority of Africans found themselves in an unenviable position, despised by both the whites and the majority of their own people. D. D. T. Jabavu wrote:

> If I am stranded in the rural areas I dare not go to a Boer farm speaking English and wearing boots and a collar without inviting expulsion with execration; but if I go barefooted and collarless and in rags I shall enjoy the warmest hospitality. The higher one climbs in the scale of civilization the worse things are if one be blackskinned.

And most ordinary Africans were just as suspicious as the Boers of their Europeanized brethren, whom they called

> *Ama-Kumsha* or *Ma-Kgomocha;* that is, literally—speakers of European languages, a word which, however, in the mind of a tribal

Muntu, is always associated with something of deceit, and is almost synonymous with that meaning turn-coat, cheat, or trickster.

Thus S. M. Molema, a clansman of Sol Plaatje's, who became a doctor of medicine and national treasurer of the ANC, himself very much one of these *Ma-Kgomocha*. Detached by circumstances from their tribal roots, caught up in a world culture convinced beyond debate that the old ways were doomed, they nonetheless took as their slogan *Mayibuy' i-Afrika!* (Let Africa Come Back!) Deep down they knew that African morality was superior to the ethics of apartheid, and to most of what locally represented itself as Christianity. And they believed, too, that, as John Dube's famous aphorism put it, *Lapho ake ema khona amanzi ayophinde eme futhi* (Where there was once a pool, water will collect again). Still, faced with the desperate need to act, and act at once, in the face of heartless exploitation, they turned to the very power which had overwhelmed them, to "Imperialism, not in its narrow and selfish sense, but in so far as it presents a high political morality." The 1917 SANNC conference stressed that

> The natives of this continent are loyal subjects of His Majesty King George V., and most emphatically deny that either General Smuts or the Union Government have any right to rob the natives of their human rights and guarantees of liberty and freedom under the Pax Britannica.

As was clear from the steady stream of legislation aimed at further consolidating the position of the already all-powerful whites, however, Botha and Smuts proposed to do just that. The torrent of laws and regulations devised for the purpose still flows today, fed by bottomless insecurities. Britannia neither could nor would hinder it.

It seems almost incredible that at the outbreak of World War I in 1914, the SANNC, "resolving itself at once into a patriotic demonstration, decided to hang up native grievances against the South African Parliament till a better time and to tender the authorities every assistance." The offer was conveyed to Pretoria in person by President Dube and his executive. "What is our Government doing?" wondered Sol Plaatje agitatedly. "When is it going to move? Surely our Prime Minister . . . should now postpone the constant pampering of the back-velders, hang colour prejudice for a more peaceful time, call out the loyal legions—British, Boer, and Black— and annex German South Africa [Namibia] without delay!" Such sentiments were far from unique among black South Africans. Dr. Walter Rubusana (who as Cape provincial councillor for Tembuland had official status) wrote to the minister of native affairs offering to raise "if you deem it necessary, a native levy of 5,000 able-bodied men to proceed to German South-West Africa, provided the Government is prepared to fully equip this force for the front." From Natal came an offer "to raise a crack Zulu regiment composed of men who had formerly fought for the old flag against their own people." Other offers, Plaatje wrote, came from

> the Zulu chiefs and headmen, from Chief Dalindyebo of the Tembus, Marelana of the Pondos, and from Griffiths of Basutoland. In Bechuana-land, the veteran Chief Khama and other Bechuana chiefs offered the services of native warriors as scouts in German South West Africa, and the Swazi princes offered a Swazi impi, besides undertaking to help in any other manner, as they did in the campaign against Seku-kuni in the 'seventies. The members of the native deputation in England were longing to catch the first steamer back to South Africa to join their countrymen and proceed to the front. But while all these offers were gratefully acknowledged, none were definitely accepted. Surely there must be something wrong. Is it that the wretched South African colour prejudice is exerting itself even in these critical times?

Certainly it was not British policy that the war should be kept white: black troops under British officers in West Africa had early annexed German Togoland, and Indian regiments played a major role in some theaters. In East Africa, black troops of the King's African Rifles were engaged against Von Lettow Vorbeck's predom-inantly black German forces. No, this was South African prejudice determining British policy—and not for the last time. Even the Cape "Coloured" people were rejected as cannon fodder, though they massed in Cape Town City Hall to proclaim their loyalty to King George V, and Dr. Abdurahman, president of the APO, sent the Union government an offer of a force of thousands of volunteers ready to go to the front. The Coloureds, declared the APO news-paper, had "closed their book with its ugly record against the Botha Government, and offered the Prime Minister their loyal support during the war." But the book was not to be closed so easily.

When a deputation was elected by the SANNC to accompany President John Dube to London to protest the Natives' Land Act, Sol Plaatje was the first choice of his fellow members. (Others cho-sen were Dr. Walter Rubusana, the only black man ever elected to the Cape Provincial Council, and a Xhosa by birth; T. M. Mapikela, a Fingo; and Saul Msane, a Zulu like Dube, who had been one of the founders of the Natal Native Congress.) In Cape Town the delegates met and appealed vainly to Governor General Lord Gladstone and Premier Louis Botha. Gladstone, despite expressions of "astonishment and pity," offered no hope of amelioration, and advised them to abandon their appeal to England. Botha attempted to exonerate himself with the assertion that he personally had not evicted the natives on his farm, an odd stance for the head of government to take. He protested that Parliament would think him mad if he tried to amend the law at that stage, further confirming the decision of the SANNC deputation to proceed to London without delay.

But deliverance from what Plaatje clearly saw and defined as "the Coming Servitude" was not to be found in wartime England. The delegates got sympathy and support from the Anti-Slavery and Aborigines Protection Society and various church groups, but Colonial Secretary Harcourt was less than helpful. Hearing them out, he neither took notes nor asked questions. On every point they raised, it seemed, he had "the assurance of General Botha" to the contrary. The Union premier had told him, he informed them blandly, that the natives had too much land already.

Sol Plaatje, if not Mr. Harcourt, remembered only too well that General Botha had a few years previously been commandant-general of the armies of the South African Republic—against which England had expended hundreds of millions of pounds and tens of thousands of lives. It had taken just eight years to the day from the signing of the Peace of Vereeninging to May 31, 1910, when England effectively handed over her black subjects in South Africa to her former foes. Botha's deputy, Smuts, now sat in the Imperial War Cabinet. South African troops would soon take the offensive in German South-West and East Africa, as well as in Europe. The war effort was not to be jeopardized over the question of land that belonged to powerless Africans. "If the Government of South Africa is not to be trusted in this matter they are to be trusted in nothing; and we know perfectly well that they can be trusted," Harcourt told the House of Commons.

Sol Plaatje continued to place his faith in British civilization, and to hope that one day England would "grapple with this dark blot on the Imperial emblem, the South African anomaly that compromises the justice of British rule and seems almost to belie the beauty, the sublimity and the sincerity of Christianity." In England he addressed more than fifty public meetings and published a book vividly depicting the effects of the Natives' Land Act and arguing against the injustice and sheer illogic of handing over loyal British subjects to England's enemies (such he insisted they were, and the pro-German rebellion of 1914 provided him with fresh ammunition). The position of black South Africans—"a helotage under a Boer oligarchy," he called it, in words that perhaps consciously echoed Milner's summation of the condition of the Transvaal *Uit-*

landers in 1899 *—was intolerable. He was sure, however, that a consensus of British opinion might "stay the hand of the South African Government, veto this iniquity and avert the Nemesis that would surely follow its perpetration." Having striven to extend the sphere of British influence in South Africa, he could scarcely believe that England would now betray her promises.

"Shall we appeal to you in vain?" he pleaded. "I HOPE NOT."

In 1919, the Great War over, Plaatje and another SANNC delegation (consisting of J. T. Gumede, L. T. Mvabaza, R. V. Selope Thema, and H. R. Ngcayiya) tackled British Prime Minister Lloyd George, the archbishop of Canterbury, the colonial secretary, and various members of Parliament. From London they went to Versailles, where delegations from all over the world were pressing their claims on the Peace Conference. (Among them a group of Afrikaner nationalists led by General J. B. M. Hertzog.) It was to no avail. Neither the peacemakers nor the Colonial Office would intervene in South Africa's internal affairs. The SANNC delegates were advised to go back home and submit their grievances to the Union government.

All this was long before anyone had heard of apartheid (a word which did not come into currency until the 1930s) or *baasskap.* Hendrik Frensch Verwoerd was a schoolboy; Balthazar "John" Vorster was a baby.

A number of reasons may be mooted to explain Britain's betrayal of her black South African subjects—cupidity, weakness and guilt among them. Racist sentiment—almost universal in the English-speaking world of the day, and widely believed to have scientific foundations by contemporaries—was on the rise. As to the economics of the sellout, Plaatje noted that the Witwatersrand mines had served "to maintain the credit of the Empire with a weekly output of £750,000 worth of raw gold." In the years since the opening of the Rand mines in 1886, they have produced the bulk of the world's gold supply, billions of dollars' worth, no matter what the price. The diamond fields, though not nearly as profitable as gold, were also sources of enormous wealth. The political power of several hundred thousand black miners who risked their lives underground for a pittance was negligible compared to that of the skilled white mineworkers, let alone the mine owners.

* In his famous telegram to Chamberlain of May 4, 1899, Milner had declared that "The spectacle of thousands of British subjects kept permanently in the position of *helots,* constantly chafing under undoubted grievances, and calling vainly to her Majesty's Government for redress, does steadily undermine the influence and reputation of Great Britain and the respect for the British Government within its own dominions."

Another significant factor was liberal opinion. Campbell-Bannerman's government in England was bent on conciliating the Afrikaner. After Mafeking Night, the pendulum had swung in the opposite direction. The "methods of barbarism" by which Kitchener had forced peace on the Boers, including the invention of the concentration camp, filled the British intelligentsia with revulsion. Over 26,000 women and children—an eighth of the Boer population of the two republics—had died of disease in the camps. These victims became a lever with which to pry independence from Downing Street.

In any case, Milner had from the outset perceived the goal of British policy as "a self-governing white Community, supported by *well-treated* and *justly governed* black labour from Cape Town to Zambesi." His successor, the second earl of Selborne, was personally opposed to restraints like the pass laws and the industrial color bar, and believed that "the worst form of government for natives is direct government by a Parliament of white men." Nonetheless, he thought blacks "absolutely incapable of rivalling the white man. . . . No one can have any experience of the two races without feeling the intrinsic superiority of the white man. All history in addition proves it." This was by and large what liberal opinion in London amounted to. "Imperial Britain, as represented by Lord Selborne, had by now absorbed pretty thoroughly the ideas of the conquered Boers," observes W. K. Hancock.

To Milner and his fellows, Afrikaner nationalism was an anachronism which ought to be stamped out. (It is doubtful whether they even conceived of an African nationalism.) Progress lay in the creation of an English-speaking greater South Africa under the crown. Milner had envisaged massive immigration from the British Isles after the Anglo-Boer war, but the expected wave of new settlers failed to materialize. Afrikaners remained more than half of the white population of South Africa, and hence the controlling element in an oligarchy based on limited franchise.

Writing during the Boer War, J. A. Hobson, whose work *Imperialism* (1902) was subsequently adapted by Lenin in one of the most influential pamphlets of all time, predicted that in the postwar period Downing Street would be obliged to choose between "an oligarchy of financial Jews, and the restoration of Boer domination," since there was no other basis for a government in South Africa. Hobson was wrong. The Imperial government could, and did, choose both. The new realities were clearly stated by Winston Churchill, the undersecretary of state for the colonies, who observed that "British authority in South Africa must stand on two legs." Political power was reconstructed on a basis of modified Afrikaner nationalism plus Chamber of Mines financial clout. White populism was perceived

as a restraint on the magnates of the Rand, who would be less overwhelming in the context of a broader union. "If Hoggenheimer has
to do, not only with the crippled population of the Transvaal, but
with the people of South Africa, there will be some chance of keeping him in his right place politically," Smuts wrote to John X. Merriman in 1906.

Kitchener's mighty army faded away. Early in 1907 Louis
Botha formed a government in the Transvaal, his Het Volk party
having won more than half the seats in the new Legislative Assembly. Botha wooed the white mine workers of the Rand, "stressing
the identity of material interests between farmers and artisans, in
the face of the capitalist threat." Needless to say, the alliance of
Boer and *Uitlander* against the "Hoggenheimers" was as much a
temporary marriage of convenience as the earlier alliance of *Uitlander* and capitalist against the Boers had been. If there was a consolidating factor it was racism and antisemitism. (Hobson had earlier
noted the presence in Johannesburg of a disproportionate element of
German and Russian Jews who "Anglicised their names after true
parasitic fashion," and whose "real strength," he said, could be
gauged from the fact that "the directory of Johannesburg shows 68
Cowens against 21 Jones and 53 Browns.") Milner was not wrong
when he contemptuously dismissed "the socialism of Johannesburg" as "the hollowest sham in the World."

Milner's own creed was imperialism pure and simple; not, he
would have it understood, in the narrow old sense, but as an ideal of
British fraternity throughout the white, English-speaking world (including the United States). Clearly it was racial fraternity that was
meant. Thus Milner argued against Dominion status for India, inasmuch as there did not exist "the same *natural* affinities between
Great Britain and India as there were between Great Britain and
Canada, for example." In due course the nations of the "Dependent
Empire" would doubtless receive their independence, and as free
peoples they might be admitted into the grand "British Alliance,"
but never to the inner circle of kith and kin. In this vision one may
perhaps dimly trace the precursor of the Bantustan policies of Verwoerd and Vorster. "The true imperialist is also the best South
African," said Milner, and South Africans would go on demonstrat-
ing the proposition long after he and the empire were defunct.

Before he left South Africa, Milner took care to place his pro-
tégés, mostly young Oxford men, in high administrative positions
from which they could further his policy. "Milner's Kindergarten,"
as the group came to be called, included such famous names as
Geoffrey Dawson, later editor of the London *Times*; Philip Kerr,
later Lord Lothian, who was British ambassador to Washington at

A quartet of Afrikaans writers: Andre Brink, Jan Rabie, Breyten Breytenbach (looking into camera), and Uys Krige.

Selby Semela in California, 1979.

The official version—an artist's idealized conception of the landing of Jan van Riebeeck at Table Bay in 1652.

Boer Commandos.

"After the fray."

Rhodes, the colossus, straddles Africa from Cape Town to Cairo, holding up the transcontinental telegraph line.

(Above, left) Baden-Powell during the Matabele War, sketched by himself. "Skirt dancing teaches one to have perfect command over one's feet, and the importance of this accomplishment can well be realized when one is being hunted over bad ground in the Matoppos by Matabele," he wrote in his diaries.

(Above, right) London celebrates Mafeking Night; Piccadilly Circus, May 18, 1900.

(Below) The Court of Summary Jurisdiction at Mafeking, March 1900. Seated are Lord Edward Cecil (with black armband) and Magistrate C.G.H. Bell. Interpreter Sol Plaatje stands on Cecil's right, with arms akimbo. The bare-headed prisoner, charged with stealing a goat, faces the table, while the Barolong chief, Molema, looks on. The defendant, "Jan" ("alias George Mahombe") was sentenced to death, and was shot a few days later, on April 2.

Gandhi (seated center) before his Johannesburg law offices, surrounded by his staff, around 1902.

Field Marshal Jan Christiaan Smuts and Sir Winston Churchill at the Casablanca Conference in 1943. Behind them stand Sir Arthur Tedder and Sir Alan Brooke.

Soweto, 16 June 1976. The first to die, a 13-year-old schoolboy named Hector Peterson, is carried away after being shot in the back by a policeman outside Orlando West High School.

OR FREEDOM WE SHALL
Y DOWN OUR LIVES.
HE STRUGGLE CONTINUES

WIDE WORLD

Soweto, 1976.

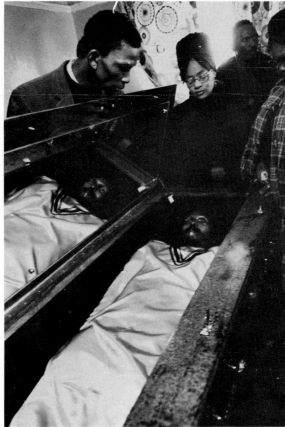

At the funeral of Steve
Biko, 1977.

Robert Mangaliso So-
bukwe, leader of the Pan
Africanist Congress.

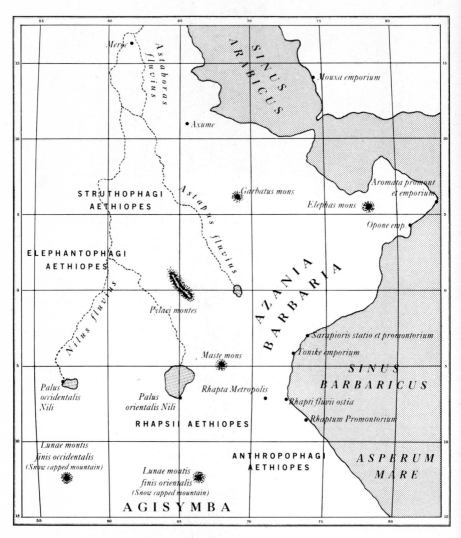

Ptolemy's Azania (adapted from the proceedings of the Royal Geographical Society, 1891).

the outbreak of World War II; John Buchan, later Lord Tweedsmuir, the author of *The Thirty-Nine Steps* and governor-general of Canada; Robert Brand, later First Baron Brand; and the dynamic Lionel Curtis, prophet of a World Federation to be founded on the entente between the British Empire and the United States.*

After World War I, Curtis and the other *Kinder* threw their support to the League of Nations. Milner himself "greatly regretted this," Lady Milner wrote after his death. "He thought they dropped the substance for the shadow." In the years between the wars, Curtis, Kerr, Dawson, and Brand were all members of the famous "Cliveden Set" associated with Lord and Lady Astor, who owned the *Observer* and the *Times*. Here, too, converged such luminaries as George Bernard Shaw and T. E. Lawrence, as also, on at least one documented occasion, Hitler's ambassador at large and later Nazi foreign minister, Joachim von Ribbentrop.

Most prominent of the *Kinder*, as far as South Africa was concerned, was Sir Patrick Duncan, who became governor-general of the Union. (His son, Patrick Duncan, would in after years be one of the most important figures in the South African Liberal Party, and later a member of the Pan Africanist Congress.) But it can be argued that Milner actually found his foremost disciple in the former Boer guerrilla leader and gray eminence of the Botha administration, Jan Christiaan Smuts. A Cambridge graduate of exceptional brilliance (he was the first man ever to take both parts of the Law Tripos in one year), Smuts became Transvaal state attorney under President Kruger when he was only twenty-eight, and during the Boer War was one of the most daring and effective of the commando generals. He was, said John X. Merriman, who knew him very well, "a philosopher ruthless and cultivated," while Duncan observed, "I only wish I thought that his fine sentiments were more intimately hitched on to the springs which govern his actions. They do sometimes get turned on but they spend much of their time in the cupboard of his soul."

After the signing of the Peace of Vereeniging, Smuts almost immediately shifted the focus of Afrikaner nationalism from the military to the political front and took advantage of changing British public opinion to clasp the English to his bosom. As we have seen, a mere fifteen years after he had led his ragged guerrillas deep into the Cape heartland, he sat alongside his old enemy Milner in Lloyd

---

* The seat of this "federated Super-State," which was to include the democracies of Western Europe, was envisaged as Quebec. Winston Churchill (no Kindergartener he!) preferred a more exclusive commonwealth, guided perhaps by a "Council of Empire," to sit alternatively at London, Ottawa, Sydney, and Cape Town.

George's Imperial War Cabinet. In May 1917, with Milner (now British secretary for war) seated on his right hand, Smuts made a momentous speech at a banquet given in his honor in the Royal Gallery of the House of Lords in which the term "the British Commonwealth of Nations" was used for the first time. The worldwide influence of the two men is hardly calculable. Both, for example, were party to the drafting of the Balfour Declaration, which laid the basis for a Jewish state in Palestine, and Smuts played a key role in the founding of the United Nations. An enigmatic genius who mixed politics with philosophy, Smuts coined the word "holism" as early as 1912, and used it in his book *Holism and Evolution* (1926) to designate the alternative to scientific reductionism. But if he rejected reductionism in science, Smuts was ruthlessly reductionist in statecraft. Thus when the "bitter-ender" Boers rose in rebellion in 1914, he did not hesitate to crush them, former comrades in arms though they were. He moved with equal force against Mgijima's Israelites at Bulhoek, against the Namibian Bondelzwarts, and against the rebel white miners of the 1922 "Red Revolt" on the Witwatersrand.

Enoch Mgijima was a religious leader in the Queenstown district of the Cape whose teaching was distinguished by two visions he had had. In one, a stone rolled down a mountain and crushed the people at its foot; in the other, two white goats fought until a baboon which had been watching stepped in and crushed them both. In his interpretation, the goats represented the Boers and English, the ape, the blacks who were destined to overcome them. In 1921 a large force of police and troops was sent to disperse his followers, who had settled on common ground in the Bulhoek location outside Queenstown, where Mgijima held title to a small plot of land. When the Israelites, as they called themselves, attacked with homemade swords and spears, they were cut down by rifle and machine-gun fire; 163 were killed and 129 wounded. The impact of this massacre on black opinion is evident; years later it was still commemorated in a popular song in distant Zululand. The religious overtones do not obscure the essentially political content of Mgijima's stand and the state's reaction.

"The Bondelzwarts affair," which took place a year later, showed even more blatantly the degree to which the Union government relied on force. The Bondelzwarts, a Christian, Afrikaans-speaking clan of mixed Khoikhoi-Boer descent living across the Orange River in the mandated territory of South West Africa had long fought German colonial rule. When Smuts and Botha invaded in 1915, they had welcomed the South Africans (actually their blood relatives) as liberators. They were soon disillusioned, and matters came to a head when the new administration attempted to impose an exorbitant graduated dog tax, basically another device for forcing "natives" from subsistance living—hunting and cattle-herding in the Bondelzwarts' case—into white employ. Defiance was met with massive retaliation, including the use of bombers, and 115 Bondelzwarts died, while many more were injured. When Smuts's *Holism and Evolution* appeared a few years later, the South African poet Roy Campbell wrote sardonically:

> *The love of Nature burning in his heart,*
> *Our new Saint Francis offers us his book—*
> *The saint who fed the birds at Bondleswaart*
> *And fattened up the vultures at Bull Hoek.*

If Bulhoek and Bondelzwarts demonstrated the nature of white reaction, the 1922 "Red Revolt" did the same for white radicalism. The rebel miners elucidated their position by raising a banner that read, *Workers of the World, Fight and Unite for a White South Africa.* Though this has been dismissed as an aberration, it probably represented the sentiments of most of the strikers (three-quarters of whom were Afrikaners) with fair accuracy. What they were striking against was the use of African labor in skilled capacities in the mines. This was emphasized when strikers attacked Africans gratuitously and killed a number of them. The Communist party brought out a pamphlet titled "The Fight to a Finish," offering assistance to the strike committee, though "without necessarily identifying itself with every slogan heard in the strike." While calling for alliance with "our fellow workers—irrespective of race or colour," the communists remained trapped by their own assumptions. "To maintain the 'white standard' to build 'a white South Africa', is impossible under capitalism, whose nature is to degrade every class it employs," they declared. As unimpressed, no doubt, as Milner had been with "the socialism of Johannesburg," Smuts, now prime minister (Botha had died in late 1919), personally led troops to crush the rebellion, bringing in bombers, tanks, and artillery. The official death toll was a hundred and fifty-three, half of them soldiers and police. Over a thousand arrests were made, and four of the white communists were sentenced to death. Three eventually went to the gallows on November 17, 1922, singing "The Red Flag." These events were to leave their mark on the Communist party, reinforcing the desire of its white leadership to see the struggle in South Africa as primarily one of class, not race.

After Union, Africans were entirely left out of the calculus of power. Their only conceded role was as labor. Harsh laws controlled every detail of their lives, simultaneously placating the racism of the "backvelders" (and almost every white South African had a touch of the backvelder), giving employment to opportunistic politicians, and supplying the insatiable labor needs of the mines. Only by rigorous compulsion could hundreds of thousands of blacks be forced off their land to work for nominal payment on the "deep levels," thousands of feet underground, where rock falls and miners' phthisis were only the most familiar of the dangers.

It is tempting today to see the stance of the SANNC and APO leaders as at best undignified, treasonable at worst. Indeed, some saw them so at the time. Writing the obituary of his colleague Saul Msane (c. 1850–1919), Sol Plaatje summed up the dilemma in which they found themselves: "During the past year or so Mr. Msane became very unpopular among the younger native workers on the Reef," he noted.

> A small band of white men, the Industrial Workers of the World, boldly and openly sympathised with the natives in the long hours they have to work and on the niggardly pay as well as the bad housing conditions on the Witwatersrand. Naturally, their programme appealed to the native labourers. But, rightly or wrongly, Mr. Msane held that it would be suicidal for the helpless natives to ally themselves with an insignificant body of white extremists who are in the bad books of the Government and very unpopular with Boers and English alike: and each time there was a clash Mr. Msane threw the whole weight of his influence on the side of the authorities, and earned thereby the name among the labourers of "Isita- sa Bantu" ("Enemy of the Natives").

Before we pass judgment on Msane and men like him, it is as well to recollect the context—so different from our own—in which they lived, thought, and felt. White hegemony had been established not only throughout South Africa but over the greater part of the earth's surface. (It was disturbed briefly by the distant thunder of the 1904–5 Russo-Japanese war. "After the Japanese victory we felt an immense elation, a sort of reassurance in the face of Europeans, and an immense sense of gratitude and hero-worship for the Japanese," wrote Nirad Chaudhuri, speaking as it were for the gallery.) This was the outcome of circumstances stretching back centuries into the past. What history had wrought, only time would undo.

At the time of Sol Plaatje's birth, such blacks as retained a semblance of independence in South Africa had been reduced to the role of pawns in the internecine struggles of the whites: territorial jockeying between the Natal and Cape colonists in Pondoland and Griqualand, for example, and at the other extreme the ongoing contest between Boer and Briton that flashed into war in 1880–1 and again in 1899–1902. The era in which African societies had been able to treat with the white world as equals had temporarily drawn to a close, even on the remotest frontier. To challenge these brute realities, whether as an individual or as an organization, was to court martyrdom. The mythology of white superiority barely countenanced the survival of independent nonwhite states outside the overlapping "spheres of influence" which now covered the globe. Even the ancient Ethiopian empire was living on borrowed time. The war which finally reduced it to an Italian colony came as a surprise to many who had not realized that an independent African state still existed. "It was the only political event that had roused the Africans for many years," says Eddie Roux. "The reaction, when it finally became clear that the Ethiopians were defeated, was terrible."

Sol Plaatje's first book, a Sechuana phonetic reader, done in collaboration with the great phoneticist Daniel Jones, was published by the University of London Press in 1915. His *Sechuana Proverbs* appeared the following year, and *Native Life in South Africa*, primarily a protest against the land act, came not long afterward, running into five editions. In early 1917 he was back in Kimberley, where he established a branch of the Brotherhood Movement, with which he had come in contact in England. (It represented, he said, "that practical Christianity which bears no distinction of colour or artificial boundaries between nations.") He was successful in obtaining an old tram shed from the De Beers Company as a meeting place for Africans at an annual rent of one shilling, and also got the company to contribute to its renovation. The new assembly hall was opened with much ceremony by the governor-general—at the instance of Prime Minister Botha himself. Significantly, too, De Beers presently became the only South African company to make a substantial cash contribution to the new South African Native College at Fort Hare.

In 1919, in addition to joining the new SANNC deputation to Whitehall and Versailles, Plaatje attended the First World Brotherhood Congress in London, and the Pan-African Congress organized in Paris by Dr. W. E. B. Du Bois. Altogether he would be away for four years, traveling to the United States and Canada on a speaking tour which he financed partly by sale of a booklet titled *The Mote and the Beam: An Epic on Sex-Relationship 'Twixt White and Black in British South Africa.* Appearing in 1921, it eventually sold some 18,000 copies. It was, he said, "a disquisition on a delicate social problem known to Europeans in South Africa as the *Black Peril* and to the Bantu as the *White Peril.*"

A few months before his departure for Europe, as he was about to go to a service dedicating the new assembly hall to Brotherhood meetings and African education, he received a message from the Rand: "The mounted police just charged a crowd of men and women, five killed by horses' hoofs, scores of men and women maimed. Most of the victims were singing and praying when police charged." He rejoiced that by contrast he and his people on the Diamond Fields were able to assemble at a peaceful service conducted by the Bishop of Kimberley, presided over by the city magistrate, and supported by the mayor and city council. Here, surely, was evidence that conciliation worked better than confrontation, that the way of Brotherhood was likely to be more effective than that of the "black Bolsheviks of Johannesburg."

When he returned to South Africa in late 1923, Plaatje continued to labor for what had now become the African National Congress, monitoring the debates in Cape Town's all-white Parliament, and taking part in efforts to create a united front of oppressed South Africans, like the Non-European Conference of 1927. He also found time to translate Shakespeare—*Julius Caesar, The Comedy of Errors, The Merchant of Venice, Othello,* and *Much Ado About Nothing*—into his native Sechuana, and to write *Mhudi,* his historical novel set in the days of Moroka and Mzilikazi. The image of the self-conscious "Black Englishman" is counterbalanced by his sallies, which reveal an intelligence unclouded by illusions. Once, recalled Vere Stent, his sometime employer and Reuters correspondent in besieged Mafeking, Plaatje responded to a government representative who admonished him to remember "all the blessings the white man has bestowed upon you," by rejoining, "I do; I always do—especially brandy and syphilis." Blacks, he observed to the 1927 Non-European Conference, were regarded more as "British objects" than as British subjects.

Having virtually pauperized himself working for African education and welfare, Sol Plaatje died in Johannesburg in 1932, of pneumonia, still only in his mid-fifties.

4

HOPES AND ENEMIES

Come, Holy Spirit:
End these wars and miseries.
Lord save us —
The nation of Africa.

A Pawn to Be Played

In July 1921, the Communist Party of South Africa was formed by fusion of a number of preexisting organizations, among them the International Socialist League (S.A.), the Social Democratic Federation of Cape Town, the Communist party of Cape Town, the Jewish Socialist Society of Cape Town, the Jewish Socialist Society (Poalei Zion) of Johannesburg, and the Marxian Club of Durban. Despite their impressive titles, these organizations had between them comparatively few members. These were predominantly foreign-born—British radicals and eastern European Jews (chiefly Lithuanians). The party was in its early years entirely white, or virtually so.

The founding father of South African communism, Sidney Bunting, had come to the country on military service during the Boer War, and remained to practice law in Johannesburg. Almost alone among the leaders of the CPSA, Bunting tried to persuade his comrades that their task was "to organise the non-whites for revolution." The manifesto issued at the party's inaugural conference made its appeal "to all South African workers, organised and unorganised, white and black," but it rapidly became apparent that the prospect of alliance with their black underlings did not in the least appeal to the privileged white workers. Indeed, Bunting soon had occasion to note, the Communists were sometimes "spat upon and

mobbed by the infatuated workers themselves." An occasional Afrikaner maverick was attracted to the movement, but these were
special cases, men like Gideon Botha, who had ridden the rails as a
hobo in the United States and known Jack London; or Eddie Roux,
a young scientist who was subsequently to write a pioneer history
of the struggle. Roux's father had proclaimed himself a Bolshevik in
1918, but was of that peculiarly South African breed of socialist who
managed to exclude Africans from consideration. ("After the revolution," his son recalled his saying, "they will be segregated in their
own territories where they will grow food under expert guidance.")

The deep contradictions in the Communist position came to a
head early, when the party was confronted with the 1922 "Red Revolt" on the Witwatersrand, a would-be Marxist revolution organized by and on behalf of the white workers, whose specific goal
was to prevent the Chamber of Mines from introducing black labor
in skilled capacities in the mines. Party policy now led the Communists "into horrifying[ly] close collusion with white working-
class nationalism and racialism." This was later justified by a Communist writer as follows:

> Although the cry for a "White South Africa", which became the chief
> slogan in the dispute, appears reactionary on the surface, it was never-
> theless founded on a sound working class instinct. The "White South
> Africa" slogan embodied a defence against capitalist aggression and
> was a challenge against the capitalist class. That the White workers
> saw no identity of interest with the Black workers and were not pre-
> pared to co-operate with them was a concrete reality of the time, and
> had to find its expression.

Matters went far beyond refusal to cooperate. "During the last few
days in Johannesburg and surrounding districts attacks have been
made by certain Europeans on natives and coloured persons without
the slightest provocation," the ministers of justice and defence declared in a joint statement on March 9, 1922.

> The Government has information that these deliberate and unpro-
> voked attacks, amounting in certain particular cases to wilful murder,
> are designed to give the impression throughout the country that a
> native rising on the Witwatersrand is imminent, and that the lives
> and properties of Europeans are in danger.

The leaders of the strike commandos aimed at combining *putsch* on
the Witwatersrand with uprising in the *platteland,* and racism was
the mobilizing sentiment. They might well have succeeded. When
Smuts arrived at military headquarters in Johannesburg, he found
that almost the entire Rand was in rebel hands. Calmly but ruthlessly, he moved to smash the revolt with whatever force was

needed. (Sol Plaatje's former employer, Vere Stent, who was there, described his demeanor as "that of a man playing chess.") The Weimar government in Germany might have done well to take heed. In Munich, Adolf Hitler was thinking along lines similar to those of the Rand strike junta.

"S. P. Bunting, almost alone among the communists, sought to counteract the growing anti-black feeling," says Eddie Roux. The role of the other Communist leaders was equivocal. W. H. "Comrade Bill" Andrews, a founder member and first secretary of the CPSA, was secretary of the white mineworkers' Council of Action, and its headquarters in the final stages of the strike were the headquarters of the Communist party. While it is true that the Council of Action did not control the commandos, it nonetheless collaborated closely with them.

To both Communists and Afrikaner nationalists, Smuts was "the puppet of the Goldbug," the representative of the Chamber of Mines and the empire, personifying "the brute force of the *Mailed Fist and the Iron Heel*" (to lift a phrase from the CPSA's 1921 manifesto). After 1922 the Communists accordingly threw their support behind the Afrikaner nationalist leaders, General J. B. M. Hertzog and Daniel F. Malan. With equal opportunism, the latter temporarily dissembled their racism, not, certainly, with a view to radical alliances—for that there was no need to do so—but in order to woo the Cape Native voters (whom they hoped to remove from the electoral rolls as soon as power permitted). In 1919 Hertzog had lauded the Bolsheviks:

> I say that Bolshevism is the will of the people to be free. Why do people want to oppress and kill Bolshevism? Because national freedom means death to capitalism and imperialism. . . . The idea in itself is excellent.

Now he went so far as to contribute funds to the biggest African organization of the day, Clements Kadalie's Industrial and Commercial Workers' Union. Meanwhile Malan extolled the "true patriotism" of "the Native," whom he declared "entitled to take his place side by side with the Nationalists in the common political arena." Like the Communists and every other faction in the spectrum of racist politics, the Afrikaner nationalists prized power above any principle, and in 1924 they got it. The backlash from Smuts's suppression of the miners' revolt gave them a parliamentary majority in combination with the all-white Labour party (which had three times rejected the CPSA's application for affiliation).

No sooner had General Hertzog been summoned to form a government than his true colors reasserted themselves. Simultaneously there was a turnabout in Communist policy. The Young Communist League had begun to talk about the need to "capture the Native youth." Some had favored establishing a segregated organization to contain them when captured, but this was vetoed by the Comintern when the suggestion reached Moscow. At the Party's 1924 conference, the Cape Town delegates of the YCL actually turned up with two African recruits. Bunting's "nigrophilist" line won the day. Application for affiliation to the Labour party was not renewed. Henceforth the CPSA, as Bunting had long advocated, would seek its chief support from the blacks.

Prior to 1927 the Communists were openly contemptuous of the African National Congress. By comparison, Kadalie's ICU seemed more promising. At its peak it claimed a mass membership running into six figures, which the ANC could not begin to rival, even allowing for exaggerations. Africans called it the *Keaubona*— "I See You"—and the pun perhaps acknowledged the fact that Kadalie and his lieutenants looked out for the ordinary black. By 1926 there were four Communist members on the ICU's National Executive Committee, who not only agitated for greater militancy but sought, Roux notes,

> to curb the power of the leaders, of Kadalie and some provincial secretaries, who, they declared, were acting as dictators. And, most important, they wanted the control of finance to be put on a sound basis, for it had become an open secret that scores of minor leaders in all parts of the country were helping themselves liberally to the funds of the organization.

In December 1926, Kadalie initiated a full-scale break with the Communists, charging that the CPSA was white-dominated. This was undoubtedly true, but it is also a matter of record (are these records to be trusted?) that he himself was in part acting under the countervailing influence of various white South African liberals and British social democrats (the latter presently sent out W. G. Ballinger, a Scottish trades-unionist, to help put the affairs of the ICU in order). In any event, the Communist members of the ICU were expelled, and this is said to have signaled the beginning of the end, the organization declining, in Roux's words, into "intrigue, incompetence, mismanagement and dishonesty." In this account, Kadalie could not accept the Communist challenge to his authority, and in any case shrank from the decisive confrontation sought by the militants.

But that is far too simple. For a start it overlooks, as Michael Harmel has pointed out, "the massive armory of repression" unleashed against the ICU by the white establishment, which dared not tolerate an effective African labor movement. Kadalie's famous *hamba kahle* (go carefully) policy, which the Communists liked to reproach him with, seems initially to imply a gradualism more appropriate to democracy by consensus than to an acutely polarized society like South Africa. Yet in avoiding head-on confrontation, Kadalie probably had a more imaginative grasp of the likely outcome than the militants who baited him. "All right," he told them at one point, "if you want to lead a bloody revolution, I am going to follow you, but mark you, if I do follow you I am going the whole hog."

Their bluff was called. The fact is that in South Africa for much of the century the sole option of those seeking a middle path between disaster and quiescence has been to *hamba kahle*. "It is certain that the I.C.U. in the fullness of its power, with a quarter-million of adherents all over the country [other sources tend to suggest that membership was more in the region of 100,000], could have carried out a nation-wide pass-burning and by passive resistance have abolished the system," says Eddie Roux. On the contrary, it is very far from certain. Though Kadalie's fervent oratory united Africans in hope, he was no Gandhi. (He was essentially a poet, thought Roux, who remembered him reading Swinburne aloud in a gentle, high-pitched voice.) And the likelihood is that the outcome of a frontal assault at this time on the pass system, the basis not only of white control but of contemporary South African capitalism itself, would have been holocaust. As it was, scores had died in confrontations with the police in the first few years of the ICU's existence. The 1920s were no time for blacks to challenge white South Africa to open warfare. The results would have been much what they were in Bambata's day, on a larger scale, and on the evidence of subsequent events in Abyssinia, Manchuria, and Spain, the "civilized" world would have stood cheerfully, if not cheering, on the sidelines.

Waged as the Communists wanted it to be, the struggle would have turned into a series of massacres, and most of the victims would certainly have been Africans. Far more deadly than the whites' dominance in the CPSA apparatus—an organization in which membership was, after all, both voluntarily assumed and resignable—were the romantic "radical" fantasies in the name of which they set out like so many Marxist-Leninist Columbuses and Van Riebeecks to colonize the African soul.

It may have been coincidence that, in February 1927, within weeks of Kadalie's break with the Communists, the newly elected Zulu president-general of the African National Congress, Josiah Gumede, was found attending a conference in Brussels of a Comintern front organization called the League Against Imperialism. It was only a few years since Gumede had publicly argued that "the African will be made a slave if Bolsheviks take over the government," admittedly perhaps with General Hertzog's endorsement of them in mind. Now he visited Moscow in the company of Jimmy La Guma, one of those recently purged by the ICU, and held discussions with Bukharin himself. He was treated to the standard Potemkin tour, with special detours to the Turkic republics of the Soviet Union, where he saw that "non-Europeans, some of them as dark-skinned as he was himself, enjoyed the same political and social rights as Europeans." Though undoubtedly of somewhat malleable disposition, Gumede can perhaps be forgiven for falling for a bill of goods successfully sold to the cream of the Western intelligentsia. Like them, Gumede wanted, needed, to believe. He returned to South Africa in early 1928 an enthusiastic Communist supporter. ANC Secretary-General E. J. Khaile was also a Communist, and the organization for the first time passed into the shadow of the party.

The CPSA seemed to be going from strength to strength, with some 3,000 members registered in 1929. But this was to be a crucial year for the Communists. In January the seventh annual conference of the CPSA adopted a new program, embodied in the Moscow-dictated slogan "A South African Native Republic as a stage towards a Workers' and Peasants' Government with full protection and equal rights for all national minorities."

Roux and Bunting, as delegates to the sixth congress of the Comintern in the summer of 1928, had argued against this, and in so doing probably represented the majority of the South African party, which still had "no wish to antagonize the white workers as a whole in particular the white trade unionists." But the matter had already been decided in advance by the Comintern's Anglo-American Secretariat (which significantly enough was given charge of Africa). Objections were brushed aside by the Comintern apparatchiks ("a hard-bitten gang of bureaucrats," thought Roux) and like good Marxist-Leninists the South Africans set about making the best of their new orders.

Much as one sympathizes with them in their resentment at being steamrollered by Moscow, the fact was that the "Black Republic" thesis, as it was called, represented a genuine attempt to come to grips with the realities. The new policy seems to have evolved out of the discussions the year before between Bukharin and other Comintern leaders and Gumede and La Guma. And at least Gumede and La Guma (the latter of French-Madagascan descent, and by racial classification a Cape "Coloured") had lived as blacks in South

Africa, an experience not calculated to promote a feeling of fellowship with the white South African working class. They knew that, quite irrespective of theory, the white workers were as a class the enemies, and not potential allies, of black liberation. (As Legassick puts it, "Whites were already structurally alienated from the national revolution in South Africa.") This was a matter of bitter experience to which white Communists were not privy.

To complicate matters, a power struggle was soon under way within the CPSA, seemingly a matter of personalities, but in fact mirroring events in Russia. Confronted with the struggle between Stalin and the Left Opposition and worldwide Trotskyism, Communist parties everywhere were going into mimetic convulsions. ("It was unfortunate that the injection of a 'national revolutionary' analysis into the South African Marxist scene coincided with the leftward swing of the Comintern in 1928 and after," says Legassick.)

As the South Africans understood it, the Moscow line was that the party should function as an elite group working through larger mass organizations like the ICU or ANC to achieve a "bourgeois democratic" revolution in the shape of the "Native Republic." The Communist revolution proper would come later. On this basis a new organization called the League of African Rights was called into being in August 1929 under Gumede's chairmanship. The latter had been relatively unsuccessful in propagating his new-found communism in the ANC. Opposition there came from the chiefs, who formed a sort of "upper house," the organization having been modeled on the British parliamentary pattern. "The Tsar was a great man in his country, of royal blood like us chiefs, and where is he now?" asked one, protesting the increasing "fraternization" with the Communists.

Initially the League of African Rights was a great success, but suddenly like a bolt from the blue a telegram from the Comintern ordered its immediate dissolution. "The communists were dumbfounded," says Roux. "But like good Leninists they obeyed orders." In fact, what had happened was that yet another policy switch had occurred. The "Native Republic," essentially a shift to the "right" (inasmuch as it contemplated alliance with a largely nonexistent black "national bourgeoisie"), had been part of the disastrous 1928 program of the Comintern, authored chiefly by the pedantic Bukharin. ("For him the first and most important step was to find some kind of scheme or formula, even though such schemes and formulas sometimes missed the most essential aspects of the matter at hand," writes Roy Medvedev.)

But in 1929 Stalin abruptly shifted "left" again, and proceeded to appropriate a number of ideas hitherto regarded as Trotskyite.

Bukharin and Rykov found themselves assailed as "right deviation-
ists" and "allies of the kulaks." In November 1929 they were expelled from the Politburo, the first step on the fatal path leading to
their show trials and execution in 1938. The new line was promul-
gated in all the national parties that accepted Comintern discipline.
Stalin, even more schematic and inflexible than the scholastic Bukharin, showed little regard for local circumstances. The official formula now precluded campaigning for such "bourgeois luxuries" as
civil rights, and the LAR accordingly had to be scuttled, notwithstanding the support it had gathered among Africans—who could
imagine little more revolutionary than the liberties which whites
took for granted. The CPSA now came under the control of its Political Bureau, dominated by a troika consisting of Douglas and Molly
Wolton and Lazar Bach. Wolton was a Yorkshireman, while his wife
and Lazar Bach were both Lithuanians. They operated by packing
the Political Bureau with an African majority prototypical of such
"representation" in the party. It was, says Eddie Roux,

> only a mechanical gesture, more a manner of speaking than a mean-
> ingful reality. The new Native members, though continually and in-
> tensively coached in the theory and practice of the new line, the fight
> against the reformist danger, were in fact bewildered and always sub-
> servient. Their presence was unreal. They said little beyond express-
> ing agreement with Wolton and Bach when called on to do so.

When in December 1930 Wolton headed a new Central Committee
including four whites and nineteen Africans, the first with an African majority, the principle was exactly the same. There was no
doubt as to who called the tune.

Waves of expulsions followed, as Bunting and the "Buntin-
gites," W. H. Andrews, Solly Sachs and other trade unionists, La
Guma and sundry noncooperative militants were read out of the
organization. These contortions were inevitably the cause of a dras-
tic decline in membership, which by 1933 had fallen as low as 150
nationwide. In part the rationale for the new shift "leftward" was
the onset of the depression of the 1930s. The worst drought in South
African history had sent thousands of impoverished Afrikaner
farm families into the cities in search of a living. The Carnegie
Commission on the Poor White Problem classified three hundred
thousand whites as "very poor" at the beginning of the 1930s
(though millions of blacks might have viewed the category as relative). Since the National party and its Labour allies were the government of the day, there was no effective opposition to mobilize these
poor whites into a political force. If the Communist party ever
hoped to win the support of the white workers, now was the time.

search for a way out of helotry. Thus Selby Msimang, trade unionist and founder-member of the African National Congress, who had been elected secretary-general of the AAC, declared himself prepared to accept "vertical territorial segregation" based on a fifty–fifty division of the country between whites and blacks if there were no other way. Half hopelessly, half ironically, he quoted Smuts himself to the effect that

> To suppose that in the modern world you can dispense with freedom in human government, that you can govern without the free consent of the governed, is to fly in the face of decent human nature as well as of the facts of history.

What was Smuts thinking of when he wrote those words? Was he, were white South Africans in general, literally schizophrenic?

As far back as 1890, when he was barely twenty, Smuts had anticipated that "the race struggle is destined to assume a magnitude on the African continent such as the world has never seen and the imagination shrinks from contemplating." History, he thought then, was "a *via dolorosa,* a path of sorrow." In 1902, treading that sorrowful path as a guerrilla general on the run at the bitter end of the Anglo-Boer war, he had declared that "the native question will never pass away; it will become more difficult as time goes on, and the day may come when the evils and horrors of this war will appear as nothing in comparison with its after effects produced on the native mind." In 1906 he wrote to John X. Merriman, who had pronounced him to be the Hamilton of the renascent Transvaal,

> I sympathize profoundly with the native races of South Africa whose land it was long before we came here to force a policy of dispossession on them. And it ought to be the policy of all parties to do justice to the natives and to take all wise and prudent measures for their civilization and improvement. But I don't believe in politics for them. Perhaps at bottom I do not believe in politics at all as a means for the attainment of the highest ends; but certainly so far as the natives are concerned politics will to my mind only have an unsettling influence. I would therefore not give them the franchise, which in any case would not affect more than a negligible number of them at present. When I consider the political future of the natives in S.A. I must say that I look into shadows and darkness; and then I feel inclined to shift the intolerable burden of solving that sphinx problem to the ampler shoulders and stronger brains of the future. Sufficient unto the day, etc. My feeling is that strong forces are at work which will transform the Africander attitude to the natives.

Three decades later, he was still prepared to wait and hope, to future deal with injustices that had by now mounted thirty

Wolton declaimed at such length about the coming collapse of capitalism that he was given the nickname "Deepening Economic Crisis" by Africans, but the CPSA failed to fill the vacuum. Given the deep-seated racism of the poor whites as a group, it is improbable that it could have done so. But to have admitted this would have shattered the core of Communist dogma. Wracked by internal strife, the party was in any case in no condition for serious action.

"I saw that to the Comintern bureaucrats the achievement of African freedom was as nothing," wrote Eddie Roux. "Our South African party was as a pawn to be played and sacrificed to the needs of central power policy." The South African Communists, Roux among them, had only themselves to blame. They had voluntarily surrendered to outsiders their right to think.

Eventually Bunting, Andrews and La Guma were all readmitted to the party. The Woltons abruptly returned to Britain in 1933, and were heard of no more. At this point, in Roux's words, the CPSA consisted "almost exclusively of paid functionaries." Even so, factional strife continued, and when Bach traveled to Moscow in 1935 to appeal against the challenging of his leadership by Roux, Moses Kotane, and John Gomas, he did not return. In the wake of the Kirov assassination, Moscow had become an extremely dangerous place in which to raise questions of policy. It seems that Bach was caught up in the purges aimed at eliminating the Zinovievite "Center" and it is rumored that he was later shot.

The All African Convention and the Beginnings of the NEUM

At the end of the twenties, the African National Congress was in organizational disarray. Early the following year Gumede was replaced as president-general by Pixley-Seme, the aging lawyer who in 1912 had been the motive force behind the establishment of the South African Native National Congress. But in the struggle between Gumede and his followers and the anti-Communists, the organization was further weakened, to the point where it became almost totally ineffective.

Late in 1930, the police attacked a peaceful meeting protesting the pass laws on Cartwright's Flats, Durban, and a number of people were killed, among them a promising young Communist leader, Johannes Nkosi. On postmortem examination, the dead were found to be terribly mutilated by the spears of the African police. No one was ever charged with the killings, but twenty-six of the demonstrators were convicted of incitement to violence and sentenced to various terms of imprisonment. It was hard to keep up the spirits of the rank and file in the face of such wanton terrorism. Morale necessarily sagged. Nkosi was a Zulu, and his people made up a song about Cartwright's Flats:

> What are we going to do?
> Today we are persecuted,
> We are made to pay money that does not help us.
> Our leaders struggle for positions.
> We don't know where to go.
> Our favorite Makhalempongo ["Billy Goat's Nose"]
>   died.
> He died with his men, the son of Bulose!
> They were fighting the special and registration passes.
> Hence we don't know where to go.

The mood of disillusionment with leadership and the despair are apparent.

The depression had had the effect of gradually reducing General Hertzog's parliamentary majority, and in February 1933 he publicly proposed a coalition government to Smuts. This paved the way for the fusion of the National party and the South African party into the United South African National party, which in later years was known simply as the United party. In the new "Fusion" government, Hertzog remained prime minister, Smuts taking the post of deputy prime minister. Dissenting was Smuts's former schoolmate Daniel F. Malan, now leader of the Cape nationalists. Unable to agree to the terms of the coalition, Malan and his followers broke away to form the Purified National party, which a decade and a half later would initiate the apartheid society.

Hertzog now had the parliamentary majority of two-thirds needed under the Constitution to amend the clause protecting the voting rights of "qualified" blacks in the Cape Province (where the "color-blind" franchise, hedged by property and educational qualifications, gave some 10,000 Africans the vote on the common role). In 1935 the Natives' Representation Bill was brought in with a view to abolishing this surviving African franchise. Though the ANC was moribund—its paper *Abantu-Batho* was obliged to close down that year—and the ICU largely defunct, African opinion could not ignore this new assault on the pitiful handful of rights remaining to blacks. ANC President-General Seme and Professor D. T. Jabavu, son of John Tengo Jabavu and the senior African academic in the country, took the lead in calling a meeting of all shades of African political conviction. This was the All African Convention, or AAC. The

word "Convention" in Xhosa (*Imbizo*) and Sesotho (*Pitso*) harks back to the traditional national gatherings of the Sutu-nguni peoples, and has a deep meaning for them (as opposed to the English "Congress"). The coming-together of the AAC in Bloemfontein in December 1935 inspired a song:

> We have heard the voice of our leaders
> Saying "The country is desolate,
> Men must unite."
> Inviting all African peoples,
> Whose different tongues are as one.
> Saying "Let them unite in Bloemfontein,
> Unite and form one organization."
> The oft-spoken-of day has come,
> The day of unity.
> Father, mothers, young men,
> Let us pray for this day.

More than four hundred delegates, including Communists like Marks and Edwin Mofutsanyana as well as churchmen and chiefs, assembled under the chairmanship of Alfred B. Xuma, tor of medicine. Clements Kadalie was among them, and it his suggestion that the AAC was placed on a permanent Though a sense of emergency pervaded the proceedings, a by the Cape Town Trotskyist Dr. Goolam Gool that "a liberation movement to fight against all the repressive established was nonetheless rejected (while in Westernize "fight" used this way means "talk," to Africans it has un Blood River). On the whole the Convention seems to conciliatory rather than aggressive, prepared to accept b ified franchise and the concept of separate developme that some sort of political consensus which included be arrived at. It was total exclusion, the loss of *all* ho simply intolerable.

Africans felt a sense of despair. Year after year t been systematically reduced, their freedoms circun opinion was contemptuous, if not downright hostile patronizing even when well-meaning. The count ministers since Union, Botha, Smuts, and Hert them scrupled to bamboozle African leadershi where they could, and to crack down ruthl couldn't. White votes counted more than Afri were always loaded against blacks, in politics as as the poor always do, they ended up paying m

Even veteran militants were now clutch

let th

years higher, to "fly in the face of decent human nature" and dispense with the scraps of consent still tolerated in the governed blacks of South Africa. In April 1936 the Representation of Natives Bill was duly enacted into law with formalities appropriate to Westminster. The African voters—only some ten thousand remained on it—were struck from the common roll in the Cape Province, losing a right that was almost a century old, and that had always represented a modicum of hope under the brass-and-iron sky of race rule. In exchange, Africans were conceded separate election of a number of *white* representatives to speak on their behalf, and a black twelve-member Natives' Representative Council to serve in an "advisory capacity" to the regime.

Was anything gained from this? Was it even remotely to be supposed that whites could now sleep more secure in the knowledge that any danger of their elected leaders being drowned in a sea of black votes had been averted? This was the argument. "It is not that we hate you, but if we give you the right to vote, within a very short space of time the whole Parliament will be controlled by Natives. I must tell you point-blank I am not prepared for this," Hertzog told the AAC deputation that came to plead with him. But in fact, when it came to suffrage in South Africa, whites were the sea, and blacks the shipwrecked. The Cape African vote had amounted to about 1 percent of the total Union electorate. Arguably, the new electoral law actually gave blacks *more* voice. Voting as a bloc on the separate roll, they would now be in a position to return candidates of their choice, even Reds, provided they were white. First, liberals like Margaret Ballinger and Donald Molteno, then Hyman Basner, a Russian-born radical and lapsed Communist party member, and finally Sam Kahn, a member, no less, of the Executive of the Central Committee of the CPSA, presently took their seats in Parliament as Natives' Representatives. And new laws had to be brought in to get rid of them.

The fact is, of course, that the Natives' Representation Act of 1936 had little to do with the question of representation as such. It was a matter of identity, of how the nation, as embodied in the electorate, was to be defined. It must be remembered that even the uniting of Boer and Briton into one people seemed wild idealism, which few could ultimately accept. For almost three centuries, color and all that was implied by color had been the parameter that distinguished Afrikaners from Africans. More, even, than language and religion, it was the standard of selfhood, a measure of identity in defense of which no irrationality was too great. These Afrikaners are a Germanic people who will sacrifice much on the altar of internal consistency. The irrational has its own integrity. Remember the words of General De Wet, arguing quixotically at the Vereeninging peace talks in 1902 for a continuation of the fighting, hopeless as it was. "I have nothing to do with facts," he said. "The entire war is a matter of faith." The logical extensions of an illogical credo demanded that the common electoral roll be scrapped; out of a total of a hundred and eighty parliamentarians, only eleven voted nay.

Though rejecting the Hertzog bills in principle, most of the AAC were nonetheless willing to compete for the Natives' Representative Council seats. ANC leaders were among those elected, including Selope Thema, Thomas Mapikela, and John Dube. Dube had expressed a qualified support for some aspects of the bills, and was hence branded a "traitor" and "Government man" by the Communists. After his death, the "Trotskyist" I. B. Tabata, in a patronizing and pompous letter of advice addressed to Nelson Mandela, called him "a willing stooge . . . principal of some secondary school in Natal." This last was, of course, the famous Ohlange Institute, which Dube had founded many years before. Dube, whatever the opinions of so-called "radicals," was and is regarded as a hero by the Zulus in particular. He was known as Mafukuzela, a title with something of the meaning of "scholar-gypsy." When he died in 1946, his praises were sung in numerous laments:

> Mafukuzela who is like the heavens,
> Sleep in your grave, Mafukuzela.
> Hush, hero of the nation of Africa.
> Earth won't get fatter because of you,
> And the mountains are quiet and still.
> Up where you are now there is no sorrow,
> There are no tears.
> We are bereft, Mafukuzela of fame.
> There is Ohlange, speaking for itself!
> There are the actions of a man among men.
> Shine forever, Mafukuzela of fame!
> You have illuminated, opened for us the way to truth,
> Mafukuzela, son of Dube, hero of heroes.

Dube was elected to the Natives' Representative Council both in 1937 and in 1942. When illness made it impossible for him to run in 1945, his seat was taken by Albert Lutuli. One of the greatest of African leaders in twentieth-century South Africa, Dube awaits the full-scale biography he deserves.

In 1937, Pixley Seme was replaced as president-general of the ANC by the Reverend Zaccheus Mahabane, a Methodist minister. But Mahabane's leadership proved no more effective, and it seemed likely that the organization might dissolve entirely. Late in 1940,

Dr. A. B. Xuma was elected president-general. One of his earliest steps was the adoption of a new constitution, which was drawn up under the guidance of Bram Fischer, the Afrikaner Communist lawyer whose underground activities and sensational trial would make headlines a quarter of a century later. The new Xuma constitution cleared the way for the ANC to become a modern political party. In contrast with the 1915 constitution, which restricted membership to those "belonging to the aboriginal races of Africa," it was non-racial, though in practice there were no whites or other minority group members. Xuma did, however, obtain a certain amount of financial support from white sources, including some money put up by the Chamber of Mines.

With the creation of a new Coloured Affairs Department in 1943, and the passage of the Asiatic Land Tenure Act in 1946 (called the "Ghetto Act" by its opponents), "Indians" and "Coloureds" were reminded that they were not exempt from the dictates of racist ideology. In the Cape, an Anti-Coloured Affairs Department movement, known as the Anti-CAD, was launched. In partnership with the All African Convention, this was to form the basis of a new umbrella organization, the Non-European Unity Movement (NEUM). The genesis of the NEUM was summed up in the 1950s by a writer well acquainted with its tortuous politics as follows:

> The history of the South African democratic movement... began with a period which was dominated by the Brahmins of "white socialism." These intellectuals failed to realize the fundamentally important role of the struggle of the oppressed people for national liberation in South Africa, and spoke patronisingly of the "Native Question."
>
> Early on already, there were small groups who rejected with contempt the racial arrogance of "White" intellectuals and struggled for a policy which would give the national liberation of the oppressed people its proper place in the forefront of the movement. It was this minority which in its fight against the "white" arrogance and patronage struggled for the "non-Europeanization" of the democratic movement. This was in fact an attempt to give the movement a fully South African character. . . .
>
> But the leaders of this new departure lacked theoretical clarity. Instead of taking possession of the democratic movement as rightful heirs, they adapted and developed their ideas as "non-Europeanism." . . . They imitated the "white" racialists who took the "non-European" question out of politics. As "non-Europeans" they would take the "white question" out of politics. *And since national affairs are in the hands of the "whites," democratic leaders tended to evade politics and contented themselves with cataloguing grievances and resentments.* [Italics added.].

The final sentence explains the sterility of a whole epoch in Cape politics, the last before the crossover into the totalitarian society which came into being after Sharpeville. As Hosea Jaffe, one of the original neo-Trotskyist mentors of the NEUM put it early on, it was "but natural that the Unity Movement itself should embody the segregationist, sectarian, isolationist outlook of the petty-bourgeois Non-Whites." Indicative of this, the movement voluntarily segregated itself into separate organizations for each of the three "races" who together comprised the "Non-Europeans." In fact only two organizations—the AAC and the Anti-CAD—ever actually existed. Both ultimately fell under the sway of a handful of radicals and opportunists: I. B. Tabata, Wycliffe Tsotsi, and N. I. Honono in the case of the AAC; Benjamin Kies, Willem van Schoor, and Hosea Jaffe in the case of the Anti-CAD. Some of these were Marxists who had, so to speak, painted themselves into a corner politically. Others were mere demagogues. A standing invitation to the South African Indian community to form a third "pillar" was never taken up. The NEUM also had its white patrons and advisers, who remained anonymously in the background.

Drawing a major part of its support from the "Coloured" Teachers' League of South Africa and the Cape African Teachers' Association, the NEUM was for much of its existence a rather parochial "talking shop." Even on this level, the fraternal organizations practiced voluntary apartheid. The chosen weapon of the "Non-Europeanists," the boycott, was over the years brandished at all manner of things, serious struggles not excluded. Dan Mokonyane has noted that at the time of the great Alexandra Bus Boycott in 1957, the local NEUM declined an invitation to send delegates to the Action Committee, giving rise to the jibe that their attachment to the boycott was so great that they boycotted everything—including the bus boycott. So successful were they in taking the "white question" out of politics that it is extremely doubtful whether more than a tiny fraction of whites, even in the Cape, had ever so much as heard of them. Nonetheless, they were to have one very significant effect, as we shall see in due course.

Assagais Against Panzers

A handful of militants aside, most blacks looked to ultimate assimilation into the established order of South African society throughout the forties and fifties. This is borne out by the fact that during World War II, as in its predecessor, they were prepared to join up and fight the enemies of white South Africa, even though restricted to unarmed roles as truck drivers, stretcher bearers and trench diggers. "We would rather fight for, and correct, the evils of our present State and incorporate in her legislation and administration all that is best for the advancement and happiness of our common humanity," said Xuma.

African boys are dying in defence of freedom, democracy, Christianity and human decency in South Africa. They are making this supreme sacrifice so that we, their Kith and Kin, may enjoy these privileges as well. . . . South Africa must play the game with the Africans now.

In the South African army, Africans were not allowed to handle firearms, and were supplied with only knopkieries (war clubs) and assagais (spears) to defend themselves against Rommel's Panzers and Stukas. Moreover, at the request of the South Africans, the Allied High Command applied this restriction to men from the High Commission territories of Basutoland (Lesotho) and Bechuanaland (Botswana) as well. Neither were Africans able to rise above the rank of sergeant, though Indians and Coloureds could do so. Orders provided, moreover, that "In the event of an emergency, any European private shall have command of the Non-European personnel irrespective of rank."

Xuma argued that black troops would serve best under officers and NCO's of their own race, and he was willing to make humiliating concessions if necessary for blacks to be commissioned. "It would be a matter of indifference to Africans whether or not they are saluted by a European," he declared. "They have no desire to inconvenience or embarrass European Officers, N.C.O.'s, or Privates."

In 1942, with the Germans and Japanese sweeping all before them, the need for a broader national consensus seemed to impinge, however vaguely, on the regime. In Cape Town City Hall, Smuts made his famous speech proclaiming that "Isolation has gone and I am afraid segregation has fallen on evil days too." If intended to influence nonwhites—as it surely was—the very wording was obtuse. The government's true coloration showed more clearly in War Measure 145, which had the effect of making "all strikes of all African workers in all circumstances illegal." Smuts himself remained trapped in the paradox, which he seems to have grasped quite clearly, of espousing both human rights *and* a white South Africa. At the United Nations, which he had done so much to bring into being, South African policies soon came under fire. "Colour queers my poor pitch everywhere," he wrote in November 1946.

But South Africans cannot understand. Colour bars are to them part of the divine order of things. But I sometimes wonder what our position in years to come will be when the whole world will be against us. And yet there is so much to be said for the South African point of view who fear getting submerged in black Africa. I can watch the feeling in my own family which is as good as the purest gold. It is a sound instinct of self preservation where the self is so good and not mere selfishness.

Though it seems possible that toward the end of his life he had begun to accept that "integration" was inevitable, he could never pass beyond the old-fashioned paternalism that was the *platteland*'s best front. In 1947, summing up his position for a deputation of Natives' Representative Council members, he said:

> We must work together. There is no other way. Providence has put both of us here. Bantu and European came to this country at the same time. . . . You came from the North by land, we came from the farther North by sea, and here we both are, and here we shall both remain. It is our country; it is your country. We must try and build up a human society that will be happy as far as human beings can be happy.

Though it was the received opinion at the time, Smuts as an amateur archaeologist, the friend of Broom and Dart and the patron of the Abbé Breuil, probably knew that the canard about whites and blacks having come to South Africa at the same time was false. But perhaps the deceit was unconscious. There are truths too important to be admitted, even to oneself. In normal logic, the question would be academic. Though social wrongs may be righted, historical wrongs are out of reach forever. Given the premises of racism, however, the matter becomes one of supreme importance. Bad history is all too often the last refuge of bigotry (to paraphrase Dr. Johnson). In responding to the prime minister, Selope Thema obliquely took up the same theme. "If there is ever a people who must be thankful for other people who came into their continent, it is the African people," he said.

> We would never be here today if the whiteman hadn't come here. And I don't think that there is a single blackman—African—who wants the European away from this Country. But we want a fair deal, a square deal. We want to feel that we belong to this nation. . . . We want to be part of this nation, we want to be part and parcel of this nation so that if other people come and invade us, we will to defend our country together with the white people of this country. We don't want to feel that the newcomers might help us against the white people of this country, but that we can be part of the same nation as the white people of this country, to defend it together with them against such newcomers. You can make us feel that way if you treat us fairly.

The subservient irony of this plea went unheeded. Thema and his colleagues probably had few illusions that there would be a new deal for Africans. Smuts was seventy-seven. His successors, Malan's Purified Nationalists (the "Malanazis," as the Communists, with their innate taste for cant, dubbed them) were waiting in the wings. For the next three decades and more, power belonged to the Broederbond. No one could tell how much worse things would have to get before they got better.

Lembede and the Youth League

The 1940s were a time of transformation for the ANC. On the one hand a new generation, feeling nationalism in its bones, and impatient with the endless delays and retreats of its elders, began to make its influence felt. On the other hand, reviving under the stimulus of the West's wartime alliance with Stalin's Russia and the fresh prestige of the Red Army, the CPSA moved to reestablish the hold that had been lost when Gumede was unseated and to prod the conservative leadership into action. These two tendencies might be thought complementary to each other. In fact they were directly contrary in thrust.

It is customary to trace the modern beginnings of Africanism in South Africa to the founding of the Youth League of the ANC on Easter Sunday 1944, under the presidency of a sickly young Zulu named Anton Lembede. Of peasant parentage, Lembede had acquired B.A. and LL.B. degrees and an M.A. in philosophy (his thesis was titled "The Conception of God as Expounded by or as It Emerges from the Writings of Great Philosophers—From Descartes to the Present Day") by correspondence. He became first articled clerk to, then law partner of, his fellow Zulu, Dr. Pixley Ka Izaka Seme, founding father of the ANC. Though he and his close friends Ashby Peter Mda and Jordan Ngubane were Catholics, their reading and thinking covered a broad ideological spectrum. In after years, Mda recalled heated debates with Lembede over Marx, Engels, Nietzsche, Ruskin, Russell and others—including Smuts and his philosophy of Holism. Of Lembede, as of Smuts, it could be said that he "felt himself summoned to strenuous and realistic combat with the philosophical dualism which had been in the ascendant among philosophers since Descartes." As Lembede saw it, the South African conflict was "one of race on the one side and one of ideals on the other." As expressed by the Youth League, the Africanist ideal was distinctly holistic in flavor:

The Whiteman regards the Universe as a gigantic machine hurtling through time and space to its final destruction: individuals in it are but tiny organisms with private lives that lead to private deaths: personal power, success and fame are the absolute measures of values; the things to live for. This outlook on life divides the Universe into a host of individual little entities which cannot help being in constant conflict thereby hastening the approach of the hour of their final destruction.

The African, on his side, regards the Universe as one composite whole; an organic entity, progressively driving towards greater harmony and unity whose individual parts exist merely as interdependent aspects of one whole realising their fullest life in the corporate life where communal contentment is the absolute measure of values. His philosophy of life strives towards unity and aggregation; towards greater social responsibility.

One wonders what the Field Marshal would have thought; but the date being March 1944, he was elsewhere preoccupied. Jordan Ngubane later articulated Africanist philosophy in terms of the ancient ethical code of the Sutu-nguni peoples called *ubuntu* or *botho* (pronounced "boo-tu"), which he defined as "the practice of being humane." Supreme virtue for the African, he says, lay in this practical humanity, in accepting others "as a part of yourself, with a right to be denied nothing that you possessed." As an ethical code, this had far-reaching implications. "The harshest judgement that the humblest African in the Sutu-nguni community can make of his neighbor is to say that he is not humane. The nearest equivalent to this value judgement in the West is to say a person is not civilized or morally developed," Ngubane observes. Christianity, he suggests, put down such deep and lasting roots among Africans precisely because its fundamental beliefs—if not the interpretations placed on them by schizoid pastors—accord so well with *botho*. The African concept of equality had its basis not in political theory but in religious belief which saw humans as aspects of *Mvelinqangi*, or First Cause (literally, "the First-to-appear"). Dying is viewed as a shedding of the physical self and a return to the ancestral realm of the spirit forms. As the essence of *Mvelinqangi* and a spirit form (*idlozi*) to be, the individual personality is held intrinsically sacred, irrespective of age, sex, or position.

In such a view, the unity of mankind is self-evident. Unlike the theoretical variety, this organic holism impinges strongly on ordinary men and women in their daily lives. For modern, alienated man, by contrast, life is riven by a terrible dualism, which simultaneously sets people apart from each other and from the world itself. Apartheid is an accurate name for it, and can in this light be seen to be not a mere sociopolitical scheme for organizing exploitation but a metaphysical principle. It was this dualism, more deadly than their cannon and muskets, that the whites had brought to South Africa. Racism and the idea that the earth could be parceled out as private property were implicit in it. For the Khoisan and the Sutunguni (as, for that matter, for native Americans, and the German tribes Caesar had encountered in his Gallic wars) life was seamless, and the earth was the patrimony of all its inhabitants. This contributed greatly to their vulnerability.

As a nationalist, Lembede reacted as negatively to manipulation by white "radicals" as he did to control of African destinies by white racists. It can be argued, too, that Communist ideology is very nearly the supreme embodiment of dualistic thinking, and hence is unlikely to appeal to a sincere Africanist. "We fear that there is a yawning gulf between your policy or philosophic outlook and ours," Ruth First was informed when she invited the Youth League to affiliate with the Communist-inspired Progressive Youth Council, of which she was secretary, in 1945.

Lembede's charismatic personality and his militant call for "Freedom in our Lifetime!" mobilized the energies of the young rebels who now came to the fore in Congress, among them Walter Sisulu, Nelson Mandela, Oliver Tambo, Wilson Conco, Duma Nokwe, Joe Matthews, and Robert Sobukwe. When he died prematurely in July 1947, aged only thirty-three, the mantle of leadership passed to Mda, in some ways the subtler intelligence of the two men. Authored chiefly by Mda, the Youth League's *Basic Policy*, probably its fundamental document, appeared in 1948.

This defined South Africa as a country of four chief nationalities, of which three—Africans, Coloureds, and Indians—suffered national oppression at the hands of the Europeans. Being the largest single population group, Africans were of necessity the key to the movement for democracy. Coloureds and Indians suffered differing degrees of oppression, but the national organizations of the three groups might cooperate on issues of common interest. The vast majority of whites, having a stake in South Africa's caste society and sharing in the spoils of exploitation, fell into the enemy camp. In the last analysis the voice of those few whites who "love Justice and condemn racial oppression" is seen to count for nothing in the councils of the ruling minority. In their struggle for freedom, therefore, "Africans will be wasting their time and deflecting their forces if they look up to the Europeans either for inspiration or for help in their political struggle." On the other hand, the "extreme and ultra revolutionary" drive-the-whites-into-the-sea brand of African nationalism was specifically rejected. "We of the Youth League take account of the concrete situation in South Africa, and realise that the different racial groups have come to stay," *Basic Policy* declares. "At all events, it is to be clearly understood that we are not against the Europeans as such—we are not against the European as a human being—but we are totally and irrevocably opposed to white domination and to oppression."

In its primary goal of taking over the helm of the ANC, the Youth League was startlingly successful, largely perhaps because of the organizational disarray into which Congress had fallen, but also because of the potency of Africanist ideas. By 1949 the Youth Leaguers had virtual control of the organization. Xuma was unseated as president-general and replaced first by Dr. James Moroka, then in December 1952 by the future Nobel Peace Prize laureate Albert Lutuli.

Battle with the Communists was joined early. The *Basic Policy* makes special mention of "certain groups which seek to impose on our struggle cut-and-dried formulae, which so far from clarifying the issues of our struggle, only serve to obscure the fundamental fact that we are oppressed not as a class, but as a people, as a Nation." This was in 1948, before the real challenge had developed.

In June 1950, anticipating the passage of the Suppression of Communism Act the following month, the CPSA announced its "voluntary dissolution." At the time the party had about 2,000 members; three-quarters are said to have been Africans, many of them also members of the ANC. It was to the Congress that their energies were now directed. Late that year the veteran Communist J. B. Marks was elected president of the Transvaal ANC, the most important of the provincial divisions. This was in line with predetermined strategy. "Immediately after dissolution, the seasoned Marxist-Leninist core came together to hammer out a course of action," says Michael Harmel. It was agreed "to participate actively in the public, legal mass movement [i.e., the ANC], and to combine this with persistent planned illegal work to rebuild and strengthen the Party as the vanguard of the most advanced class, the working class."

The ANC thus became the arena in which Africanists and Marxists contended. The latter, though perhaps more disciplined, determined, and experienced at political infighting, were always liable to trip themselves up out of opportunism. Thus, after the utter failure of the attempts of the Natives' Representative Council to intercede with the Smuts government against the brutal suppression of the great gold miners' strike of 1946 had shown the council up for the "toy telephone" it was, Lembede and the prominent black

Communist Moses Kotane jointly called for a boycott of elections to both the NRC and Natives' Representative seats in the all-white Union Parliament. The call had widespread support among politically conscious Africans, and was heeded by the incumbent Natives' Representative for Cape Western, Donald Molteno, who did not offer himself for reelection the following year. The Communists thereupon broke the boycott and put up their own candidates, Sam Kahn taking Molteno's vacant seat and Fred Carneson, another party member, being simultaneously elected to the Cape Provincial Council seat for the same constituency. Somehow Kotane and other black Communists managed to stomach this sort of thing; to the Africanists it simply shed further light on the CPSA as an organization of unscrupulous white power politicians.

Things were not, of course, always clear-cut. During the celebrated Defiance Campaign called in 1952 to coincide with the official celebration of the tercentenary of Van Riebeeck's arrival at the Cape, Communists and Africanists worked side by side, along with independents like Patrick Duncan and Manilal Gandhi, son of the Mahatma, and gained a good deal of publicity for the anti-apartheid forces. The ANC now reached its apogee, claiming some 100,000 paid-up members. But the Malan government reacted ferociously, with bullets, banning-orders and prison sentences. In the forthcoming parliamentary session, the Public Safety Act and the Criminal Law Amendment Act closed loopholes and added new powers to the already draconian panoply of the minister of justice.

If the Africanists' principles prevented them from emulating Communist opportunism, neither could they rival Communist blandishments. Youth Leaguers Walter Sisulu and Duma Nokwe, among others, were presently treated to lengthy tours of Communist countries, where they were given the full Potemkin treatment accorded Gumede a quarter of a century before. Like Gumede, they came back well steeped in Soviet mythology. The Communists worked assiduously to woo the league, and in many cases they succeeded, the most notable convert being Oliver Tambo. It was Tambo who in 1953 took the lead in conjuring up a new, all-white fraternal body, the Congress of Democrats, which now became the "legal" home of the former members of the CPSA and sundry fellow travelers. In the same year, however, underground cells and district committees having been established throughout the country, a new, secret party organization was inaugurated, styled the South African Communist Party (SACP) to distinguish it from the defunct CPSA, which "despite its great achievements and struggles . . . proved incapable of surviving under illegal conditions." Since the leaders, members, and ideology of the new underground body were virtually identical with those of the old party, however, this may be dismissed as mere sleight of hand. The CPSA *was* the SACP to all intents and purposes.

The new strategy envisaged the creation of a segregated umbrella organization modeled on the NEUM. This, the so-called Congress Movement, would consist of the Congress of Democrats, the South African Indian Congress, a tamed African National Congress, and the South African Coloured People's Organization (SACPO), now launched as a fourth "pillar" but so much an organizational fiction that to have dubbed it a "Congress" would have been risible. Firmly in control of COD, SACPO, SAIC, and the South African Congress of Trade Unions (SACTU), the apparatchiks now proceeded to the all-important task of consolidating their grip on the ANC itself. To do this it would be necessary to precipitate a split and get rid of the dissidents. Opening shots in the struggle were attempts to expel the chairman of the key Orlando (Soweto) branch, MacDonald Maseko, and Potlako Leballo, chairman of the Orlando East Youth League. The reason given for Maseko's expulsion was that he had organized a faction called the *Bafebagiya* (a Zulu word meaning "They died rejoicing"). Little seems to be known about this. The outspoken Leballo had not hesitated to denounce the Youth League leaders who had attended the 1953 World Youth Festival in Bucharest (Sisulu, Nokwe) as "eastern functionaries." He was not about to sit still for expulsion by administrative fiat, and had himself confirmed as chairman by his branch, while the Orlando ANC in its turn expelled H. G. Makgothi, Transvaal president of the Youth League, and one of those who had gone to Romania, along with the Transvaal secretary.

Despite support from the militant Witwatersrand branches like Orlando and Newclare, the Africanists were at a disadvantage. The struggle coincided with two important ANC campaigns, against the imposition of the Bantu Education Campaign and the removal of Africans from the "black spots" in the Western Areas of Johannesburg. A "Resist Apartheid Committee" was set up, the main purpose of which, according to one commentator, "seems to have been less to assist in organizing the Western Areas Campaign than to serve as another weapon of the leadership in the power struggle with the Africanists." ANC President Lutuli, ill and restricted by ban to the Natal district of Stanger, was more or less out of the picture. The campaign was conducted by the Transvaal leadership, based in Johannesburg and headed by Robert Resha. In the upshot, it was a total failure, and revealed the organization as both ineffectual and untrustworthy. "Congress," says Edward Feit, "had reached its apogee in the Defiance Campaign of 1952; it reached its nadir in the Western Areas and Bantu Education Campaign of 1955."

In June 1955, the Communists added mock ideological icing to the cake, summoning a "Congress of the People" to rubber-stamp the "Freedom Charter" which was henceforth to be the joint program of the Congresses. Lutuli's Deputy, Dr. Wilson Conco, presided; afterwards he admitted that he had seen the "Freedom Charter" for the first time at the conference, and Lutuli himself could not say who had drafted it. Upwards of 2,000 delegates were assembled at Kliptown, near Johannesburg, and harangued from a platform decorated with symbols of the fraternal organizations. Presumably adopted for the benefit of illiterates, these embodied an invidious racial stereotyping. The ANC was represented by an elephant, SACPO by a horse, the SAIC by a fox, and COD—*vanitas vanitatum*—by an owl.

Though exuding a pungent whiff of prefabrication, the "Freedom Charter" was on the face of it a document that few social democrats would take exception to. In addition to rights and liberties generally reckoned "bourgeois," it called for nationalization of the mines, banks and monopoly industry, and redistribution of the land, thus throwing down the gauntlet to the entire spectrum of capitalist interests in South Africa and overseas. Bravado of this sort in some ways maximized the obstacles in the face of the democratic movement by defining the enemy to include some of the most potent forces in the world. More significant, however, was the built-in multiracialism of the manifesto, which asserted, inter alia, that

> There shall be equal status in the bodies of state, in the courts and in the schools for all national groups and races.

This and other clauses implied the perpetuation of the arbitrary categories of apartheid, the very system on which white *baasskap* was based. On the contrary, observed Robert Mangaliso Sobukwe, in a free, nonracial South Africa, there would be no minority groups. "All would be Africans, and all would be guaranteed human rights as individuals."

In any case, the Africanists saw the Kliptown declaration as "political bluff," not to be taken seriously. It was meaningless, Leballo pointed out, to go about proclaiming that "The people shall govern," "The people shall share" and so on, when no steps were in the offing for the realization of these ideals—or for that matter for remedying even the most basic of the injustices to which the people were daily victims. "We are merely being made tools and stooges of interested parties that are anxious to maintain the status quo," he observed bitterly.

As was undoubtedly intended, the state was only too eager to pick up the gauntlet thrown down by the Freedom Charterists. That September the Special Branch raided hundreds of homes and other premises in search of evidence of treasonable activity. For more than a year the police ruminated over their findings, Minister of Justice C. R. "Blackie" Swart notifying Parliament in July 1956 that several hundred arrests were contemplated. Finally, in December 1956, one hundred and fifty-six Congress leaders were dramatically arrested, those from distant centers being flown to Johannesburg on military aircraft. The ritual drama of the Treason Trial had begun.

More than a hundred of the accused were Africans, among them Lutuli, Sisulu, Mandela, Letele, Tambo, Nokwe, Resha, Conco, and Matthews, father and son. There were twenty-three whites, including Beyleveld, Carneson, Slovo, First, Forman, Turok, Lee-Warden (Natives' Representative in Parliament for Cape Western), Levy and Bernstein. The Indian contingent, headed by Dr. G. M. "Monty" Naicker, was almost as numerous, and the handful of Cape "Coloureds" included Alex La Guma, Reggie September, and George Peake. But the real leaders of the SACP were missing from the list, except for Moses Kotane (always a bit of a maverick). Among those who were *not* on trial were Michael Harmel, Jack Simons, Bram Fisher, Sam Kahn, Brian Bunting, J. B. Marks, Yusuf Dadoo, and Jimmy La Guma. Either considerable care had been taken to protect the big fish, or the security police were badly informed as to who called the shots on the Central Committee.*

The Treason Trial was to drag on for five years, in circumstances varying from the grotesque to the farcical. In the end all the accused would be acquitted. Had the police with malice aforethought set out to do so, they could scarcely have devised a more effective means of providing the accused with international publicity and "revolutionary" cachet. The government, observed journalist Anthony Sampson, "were not only trying the opposition, they were creating it. . . . For the greatest single upshot of the treason hearings was the emergence, both in black and white minds, of the name 'Congress' as a real force."

Notwithstanding, in this period the ANC suffered a continual draining away of confidence among the mass of Africans, particularly on the Witwatersrand. All the crafty stage-managing in the world could not compensate for the essential reluctance of the Communists to trust themselves to the tidal wave of revolution, where

---

* This does not, of course, exclude the possibility that we, too, are badly informed about this, and that the real leaders of the CPSA-SACP were always underground; some might say that they were in another country and on another continent entirely.

the people with whom they so glibly conjured might show their real will. That the African public had a mind of its own was demonstrated by the events of 1957.

Azikhwelwa!

"The history of all hitherto existing society is the history of class struggles," declared the *Communist Manifesto* in 1848. "That is, all *written* history," Engels added forty years later, conscious that humanity is neither synonymous nor synchronous with the alphabet, that literacy is itself a sign of privilege and an indication (if we adopt the Marxist perspective) of differentiation into "separate and finally antagonistic classes." For centuries in England death sentences might be commuted to transportation for life if the condemned could demonstrate a rudimentary ability to read and thus establish title to "benefit of clergy." The colonies, chiefly America and Australia, were thus improved by many a ruffianly set of genes. Even in the age of compulsory education, reading and writing—let alone reading and writing history—sets one apart from the great mass of humankind, to whom literacy remains an esoteric and rather frightening phenomenon.

It is a truism that wars tend to be recorded from the victors' standpoint. It follows that the struggles of the deprived go unchronicled or falsely chronicled in near proportion to the degree of their deprivation. The battles won by those who have no historians of their own are either ignored or co-opted as propaganda by hostile publicists.

History is the mythology of celebrity. It is only recently that writers like Fernand Braudel have begun painstakingly to restore the lost details of the quotidian, and remind us that all was not kings and sieges. Even revolutionary history focuses on the "great." The aphorisms of Robespierre and Saint-Just are well known, but what of the anonymous mass of the Paris Commune and the *sociétés populaires*, those "mighty pressure groups of the poor," which the Jacobins supplanted with their party machine? We have no dearth of studies of the mental processes of Lenin, Trotsky, and Stalin, but know little about the feelings of the ordinary Russian peasant, or even of the militant Kronstadt sailors slaughtered by the Bolsheviks because the latter "knew well enough that no party, no matter how revolutionary it was, would be able to survive the transformation of the government into a true Soviet Republic."

Unlike the Jacobins and the Bolsheviks, the South African Communists contrived to betray the revolution even before it had happened. It was they more than anyone else who organized the demoralization of the intelligentsia by setting up their Russophile creed as the socialist shibboleth. The entire "left" thought in terms of raising popular consciousness to its own rarefied (Stalinist, Trotskyist) level, and apparently imagined that when this had taken place a revolution would follow. The idea that the ordinary people possessed far higher consciousness than the self-appointed leaders would have seemed, will no doubt seem, absurd. Yet if the history of revolutions teaches any one thing, it is that the people always know better than the leadership. Power and wisdom do not seem to mix well: privilege is naturally myopic.

In the South African context, a handful of "movement" politicos have loomed large, chiefly because they or their sponsors wrote the books (having retired from the fray to Britain or Eastern Europe). But there were other contests and other contenders, whose achievements were in every sense far more positive, and who actually won short-term victories on real issues, and gave the townships a glimmering of hope. Such a one, for example, was James "Sofasonke" ("We are all going to die") Mpanza, who led the overcrowded inhabitants of Orlando, Alexandra, and other Witwatersrand locations onto vacant municipal land in 1944 to build the great shantytown which later became known as Soweto. Such was the Alexandra bus boycott of 1957, whose slogans *Azikhwelwa!* ("We won't ride!") and *Asinamali!* ("We have no money!") were to resurface twenty years afterward in the mouths of Soweto students who did not remember what they had originally stood for—most of them not even having been born at the time—but yet associated them with victory.

A bus boycott had taken place under Africanist leadership in Evaton township in 1955–56 with some degree of success, though the Freedom Charterists held aloof, as they did from everything they could not control. As long ago as 1943 and 1944 Alexandra itself had experienced spontaneous bus boycotts, when the privately owned bus companies then operating the service attempted, with the approval of the Road Transportation Board, to raise fares beyond the slender means of most township people to pay. These boycotts were victorious, and in 1945 the bus routes were taken over by the Public Utility Transport Company (PUTCO) and the old fourpenny fare was restored.

Situated about ten miles north of Johannesburg on the main road to Pretoria, Alexandra possessed a sense of community uncommon in the newer type of township operated under a strict permit system. Population density was high: one hundred thousand people, many of them "illegals," crowded into an area of about one square mile. There was no permit system in force, and Africans could actually own their own homes. Those who did—they were called standholders—were obliged, however, to cram as many tenants as they could onto their plots to meet the exorbitant mortages they were obliged to pay. In theory at least this created a potentially divisive class distinction between landlords and renters, the former living in comparatively comfortable houses, the latter in rows of one-roomed shacks in back of them. One of the lessons of the boycott was the ability of people to transcend such differences.

Because there was electricity on only a very few streets, Alexandra was called "Dark City," and crime was rife. The brutally primitive conditions of South Africa's black "locations" were the rule here too. Open sewers ran down the unpaved roads. Smoke from tens of thousands of coal stoves polluted the air. But at least the township wasn't fenced. Neither were there fences around the three public squares, where anyone could hold a game of cricket or football or a political meeting (though at one stage the ANC had tried to enforce a monopoly on meetings). "Alexandra," writes Dan Mokonyane, "was not a paradise, but it was a haven for many."

In January 1957, PUTCO in its turn declared that because of increased costs it had no option but to raise fares to fivepence. The increase represented a very real hardship for workers, many of whom were already spending 10 percent or more of their total incomes on bus fares. The manager of the Pretoria Non-European Affairs Department later publicly admitted that most people could not afford the increase. Two-thirds of the Pretoria boycotters, he pointed out, were unskilled laborers earning barely £9 a month, and had last had a wage increase award in 1942, *fifteen years before.* The old fares had amounted to £10 a year, which would be raised to £12 by the increase.

The Standholders' Association protested vigorously, and Africans marched on the bus offices to protest under a banner inscribed with one of Mpanza's old slogans: *Asinamali!* There was nothing self-pitying about this. It was a precise and accurate statement of the facts. They had no money. The shout of *Azikhwelwa!* (which had been used in the 1944 boycott) was raised, and a new boycott commenced on January 7, the entire working population of Alexandra—perhaps forty-five thousand people—undertaking a daily walk to central Johannesburg and back of twenty miles or more. That night (that is, *after* the popular movement had begun) the Alexandra People's Transport Action Committee (APTAC) was formed to organize the struggle.

The action committee consisted of representatives of a variety of groups, some parochial, others national and even, as it happened, international. Every organization in the township was invited to send three delegates. The African National Congress delegation, including three members each from the ANC Women's League and Youth League, totaled nine representatives led by Alfred Nzo, later ANC secretary-general. There were three Africanists, the fire-eating Josiah Madzunya prominent among them. The Movement for a Democracy of Content (MDC), a neo-Marxist grouping with international ramifications, was represented by Dan Mokonyane, Arthur Magerman, Simon Noge, and temporarily by Lawrence Mayisela. Other committee members represented the Standholders' Association, the Standholders and Tenants' Association, the Vigilance Association, and the Tenants' Association. As many of the latter were also rank-and-file members of the ANC, the Nzo group could command a two-thirds majority on most issues. Mahlangu, a standholder businessman, was elected president of APTAC, and Nzo became secretary. The "extremist" opposition consisted of the Africanists and the MDC.* "From the very beginning the ANC, banking on its majority on the committee, decided to treat the decisions of the committee in a cavalier fashion, and took its instructions from the big shots in the Treason Trial," Mokonyane says. Nzo was later to be suspended for high-handedly making announcements to the press without consulting other committee members, after being censured several times. In the later stages of the boycott, Madzunya replaced Mahlangu as president, while Mokonyane became secretary.

It was the people and not the committee, however, who determined the course of the boycott. Four times a week there were mass meetings to iron out policy in one of the three public squares of Alexandra. The strike rapidly spread to Sophiatown and Lady Selborne location in Pretoria, also served by PUTCO buses. Witwatersrand townships not faced with fare increases, like Moroka and Jabavu, also came out in solidarity, as did bus riders as far away as

---

* The MDC, which was active in Britain, Germany, the United States, and elsewhere, as well as in South Africa, has inaccurately been called Trotskyist by various writers. One former member has defined it as "a non-hierarchical, antibureaucratic international movement dedicated to the achievement of a post-scarcity democracy of content, as distinguished from 'formal' democracy." For details of its program, see in particular, "The Great Utopia: Outlines for a Plan of Organization and Activity of a Democratic Movement," an unsigned article in *Contemporary Issues* 2, no. 5 (Winter 1950): 3–22, attributed to Ernst Zander. On the Witwatersrand the leading figure in the MDC was the poet Vincent Swart. Madzunya and Swart had as young men been members of the Workers' International League, a Johannesburg grouping associated with the Trotskyist Fourth International, but by the time of Azikhwelwa this was no more than a memory. Mokonyane proposed that the South African section of the MDC adopt the name "The Movement for the Reconquest of Africa," and in acronym form this did in fact appear on its banner in Alexandra.

Bloemfontein in the "Free" State, and Port Elizabeth and East London in the Cape. At the height of the movement as many as several hundred thousand people were involved nationwide.

Even the much feared *tsotsis,* or township thugs, suspended their reign of terror for the duration of the boycott, and did their bit by serving as pickets—a role in which for obvious reasons they tended to be highly effective. During the whole three-month boycott period only three serious crimes are reported to have taken place in Alexandra. African taxi drivers reduced their fares substantially, and many white motorists also rallied round to give rides to walkers whenever they could do so. The support of the whites made a deep impression. It showed, Mokonyane thought, "what is likely to happen in a movement that is decisive, has a positive direction and a clear cause. The much extolled hatred between black and white disappeared overnight."

Nonplussed, the authorities tried intimidation, always their favorite tactic. Since Malan's retirement the National party had been led by J. G. Strijdom, the so-called "Lion of the North," and a prime exponent of *kragdadigheid* (which may be roughly rendered as "powerdeededness"). "If they want a show-down they will get it," announced Minister of Transport B. J. "Ben" Schoeman. "The Government will not give way, no matter whether the boycott lasts a month or six months." Thousands of people were arrested for petty offenses. Jaywalking arrests alone soared into the hundreds. All vehicles in which blacks were traveling were stopped at six different checkpoints along the route, and regulations against overloading were strictly enforced by police wielding tape measures to check that no passenger occupied less than the prescribed minimum fifteen inches of seat space. Passes were demanded, drivers questioned, names taken down. Official spite even descended to the pettiness of deflating bicycle tires. "For once the whites had a grandstand view of the viciousness of the police," Mokonyane observes. This was significant in mobilizing whites other than the handful of politically conscious liberals and radicals. South African society is a great insulator, and many urban whites have little practical perception of the crimes committed in their name.

Aware that the government was planning a war of attrition, and that the people could not be expected to keep walking ten miles to work and ten miles back day after day indefinitely, the APTAC oppositionists planned the escalation of the struggle to a new level. To call for a general strike would have been illegal, and the police would have jumped at the opportunity of arresting them all on a serious charge, but there was nothing to stop them from urging people to "save food for a rainy Monday," and they began doing so at every opportunity. Originating early in the second week of the boycott with Mokonyane, whose mordant rhetoric resonated best with the after-work mass meeting audiences that gathered in Square Number Three, this oblique call for a stay-at-home strike was backed by the Africanists. But Nzo's Freedom Charterists seemed more intent on using the boycott and its mass meetings for collecting money for the Treason Trial Defence Fund, and it was with difficulty that they were prevented from co-opting boycott platforms to divert the people's meager resources in this way.

The implications of a mass work-stoppage some "rainy Monday" (there was already a tendency to "go slow," and support for a stay-at-home was gathering in Orlando, Pimville and other townships) began to impress themselves on the Johannesburg Chambers of Commerce and Industry, which in turn started to press for a quick settlement. For its part, however, PUTCO continued to insist that it had no option but to charge the fivepenny fare, and announced that unless the boycott ended by March 1, service would be permanently terminated. When there was no sign of a letup, PUTCO workers were dramatically given a week's notice to quit. The government, too, remained adamant. This was hardly surprising, since PUTCO was effectively a parastatal corporation, subsidized heavily on so-called "sub-economic" routes, and the obvious alternative to an increase in fares was an increase in the subsidy. And there was always *kragdadigheid*, which as so often in South African history rapidly gathered its own momentum. If the PUTCO buses were withdrawn, it was announced, no other company would be permitted to take over the service. Schoeman went so far as to bring in the Motor Carriers' Transportation Amendment Bill of 1957 to back up this absurd threat. The boycotters were unfazed. On Square Number Three men hoisted their bicycles into the air and shouted, "Goodbye PUTCO!"

So-called "hush-hush" meetings now began to take place between APTAC and representatives of the Johannesburg business community. But if the latter thought a sellout would be easy to engineer, they were to be disappointed. Delegates from the action committee attending any given "hush-hush" were elected at mass meetings, and were expected both to declare in advance exactly whom they were meeting with, and to report back in due course. First of all it was demanded that the boycott be called off as a precondition to talks, on the grounds that the South African government could not compromise its authority by negotiating under duress. This hoary tactic, dating back at least to the Smuts-Gandhi confrontation of 1906, was not going to work now, inasmuch as it was all too clear that once the boycott was called off there would be no other threat able to bring the establishment to the negotiating table.

The Reverend Ambrose Reeves, Anglican bishop of Johannesburg, deputizing for the president of the Chamber of Commerce, presently assumed the role of mediator between the businessmen and the boycotters. A string of British-born Episcopalian clerics have played a key role in legitimizing the Congress Movement. Reeves, chairman of the Treason Trial Defence Fund, was thick as thieves with the CODites. Members of COD would later stand in for him at meetings, "and so it was that religion, Stalinism and commerce joined hands against those they called extremist leaders," in Mokonyane's telling phrase.

The fact was that the Congress brass now wanted the boycott called off at all costs. It was diverting public attention from the Treason Trial "spectacular" which they had so carefully organized, and undermining the ANC's credibility—overseas and among whites— as the vanguard African movement in South Africa. Moreover, there was always the unspeakable fear that it might get out of hand and develop into a true revolutionary upsurge in which the puppet "leaders" were likely to be swept away, like much else that was familiar on petit-bourgeois horizons. "The Chamber of Commerce and the liberal Europeans remained desperately anxious to stop the boycott," says Anthony Sampson. Closest of all whites, save a handful, to the chthonic forces of black rage, the CODites probably knew the dangers better even than their nominal adversaries in the Special Branch. Historically they had always played a far more significant role than the police in braking and diffusing forces making for real changes. Their effectiveness lay, perhaps, in the fact that all but a handful of them were sleepwalkers, unconscious of their own ends. Backed by the authority of the state, Special Branch bullyboys indulged in crude schoolboy power hunger. But the Communists were acting out subtler longings, fantasies of omnipotence with sources in the infinitely vaster power of the dream. Revolution was their study. Since their real but unadmitted class interests inhibited them from actually making one, what could be more natural —perhaps inevitable—than that they should act as wreckers?

All the stops were now pulled out. At some personal risk (or, it was suggested, having obtained permission from an examining magistrate) Treason Trial defendants Oliver Tambo, Joe Matthews, and Arthur Letele came in person to confer with the stubborn "extremists" of Alexandra. Author Alan Paton, leader of the Liberal party, which had been formed by non-communist radicals and liberals around the same time as COD, also stepped forward as intermediary. Paton and Patrick Duncan met the boycott representatives at a house in the white Johannesburg suburb of Orange Grove. Paton's first ploy was to call in a black mouthpiece, that favorite liberal device, the Responsible African Leader (in Algeria the French called them *interlocuteurs valables*). "Do you know my friend Dr. Xuma?" he asked. This in itself struck the boycott leaders as patronizing. Everyone knew *of* Dr. Xuma, president-general of the ANC from 1940 to 1949, and one of the most prominent black professional men in South Africa, whose name "was celebrated in a song which most of us had sung as school children." They were obliged to admit that they did, and without further ado Paton picked up the telephone and summoned Xuma to join the talks.

But for all his celebrity, Xuma had acquired a reputation as a compromiser. In any case, having largely retired from active politics, he had nothing to do with the bus boycott. The action committee would not concede his right to intervene, and refused even to discuss the subject with him, so that he was obliged to leave again without ceremony. "You can always bank on the white man not to try and find out what is happening, but to try and impose his solution," commented Patrick Duncan, one of the very few whites who could sometimes see things from the African point of view.

The scheme being proposed by the would-be mediators was odd to say the least. Riders would still pay the fivepenny fare, but on reaching their destinations they would line up again to have a penny refunded out of a special Chamber of Commerce fund of twenty-five thousand pounds. This was a stopgap and would last only until July 1. Moreover, it excluded fellow boycotters in Lady Selborne, inasmuch as the Pretoria Chamber of Commerce was not willing to follow the example of its Johannesburg counterpart and put up the money. It was obvious that the motive could only be to defuse the boycott and condition people to accepting the increased fare—which they would find themselves paying in full once the subsidy was used up. Township bus queues, in any case, had to be experienced to be believed, and now it was proposed to add yet another weary line at the beginning and end of each workday.

On the action committee, however, only Mokonyane, Madzunya, Mathopa, and Magerman opposed this cruel fraud. The Congress steamroller went into action. Protocol entitled the oppositionists to make a minority report to the mass meeting, but every effort was made to dissuade them from doing so, and they were "physically excluded" from making a statement to the press. But the fact that the president and secretary of APTAC, Madzunya and Mokonyane, were being silenced could not be concealed. It was obvious to experienced journalists that a horse-deal was under way.

Mahlangu, of all people, was chosen to lay the Chamber of

Commerce scheme before the people of Alexandra. By six o'clock on the evening of March 1, a crowd of more than ten thousand had gathered on Number Three Square, and it continued to grow. Mahlangu got up to speak, only to be greeted with shouts of "*Azikhwelwa!*" "Tell us the truth—how much did you get?" and "Let Mokonyane speak!" The crowd surged around the platform—a rickety table—and Mahlangu ducked for cover. Mokonyane jumped onto the platform; Madzunya handed him the mock-up of the proposal prepared by the oppositionists, and he set fire to it. "The pretensions of the ANC boycott leaders and the Standholders' Associations disappeared with the ashes," he later wrote. "Henceforth they cooperated with every reactionary including PUTCO drivers and conductors to smash Azikhwelwa."

It was difficult for white radicals, even the best of them, to grasp the motives that made the people of Alexandra persist in their struggle. "Many thought that the boycott would fizzle out," wrote Eddie Roux. "The intransigents had virtually won their victory; the fare was back at 4d. But they would not agree to queue. Strangely enough the boycott continued." A new scheme was put together by the Chamber of Commerce in conjunction with the Freedom Charterists. Fivepenny tickets would be sold for fourpence. The difference would be made up out of the Chamber of Commerce fund, with assistance from the Johannesburg municipality. This still excluded the Pretoria walkers, and begged the question of what would happen when the fund ran out, and the mass meeting called to discuss it rejected it. "But the next day the buses appeared again," writes Anthony Sampson,

> and Congress, throwing all its influence into ending the impasse, showered Alexandra with leaflets urging the people to ride, promising a new campaign to win higher wages. The committee was split, and for a week the boycott hung in the balance, some of the people riding, others walking. Confusion, vagueness and cross-purposes weakened the politics of Alexandra, *and there was a danger that the leadership might lose control altogether.* [Italics added.]

Mokonyane phrases it somewhat differently. "The ANC issued two cowardly leaflets calling for people to ride the buses," he says. "As a consequence they were not allowed to hold any meeting in Alexandra Township for at least nine months."

With tickets on sale for fourpence, and the boycott platform well and truly sabotaged by the Congressites, the tired walkers of Alexandra gradually drifted back to the buses. Still the action committee, now led by the oppositionists, held meetings every Sunday to keep up the threat of a "rainy Monday." Victory was consolidated later in the year, when Schoeman introduced the Native Services Transport Bill in Parliament, empowering the government to levy the necessary subsidy from the employers. As Sampson points out, it was the first act of Parliament in the history of the Union to pass in response to African pressure. The Congress Movement could claim no part in this victory, as even President-General Lutuli admitted. "The boycott was essentially a movement of the common people," he afterward wrote. "The African National Congress had no part in organizing it." On the contrary, it had done everything in its power to break it, and would undoubtedly have succeeded but for the vigilance of Mokonyane, Madzunya and the other oppositionists on the action committee, and the steadfastness of the great majority of ordinary township dwellers, who in the three months of the boycott walked an extra 1500 miles for their penny.

5

THE SHAPES OF THE LIE

The last temptation is the greatest treason:
To do the right deed for the wrong reason.
T.S. ELIOT

Nothing resembles virtue so much as a great crime.
SAINT-JUST

To Sharpeville and Beyond

As EARLY AS 1954 Mda and Leballo had formed the Africanist Central Committee ("Cencom") and begun publishing their own journal, *The Africanist*. From this point on a decisive clash with the leadership of the Congress movement became more or less inevitable. The same umbrella could not comfortably shelter both multiracialists and Africanists.

Trouble was sparked at the Transvaal provincial conference of the ANC in October 1957, when the executive staged a return to office *en bloc* under the Treason Trial rallying cry "We stand by our leaders!" The puppet strings seem to have been a little too visible, and in any case it was a bad time to test the docility of the rank and file. Azikhwelwa and its aftermath had shaken Congress support in the townships. As Mokonyane noted, the ANC could not so much as hold a public meeting in Alexandra at this point.

At a special conference, held early the following year to deal with grievances, Leballo called for new elections. "Enthusiastic applause welcomed the motion," says Gerhart. "But just as it seemed that the dissidents would prevail—opening the possibility that the Africanists might gain a bridgehead in the Transvaal provincial executive—the chairman declared the meeting closed because time had expired for use of the hall. Loyal delegates rose and broke into strains of 'Nkosi Sikelel i-Afrika,' the ANC anthem, but most people present remained seated in confusion and protest."

A few weeks later, the leadership plunged into a new adventure, proclaiming a week-long stay-at-home to coincide with the white general election on April 16, 1958. Opposed by the Africanists —reasonably enough, since the organization was in a state of confusion and no adequate preparation had been made—the stay-at-home was a fiasco, and had to be called off after the first day. The executive used this as a pretext to expel Madzunya and Leballo (the latter for the second time) on the grounds that they were "disrupters" who had sabotaged the work stoppage.

The formal split came in November, when in outright challenge the Africanists put up Madzunya for election to the office of Transvaal president. A credentials fight developed, in which the ultimate sanction of both sides was the threat of violence. On the second day, the Africanists found themselves denied admission to the conference hall by "volunteers" armed with knopkieries and iron bars. Rather than attempt to enter forcibly, they adjourned and met separately in a school nearby, where they drew up a letter disassociating themselves from the conference and also from the ANC "as it is constituted at present in the Transvaal." The formation of a new organization was announced. "We are launching out, openly, on our own, as the custodians of the A.N.C. policy as it was formulated in 1912 and pursued up to the time of the Congress Alliances," the letter concluded. Confident of having won, the executive under Oliver Tambo would not even allow it to be delivered, and the Africanist delegated to do so, Rosetta Nziba, "was sent flying," in Mokonyane's words.

But the Africanist heresy was more vigorous than the Freedom Charterists knew. In April 1959 at a conference in the Orlando Communal Hall the Pan Africanist Congress (PAC) was formally launched. Sobukwe was chairman, Leballo was national secretary. In a surprising omission, Madzunya did not so much as win election to the newly formed National Executive Committee. Mokonyane later averred that the PAC hierarchy had imitated its multiracialist enemies and simply picked itself. "The so-called conference . . . was a rubber stamp—typical Stalinist behavior," he writes.

Much controversy had always revolved around Madzunya, a fifty-year-old Venda from the northern Transvaal, whose beard and tattered black overcoat supplied the white press with a suitably spine-chilling image of black nationalism. Gerhart, calling him "a street peddler with a flamboyant personality and an elementary school education," asserts that "he was in fact only on the periphery of the Africanist movement," and that he played the part of fire-eater "largely unaware that the Africanists considered him a politically dispensable stalking-horse." Mokonyane, who had the advantage of knowing Madzunya and who worked closely with him during the Alexandra bus boycott, presents a picture that is quite different. "The only Africanist group that existed and functioned independently was the Alexandra one under Madzunya," he says.

> There is no doubt that, for a long time, he was the mainstay of the Africanist movement . . . both courageous and consequent, whereas Leballo in Orlando Township was more wind and piss than anything else. . . . Madzunya was not anti-white as such but one could not say the same of opportunists like Potlako Leballo. . . . I was with Madzunya when the so-called Conference finished. The press interviewed him about not being on the Executive. He said characteristically that he was willing to serve under any leadership of PAC. Needless to say I refused to be part of the Conference because it was demanded of me that I should take out a membership before I could take part in the proceedings—a membership of something that was not even named, for the PAC was only named that day.

In fact, as with the ANC, the PAC leadership on the Witwatersrand consisted mostly of professionals and students. Both organizations, significantly, ended up expelling Madzunya, one of the few whose claims to popular support had been validated in action, whatever his subsequent aberrations.

Inasmuch as black power was likely to draw down the full fury of the police, subterfuge became part of the PAC stance. The drive-the-white-man-into-the-sea line appealed to many, Peter 'Molotsi admitted to Gerhart. "But we didn't want to go down on paper. . . . We wanted a lease of life to continue—to get the bloody bastards, that's all!" Some months after the founding of the breakaway Congress, however, several members of the Movement for a Democracy of Content who happened to be white, Vincent Swart among them, were excluded from a PAC meeting in Orlando's Donaldson Hall, "which maintained it was communing with the African forefathers," Mokonyane notes sardonically. "From that time onwards PAC began to play a shortened version of all the mistakes of the ANC." Still, Mokonyane believed, men like Sobukwe, 'Molotsi and Nana Mahomo were not fundamentally antiwhite.

In the late fifties South African oppositionists operated in a twilight zone of semilegality which imposed its own rules. *Kragdadigheid* was already tending to stifle public discussion. Illegality was just over the horizon. I was not overly surprised when around this time Patrick Duncan proposed that I undertake a mission to explore the Botswana border for potential escape routes. Even the Liberal party was beginning to realize that the next stage of the struggle would probably be underground.

But the question of who was to wage this struggle remained

unresolved. Undoubtedly the Communists had their plans, but the credibility of the Congress Movement was declining fast. The PAC, whatever its faults, had youth and mass appeal on its side. The Liberal party was vigorous, and the breakaway of old mossbacks like Oscar Wolheim and Donald Molteno to join the newly formed Progressive party in 1959 had had the effect of clearing the air. Though the number of active members who identified with African aspirations was small, an *ad hoc* collaboration between the radical Liberals and the Africanists developed, especially in the Cape. In part it was prompted by the strong distaste both groups felt for the CODite arbiters of Congress Movement policy. Key figures in this cooperation were Jordan Ngubane, who joined the Liberal party and became its vice-president, and Patrick Duncan, editor and publisher of the magazine *Contact*, who in years to come was to renounce nonviolence as espoused by the Liberals and join the PAC.*

Early in 1960 the PAC, over the objections of Madzunya, Mda, and Ngubane, embarked on a campaign for a minimum wage and the abolition of passes for which it was ill prepared. This culminated in the Sharpeville massacre on March 21, when at least sixty-seven demonstrators were shot dead by police in a Transvaal township, and almost two hundred more were wounded. Sharpeville, a watershed in South African history, has been described many times, and need not be rehearsed here. In the aftermath, Sobukwe, Leballo, and most of the PAC leadership were jailed, and both the PAC and the ANC were banned under the hastily introduced Unlawful Organizations Act. Even though the Liberal party and the NEUM remained legal, there could be scant doubt that the state would no longer tolerate open attempts to organize mass opposition to its policies.

Len Lee-Warden, M.P., the CODite Natives' Representative for Cape Western, now committed the signal indecency of pleading in Parliament that the government ban only the PAC. "If ever there was a need, it exists today for the Government to realize that it has in the ANC a friend and not an enemy, because these two organizations that we are asked to ban are so diametrically opposed that the Government should seize the opportunity of appealing to the

---

* "Among Liberals he was known as an emotional anticommunist," says Gail Gerhart in "Political Profiles, 1882–1964," vol. 4 of Thomas Karis and Gwendolen M. Carter, eds., *From Protest to Challenge: A Documentary History of African Politics in South Africa, 1882–1964* (Stanford: Hoover Institution Press, 1972–77), p. 26. I worked closely with Duncan during the late 1950s, and in my opinion he was one of the most hard-headed of the Liberals, and more than anyone else responsible for turning the Liberal party away from sectional white politics toward a genuine involvement in the destiny of the African majority.

ANC to assist it to restore peace and order in South Africa," Lee-Warden declared. Later that year an ungrateful Dr. Verwoerd did away with such anomalies as Natives' Representatives altogether, and Lee-Warden's seat in Parliament with them.

Though the Liberal party in the Cape lent the PAC campaign its active support, trucking in large amounts of food for the stay-at-home strikers, its psychology was scarcely revolutionary. Neither was the PAC itself capable of supplying the leadership and organization called for by the volcanic popular energies seething in the key Cape townships of Langa and Nyanga. It has been contended that the ultimate role of both the Liberals and the PAC leaders was to divert the struggle into relatively innocuous channels. Little or no part was played by the traditional "left" as represented by the SACP/COD ("Stalinists") and the Non-European Unity Movement ("Trotskyists"). They were, Patrick Duncan noted in his diary, "totally isolated." By contrast Liberal party morale had never been so high, and its offices were a "tremendous hive of activity." The Cape "Coloured" population, a majority in the peninsula, held aloof. Its intelligentsia, which should have given the lead, had been depoliticized by years of exposure to the negativity of the Anti-COD pillar of the NEUM; in any case, its feelings towards the "natives" were highly ambivalent at best.

Despite the terrible news from Sharpeville, the struggle in the Cape mounted in intensity. (This is an important point: it was not so much the fear of police bullets as the stance of the political "vanguard" that defused the crisis.) By March 25 fully half the African workforce was staying home. The police found themselves unable to cope with the thousands of passive resisters appearing outside police stations to surrender themselves for being without passes, and a temporary suspension of the pass laws in the Cape Town area was announced by the local commander, Colonel I. B. S. Terblanche. Later that day it was extended to the whole country by order of Minister of Justice Erasmus and General Rademeyer, the head of the police force. "For nearly two weeks no one was to be arrested under the pass laws," writes Tom Lodge. "It was the first time that a Nationalist government in South Africa had given way to an African political initiative [except, one should add, for Azikhwelwa] and the action reflected the uncertainty of the government's handling of the crisis."

By March 30 the stay-at-home was 95 percent effective in Langa and Nyanga, according to some sources; at Worcester it was reported that Coloured workers were joining the strike. That day the police conducted massive and brutal raids on the townships to force the people back to work, and a national state of emergency was declared. Duncan noted in his diary that Erasmus had ordered the arrest of the Liberal leadership "but that Terblanche had told him that he could not, in that case, guarantee law and order in the townships, as the Liberal Party was his only link with the people." It was an ironic, albeit unconscious, summation of the traditional left-wing stereotype of the liberal role.

There now occurred one of those rare spontaneous popular initiatives that leave all political leadership behind. Great crowds of blacks assembled in Langa and Nyanga and began to march on Cape Town in orderly fashion. "Whatever plans had been made beforehand, the PAC leaders were taken aback when it began," notes Lodge. Philip Kgosana, the twenty-three-year-old University of Cape Town student who was PAC regional secretary for the Western Cape, later widely believed to be the leader of the march, has conceded that he was actually in bed when he got news of it. A reporter gave him a lift, and he hastened to the head of the procession, where he was told that the march was to protest to the police about the attacks that morning. At Caledon Square police headquarters, a crowd variously estimated as involving between fifteen thousand and thirty thousand gathered.* Kgosana met with Terblanche, who promised him an interview with the minister of justice if he would get the marchers to disperse. Though the Liberals reportedly advised him not to keep the appointment, he did so, and was promptly arrested. "Whatever the marchers might have achieved by staying in Cape Town that day, one thing is certain: they lost everything by going home," Lodge observes. "One has a feeling that throughout the crisis there was a four-cornered relationship: the police chiefs, the *Contact* Liberals, the Kgosana group and finally the people of Langa and Nyanga. It was these last who had least say in the decisions." Police and military units now swiftly sealed off the townships, food supplies were halted, and a barrage of brutality was unleashed to force people to give up the strike. Within a week, the crisis was at an end.

Though it continued to exist until 1968, when the Prohibition of Political Interference Act made the existence of nonracial political bodies illegal, and imposed a cruel choice between segregation and dissolution, the Liberal party had essentially run its course. The age of law and order had come to an end. The state of siege had

---

* There is a tendency for such figures to be wildly inflated. For example, in R. W. Johnson's *How Long Will South Africa Survive?* (New York: Oxford University Press, 1977), p. 19, it is asserted that "perhaps 100,000 Africans marched to the city center." The fact is that the entire African population of the Cape Peninsula barely totaled 100,000 at the time.

begun, and in war a party committed to nonviolence could provide only martyrs.

In 1961, Albert Lutuli was given the Nobel Peace Prize. In 1962 the Sabotage Act—aimed, according to B. J. Vorster, the new minister of justice, primarily at whites—signaled the end of free speech on all the vital issues. That year, too, Potlako Kitchener Leballo emerged from prison, and the PAC's guerrilla wing, called Poqo (meaning "standing alone" in Xhosa, with the implication *Ama-Afrika Poqo,* "the independent people of Africa") was set up. From the relative safety of Basutoland (now Lesotho), Leballo indulged in a great deal of bombast concerning the imminence of revolution, scheduled according to him for April 1963. This provoked a preemptive initiative from the South African authorities. On April 1 Basutoland police swooped onto PAC offices in Maseru and seized extensive membership lists, which evidently found their way into the hands of the South African police almost at once. Mass arrests followed which effectively crushed the PAC-Poqo organization inside the Republic. Sobukwe remained in detention until 1969, and was under banning order until his death; Kgosana and Madzunya were both expelled from the PAC under various pretexts; Leballo continued his activities abroad.

Around the time of Lutuli's Peace Prize Award, the ANC too decided to form a military organization. This was christened Umkhonto we Sizwe ("Spear of the Nation" in Zulu), also known to initiates as "MK." Not long after completing mopping-up operations against Poqo, the police raided Umkhonto headquarters at Rivonia near Johannesburg and arrested the entire high command of the underground organization at one blow. On May 1, 1963, the General Law Amendment Act, enacted with a view to breaking Poqo and Umkhonto, effectively did away with habeas corpus in the Republic.

Nelson Mandela, the black focus of much SACP image-building, had been arrested in August 1962 after returning from a lengthy tour overseas to enlist support (mirroring the trip to the UN and elsewhere that Leballo was making around the same time). Mandela was put on trial along with Sisulu, Mbeki, and other "Rivonia" defendants, and in June 1964 all the accused who had been found guilty were sentenced to life imprisonment. Two years later the acting chairman of the Central Committee of the SACP, Abram Louis ("Bram") Fischer, was also sentenced to life in jail. The Fischer case caused much sensation in the press. Not only was he an Afrikaner, but his father had been judge-president of the Orange Free State Supreme Court and his grandfather prime minister of the

Orange River Colony. Since that time there has been little evidence of any significant Congress Alliance organization inside South Africa. Fischer died of cancer in 1975; Mandela, Mbeki, and Sisulu are at the time of writing still imprisoned on Robben Island.

Mandela referred to "reports that my arrest has been instigated by some of my colleagues for some sinister purpose of their own" at his trial. "I dismiss these suggestions as the sensational inventions of unscrupulous journalists," he added. Nonetheless, the charge has been reiterated by one who is, at any rate, no journalist: I. B. Tabata, president of the African People's Democratic Union of Southern Africa (APDUSA), and sometime AAC and NEUM kingfish. When he returned from his trip abroad, Tabata asserts,

> Mandela realised that the existence of the so-called Congress Alliance was a barrier to African unity.... unlike Sobukwe, he thought that the ANC could still play a useful role in uniting the people, provided that the leadership of the organization was restored to the Africans who alone had the constitutional right to be members[!]. Thus Mandela fought for the disbandment of the Alliance and succeeded[!]. *For this, he paid the price of life imprisonment on Robben Island.* But this did not prevent the cynical CP from cashing in on his imprisonment. [Italics added.]

Nevertheless, it has to be observed that the multiracial structure of the alliance was not abandoned until the ANC conference held at Morogoro, Tanzania, in April 1969, which invited Indians, "Coloureds" and whites to join the ANC "on the basis of individual equality." (As indeed they had always been entitled to do in terms of the nonracial ANC constitution of 1943.) Some were to be more equal than others, it was decided at Morogoro: membership on the National Executive Committee was reserved to Africans (i.e., those defined by the regime as "Bantu").

Among the documents seized by the police at Rivonia was an outline of a plan entitled "Operation Mayibuye," which prosecutor Percy Yutar called "the corner-stone of the State case." Noting that "very little, if any, scope exists for the smashing of white supremacy other than by means of mass revolutionary action, the main content of which is armed resistance leading to victory by military means," it went into some detail on the subject of preparations for guerrilla war. "The objective military conditions in which the movement finds itself makes the possibility of a general uprising leading to direct military struggle an unlikely one," the writers conceded. "Rather, as in Cuba, the general uprising must be sparked off by organized and well prepared guerrilla operations during the course of which the masses of the people will be drawn in and armed."

Lack of equipment and trained guerrillas would be made up for by "proper organization of the almost unlimited assistance which we can obtain from friendly Governments."

At his trial in 1966, Bram Fischer dismissed this as "an entirely unrealistic brainchild of some youthful and adventurous imagination. . . . it could achieve nothing but disaster." It would appear, however, that in the years following the incarceration of Fischer, Mandela, and other leaders, some such plan was embarked on. This much was indicated by J. B. Marks, in a speech he made to the international meeting of Communist and Workers' Parties in Moscow in his capacity of chairman of the SACP and leader of the South African delegation. *

On the evidence, either the South African security police were phenomenally effective, or the "guerrillas" being sent into the Republic were singularly ill prepared and led. One of the more widely publicized—and bloody—incidents was, for example, the so-called "Goch Street Case," in which two whites were killed in a warehouse by young blacks alleged to be members of the ANC who had left the country illegally to receive military training abroad. After the attack, two of the assailants were captured. One suffered brain damage at the hands of the police, which made it impossible to bring him to trial; the other, Solomon Mahlangu, was hanged in April 1979, almost two years later. Not long after the Goch Street shootings, however, a high-ranking South African police officer gave a television interview screened in the United States and elsewhere in which they were cited as proof of the existence of a widespread ANC menace. Alas, numerous trials and convictions, followed by draconian sentences, seem to suggest that the menace is more to young ANC cadres ("sacrificial lambs" might be a better term for them) than to the South African regime. One has only to compare the activities of "M.K." with the daily bombings and shootings carried out with ruthless efficiency by the *moudjahiddine* of the FLN during Algeria's struggle for independence. The FLN, unlike Umkhonto we Sizwe, could by no means count on "almost unlimited assistance" from friendly governments, inasmuch as Moscow backed the French Communist party, which for a long time clung to the principle of *Algérie française*. Obtaining arms was one of the *moudjahid*'s primary goals, and mostly he got them the hard way

---

* Marks took time out to reproach critics of the Soviet invasion of Czechoslovakia who spoke up at the conference for their "special and rather strange point of view," and to condemn "border provocations committed against the Soviet Union, the citadel of socialism and mainstay of anti-imperialist forces everywhere" (i.e., by China), and to denounce the subsidizing "and actually preserving from complete collapse of a group of right-wing renegades from our struggle" (i.e., the PAC) by the Maoists.

—from the enemy. The FLN had, moreover, to fight long and hard for the kind of recognition at the United Nations which the ANC can take for granted. Despite all this, in seven and a half years of war, the Algerian guerrillas tied down a French army numbering half a million men and more, and inflicted casualties that included more than twenty thousand French military and civilian dead. Algerian losses have been estimated as anything between three hundred thousand and one million dead. In fact, actual acts of sabotage performed by the ANC are few, even in comparison with those carried out by SWAPO in Namibia (South West Africa) against the selfsame South African forces.*

The ANC in exile has long been wracked by substantial disaffection, and afflicted by expulsions and splits. Demoralization may have gone even further. In 1971, Brigadier P. J. Venter of the South African security police claimed that in the preceding four years thirteen ANC members had returned to the Republic to surrender themselves, thereafter becoming police agents.

Nonetheless, with the support of Eastern European regimes, of the United Nations' bureaucracy, of sundry elements of the Western and African establishments, and such bodies as the World Council of Churches and the International Universities Exchange Fund (IUEF), the Congressites have managed to keep up a facade of credibility. This has been bolstered substantially by the readiness—indeed eagerness—of the South African regime to identify its enemies as the ANC and its Communist masters. This bill of goods goes down as well with United States Republicans, British Tories, and nervous reactionaries everywhere as it does with the white electorate in South Africa. A large element of self-deception is no doubt involved. White South Africans need to believe, for example, that "Communists" and "outside agitators" were behind the Soweto uprisings of 1976–77. (In fact there is no evidence to suggest that either the ANC or the SACP was involved, or even, in the latter case, represented in Soweto at the time.) The alternative explanation—that these events were a primal expression of African desperation and rage against whites—is too threatening.

Over and above all this, however, and perhaps most important of all, there has been a wholesale surrender of Western "radicals" from Stockholm to San Francisco in the face of the moral blackmail

* It should be kept in mind that SWAPO claims to represent fewer than a million Namibians, as against the twenty million and more South Africans on whose behalf the ANC speaks—yet, as reported in *Jeune Afrique,* cited in *A Survey of Race Relations in South Africa, 1971* (Johannesburg: South African Institute of Race Relations, 1972), p. 95, SWAPO actually had at that time more branches abroad than the ANC.

—the word is very apt—of the ANC-SACP lobby and its proxies. This is, of course, an epiphenomenon of the general abdication of the Western radical intelligentsia in the wake of the 1917 Bolshevik revolution, the implications of which are global, and not merely South African. Upon examination, the role played by the Congress Movement's supporters in the West will be found to parallel and complement the functions performed by the CPSA and the Congress of Democrats in South Africa at earlier periods. It probably derives from a very similar psychology. Similarly, too, it is fundamentally at odds with African freedom. Analysis of this factor calls for a book all on its own, but one case will give a glimpse of its workings.

In the issue of the British "underground" paper *The Black Dwarf* dated November 26, 1969, an article appeared under the title "Southern Africa: A Betrayal." The editors supplied the following preamble:

> For the last few months we have been receiving a mass of material related to the struggle in Southern Africa. Much of this material was of a controversial nature and there was no way for us to ascertain its veracity. Last month, however, we received what we regard as an extremely important document. We have had it verified by our contacts in Africa and in London. We are satisfied that the general line taken by this document is correct, though we have not been able to check every small detail. We are printing it below because we believe that it is time that many African militants were told the truth and that the facade of lies which we have all been told was stripped away. In the past *The Black Dwarf* itself has published articles on Southern Africa which only helped to mystify the situation further. For this we apologise to our readers and hope that the document below will wipe out the stains of the past. The authors of this document are both guerrilla fighters. We have proof of this, but for obvious reasons they do not wish their names to be known.

An honest enough statement, and all honor to those who wrote it. But the truth was not to be known so easily. As I write, I have before me two copies of the issue of *The Black Dwarf* in question. Both advert to "Southern Africa: A Betrayal" on the first page. One copy contains the article; the second carries the entire two-page center-spread it occupied blanked out. These two blank pages testify eloquently to the pressure the Congress Movement bureaucracy was able to wield in Great Britain in that year in defense of its interests. Tariq Ali, editor of *The Black Dwarf*, and very much its moving spirit, reportedly resigned over this blatant self-censorship forced on him by his editorial board, and the paper expired not long afterward. (Ali went on to found *The Red Mole*.) The censors were just a fraction too slow. Some few copies of this unique statement in the carefully closeted annals of the ANC did reach the streets.

The anonymous authors set out to explain their reasons for leaving Umkhonto we Sizwe. They know perfectly well, they say, that their statement may be taken up by the propaganda organizations of the South African government. They know, too, that "the ANC profiteers will make this continent hot for us with the kind of propaganda which still gets heard despite their total failure in the struggle." But they can no longer remain silent.

Among the incidents which have moved them to speak out, they cite the so-called Wankie Affair, a guerrilla operation in which a band of ANC oppositionists were deliberately sent to their deaths in Rhodesia-Zimbabwe in August 1967. "We have proof that the Smith government was alerted of the attempt to infiltrate into Rhodesia by some of the leaders in ANC or ZAPU," they write.

> The men who were sent down to Wankie were under duress; they were forced, on one occasion at gun-point, to cross the Zambesi into Rhodesia: a terrain which they did not know, and amongst a people whose languages they had not been taught to speak. . . . Little does the "progressive world" suspect that Wankie was staged for two reasons alone: to get rid of unwanted dissenters, and to press fund-giving organisations into giving more money for the "heroic" cause. [Italics in original.]

The blood of the martyrs, it has been observed, is the seed of the church. In this case it is also the seed of international funding for the Congress bureaucrats. It has been reported that ZAPU militants sent into Rhodesia were ordered always to carry their party cards, so that when the body count was made it would be known who was "in the forefront of the struggle." They were also sent in in full battle dress, equipped with heavy weapons unsuitable for guerrilla purposes. In the Wankie Affair, it would seem, they were betrayed into the bargain. All the evidence would indicate that this was no isolated incident either.

"Southern Africa: A Betrayal" goes on to paint a mind-wrenching portrait of Congress Stalinism in action. We read of assaults, beatings and stabbings of protesters "officially sanctioned by the Tambo-Kotane-Modise group, both in Tanzania and in Zambia"; of murders carried out in Zambia by strong-arm men trained at the Lumumba Institute in Moscow; of the favoritism and nepotism which pervade the organization. There is systematic slandering of those who oppose the Moscow line:

> The ANC leadership found itself involved "reluctantly" in the Sino-Soviet dispute. Men who had been trained in China were looked upon

with scorn and distrust. Whoever spoke against the Kremlin and its policies was branded as a "deviate Maoist and revisionist," or alternatively, "an Imperialist tool," and such persons were marked and termed "fifth column elements that were against the liberation of South Africa."

Tanzanian law-enforcement agencies are used against those who threaten the bureaucrats:

> To stifle, and finally eliminate opposition in the camps, particularly in the main Kongwa camp where rebellion was imminent, the clique brought into play the legal institutions of the Tanzanian government. The reason given—when fourteen men were detained indefinitely—was that these men were a potential danger to both the liberation movement (ANC) and the freedom of the South African people. In fact, however, these were the men who dared to expose the myth.

Terrorist trials by tribunals set up by the dominant clique are used to break down the opposition. Some, after being subjected to psychological coercion greater than they could bear, were interned in the Mrembe Hospital—a mental asylum—in Dodoma, Tanzania. The writers note at least one suicide, and a number of attempted suicides in all the camps, and particularly in Kongwa. Discipline in the camps is maintained by platoons of young thugs, who administer beatings with lengths of hose. There is a division of the men into ethnic and tribal groups reminiscent of South Africa's Bantu Affairs Department:

> To this day, both in Zambia and Tanzania, the enmity amongst the men of different tribal groups surpasses that which they feel for the South African government. Such is the state of disintegration within the camps, a situation which has been deliberately engineered.

These, the writers say, "are only a few of the atrocities we have gone through and escaped from, but which our compatriots are still suffering right now, in the camps." However, they add,

> We shall struggle against and resist all attempts to make the South African revolutionaries members of the South African "Communist" Party against their will, or the African National Congress a branch of the "Communist" Party of the Soviet Union. Our struggle shall not be directed from Moscow. We recognize that ultimately it is not in the interest of Moscow, as it is not in the interest of the United States, Britain, West Germany or France, that there be a major upheaval in Southern Africa.

The credulous and willing acceptance of the lies of the SACP–ANC hierarchy by the West's "compulsive ignoramuses" (to borrow a phrase from Robert Conquest) is undoubtedly greatly to be blamed for this betrayal.

Stalinism and Racism

Until such time as ideological polarization wrecks the status quo, it will tend to reinforce it. And from the wreckage a new order strongly resembling the old is likely to arise. "He who fights too long against dragons becomes a dragon himself: and if thou gaze too long into the abyss, the abyss will gaze into thee," says Nietzsche.

Threatened with annihilation, oligarchies either close ranks or crack. There was never until quite recently any reason to suppose that white South Africa was likely to crack in the foreseeable future. (And it remains possible that the reasons given now are specious.) Until 1976 each year that passed left the regime more powerful, and its opponents in greater disarray. Those who wielded the rhetoric of "communism" were objectively (and how reverently they, in particular, had always spoken of "objectivity") supplying the state with its justifications. This is one lesson of the CPSA–SACP's "Fifty Fighting Years," and of South African "left-wing" politics in general.

It was only when the tide of international opinion had swung about that the protagonists of apartheid and *baasskap* were given pause. By then they had entirely obliterated the internal political opposition (though not the undying opposition of the great masses of the South African people). The "opposition in exile" had taken up its stance as an agency of Russian foreign policy and the KGB. A totalitarian solution to the South African predicament: this had always been where it really stood. The activities of the CPSA since the 1930s and before make its hostility to popular power, and hence to any genuine revolution, all too apparent. "The word 'revolutionary' can be applied only to revolutions whose aim is freedom," Condorcet observed almost two centuries ago. But it is to be doubted whether these South African "revolutionaries" even know the meaning of the word. They look to Russian tanks to solve their problems:

> Shall we shed our tears in a shower?
> Stalin is now the most live of all living,
> Our weapon, our knowledge, our power,

declared their organ, *New Age*, in the year of the Hungarian Revolution. After Khrushchev's revelations at the famous Twentieth Congress of the Communist Party of the Soviet Union in 1956, most Communist parties were found to contain some members with the courage to recant. None did so in the case of the South African party. This loyalty to an alien despotism was not merely bizarre; it exactly reflected their domestic policies.

Racist violence and intransigence were the only things which could supply the morally bankrupt CPSA with credibility. They had, accordingly, to be provoked wherever possible. Oswald Pirow and Lazar Bach, Michael Harmel and Hendrik Verwoerd both needed each other and deserved each other. Despite the differences between the Calvinist and Leninist forms of puritanism, they were essentially products of the same society. It was a society which, to use Hannah Arendt's phrase, "perverted all virtues into social values." For both, the end justified any means, and the means finally became the end. In white-ruled South Africa, power has always been sanctioned, in the words of Jan van Riebeeck's diary of the 1650s, "by the sword and the laws of war." Of course it may be argued that force is fundamental to every social order. "All laws started with arbitrariness and revenge," asserts a writer on Roman jurisprudence. In South Africa, however, the arbitrariness and basic injustice of the law are simply too obvious to be hidden under the shroud of custom.

A cruel irony lay in store for the Stalinists. The racism they had pandered to returned to haunt them. At Morogoro in 1969 "other races" were admitted to membership of the African National Congress in exile (but, significantly, not to the "internal" ANC). On the face of it, this was a step toward democratization. If in the period of legality the multiracial structure of the Congress Alliance had served to enable the CPSA–SACP to "exercise its vanguard role," surely open membership might be expected to neutralize the influence of the "non-Africans" alleged to dominate the alliance? Would they not, in a democratic context, simply have to submit to majority decisions?

The drive for open membership in the African National Congress had evidently begun as early as 1965, when Tambo, Resha, Kunene, and Kgogong met the Slovos, Dadoo, Harmel, and other SACP leaders at the Slovos' house in England. Resha now emerged as the leader of the opposition to the proposal, "and openly stated that these non-Africans wanted membership because they wanted power in the ANC." And at Morogoro, when the so-called Revolutionary Council was set up to direct the alliance, Resha is also said to have been the main opponent of the new policy. Clearly, however, he was outgunned and outmaneuvered, and in the last years of his life (he died in 1973) he was evidently made to pay dearly for his disobedience. His former comrades, it is said, "politically isolated him into his grave." (Worse, they evidently cut off his income!)

The overwhelming majority on the Revolutionary Council, the Communists protested, were Africans! It included "only one Indian, one Coloured and one White" (Yusuf Dadoo, Reggie September and Joe Slovo). How could this put it "under the hegemony" of a "clique of non-Africans"?

How indeed? The "African Nationalist" opposition responded by citing Eddie Roux on the subject of phony majorities. And in any case, they asserted vehemently, *"The Slovos and the Carnesons have no right even to attend meetings of Africans where plans to overthrow White domination are discussed."* [Italics in original.]

The chickens had come home to roost, and with a vengeance. But one thing inevitably remains puzzling to the outsider. Why, since the "non-Africans" are by definition a minority, is the Congress opposition so fearful of their power? Slovo, September, and Dadoo are scarcely so terrible a trio as to put the wind up any reasonably resolute body of revolutionists. Mao Tse-tung or Algeria's Houari Boumedienne would probably have polished them off before breakfast.

Let us concede that the minority hierarchy keeps tight control of cash flow from Moscow. Does this mean that the rest are up for sale? Can it be that the almost superhuman ability to corrupt attributed to the "non-Africans" is explicable in terms of the desperate need of the accusers to justify their own failure to resist? The surrender that the contemporary inheritors of the ANC have made is above all a surrender to racist and totalitarian ideas—of which the Slovos were, and are, merely the local pawns. It is a surrender to the lie of power and the power of the lie. This is a battle each of us must fight for himself, and skin color has nothing to do with it.

The Yugoslavian dissident Mihajlo Mihajlov has identified "the belief that power gives freedom" as the innermost essence of all totalitarianism. "Against this belief in power can only be set the belief that all power enslaves, and enslaves primarily him who wields that power, and that to suffer violence without resistance is just as wrong as to commit it," Mihajlov writes. Stalinism and racism alike are diseases of the soul, and here lies their common origin.

6

THE HUMAN DIMENSION

Black man, you are on your own!
SASO

THE HIATUS OF THE MID-SIXTIES
was ended by the meteoric rise to national prominence of the new
politics of Black Consciousness. The movement had taken shape in
the South African Students' Organization (SASO), formed under the
leadership of Stephen Bantu Biko in the years 1968–69 as an alternative to the nonracial National Union of South African Students
(NUSAS), long seen by its supporters and its enemies as the most
radical legal body on the South African scene. On the contrary, Biko
asserted, the sort of token integration represented by NUSAS
merely served as salve for the guilty consciences of a handful of
liberal whites, while creating the false impression that something
was being accomplished. A truly nonracial society could emerge
only after the overhaul of the whole system. "The biggest mistake
the black world ever made was to assume that whoever opposed
apartheid was an ally," wrote Biko.

> I am not sneering at the liberals and their involvement. . . . Rather I
> am illustrating the fundamental fact that total identification with an
> oppressed group in a system that forces one group to enjoy privilege
> and to live on the sweat of another is impossible. . . . The liberals
> must fight on their own and for themselves. If they are true liberals
> they must realize that they themselves are oppressed, and that they
> must fight for their own freedom, and not that of the blacks with
> whom they can hardly claim identification.

187

In 1972 the Black People's Convention (BPC) was founded to provide Black Consciousness with a broader organizational base. Four years later the explosion of the students of Soweto in wave upon wave of unprecedented assault on the whole system of white rule testified to the far-reaching influence and power of Black Consciousness ideas.

Steve Biko's career and his murder by the South African police in September 1977—surely one of the most imbecilic crimes ever committed in the name of white South Africa—have been documented in a spate of books, and even a play. His story captured the imagination of people around the world. Only thirty years old at the time of his death, he had shown every sign of becoming one of the outstanding leaders of the twentieth century. As Conor Cruise O'Brien summed it up:

> Many people hailed as martyrs, and almost all would-be-martyrs, have been more or less crazy. Stephen Biko was as far from crazy as it is possible to be, and he neither wanted nor even expected martyrdom. He became a martyr none the less: one who bore witness, both through his life and through his death, to the faith and love that were in him.
>
> If we can assume the existence of a God who is Love, Biko is a martyr in the full, traditional, spiritual meaning of the word. Without that assumption, and extending the word in a legitimate secular sense, Biko remains a martyr: not just a passive victim, but one whose life-and-death testimony goes out to the world and changes it.

Biko spoke, above all, for millions of young black South Africans. Though these young people are numerically far and away the greatest human dimension of apartheid, the reality of their life experience remains unknown to the outside world. This chapter attempts, however inadequately, to convey something of the story of one of them, Selby Semela.

Out of Soweto

"Soweto" is an acronym for *South Western To*wnships. Southwest, that is, of Johannesburg, the economic core of the Republic of South Africa. Selby Semela was born in Pimville, one of the oldest and rottenest of these townships, on January 23, 1958.

What did the future portend for a child born in Soweto that year? Not much at best, and in all probability a swift descent into an early grave. One estimate, perhaps on the high side, suggests that as many as 60 percent of African children in the Johannesburg area die before they reach age one. Malnutrition is chronic and almost universal. The brains of small children are especially vulnerable, since during the first four years of life the brain attains 90 percent of its adult weight, while the rest of the body reaches only about 20 percent. It has been known for sixty years that there is a correlation between low birth weight and mental retardation, and one expert in brain development suggests that early-life malnutrition can lower the IQ by as much as fifty points. Though the Sutu-nguni peoples are historically tall and powerfully built, the children of Soweto are mostly puny.

In 1958 South Africa is still a British dominion within the Commonwealth of Nations to which Jan Smuts gave a name, and the government of the Afrikaner National Party is coming up for its third term in office. A new star is rising, that of the charismatic "architect of apartheid," Dr. Hendrik Frensch Verwoerd, who is about to be elevated to the office of prime minister. A man of amiable appearance (he looked rather like Kriss Kringle, thought an American journalist), Dr. Verwoerd is fifty-seven. The people of Soweto have made his acquaintance during his tenure as their "Great Induna" in the office of minister of native affairs.

Britain in 1958 is led by Tory Prime Minister Harold Macmillan. In France General de Gaulle's fledgling Fifth Republic is gathering its strength for a showdown with *Algérie française.* The events of Suez, old-style colonialism's last binge, are already two years in the past. In the United States it is the age of Eisenhower and of John Foster Dulles. The forcible desegregation of Little Rock has been carried through. Sputnik I has been launched, creating a furor over the alleged existence of a "missile gap" that some take more seriously than others. ("If they knew what we know, they'd be behind too," said Bob Hope of this phenomenon, a wisecrack that seems to gather profundity with each year that passes.) Though the preceding twelve months were a period of economic recession, John Kenneth Galbraith has written an influential book titled *The Affluent Society.* No one has seriously disagreed with that description.

The black townships of South Africa are not commonly dignified with any of the terms used in English to designate places of human habitation. They are called, quite simply, "locations" (a word naturalized by those who live in them as *elokishini*). Such "locations" are to be found outside every South African city or town. This is to be expected, for what is located in them is labor: the millions of black workers on whose toil South African industry, big and small, modern and primitive, depends. Soweto itself is nothing but a vast huddle of locations—several dozen of them. In all, as befits the status of Jo'burg, a kind of megalocation.

E Goli, city of gold, vortex of labor and money, Johannesburg sits at the heart of the Reef, the string of industrial cities—Benoni, Brakpan, Carltonville, Edenvale, Germiston, Krugersdorp, Randfontein, Roodepoort, Springs—built on and around the Witwatersrand ridge. Less than a century ago, as they say, "there was nothing here." The first mines were opened, the first street laid out in 1886. Eighty years later the Reef had yielded more than ten billion dollars in gold, and some of those same mines were still producing. Not for nothing is South Africa's currency, the Rand, named for the Witwatersrand —the "ridge of white waters" which sits, quite fortuitously, atop the richest auriferous deposits ever discovered. Though declining as a percentage of GNP, at least till 1979, gold remains a vital source of foreign exchange. The seven great mining finance houses— Anglo–American, Anglo–Transvaal (Anglovaal), Rand Mines, General Mining and Finance Corporation, Johannesburg Consolidated Investments (Johnnies), Gold Fields of South Africa, and Union Corporation—constitute a major focus of multinational corporate power, with holdings all over the world. "They are so closely intertwined that to conceive of them as separate entities would be entirely misleading," say Seidman and Seidman. In 1974 the assets of the largest, Anglo–American, were estimated at over $7.4 billion (despite its name, some 56 percent of Anglo–American's shares are held by South African interests). The surpluses produced by these companies have over the years been reinvested to finance South Africa's industrial development. Between 1966 and 1973 output in the manufacturing sector doubled, and it is estimated that the country produces 80 percent of its own industrial plant. Domestic industry supplies everything from transistors to heavy equipment and railroad loading stock. A recent survey has ranked South Africa eighteenth among world nations in economic capability, with a 1975 GNP of thirty billion dollars. This capability was financed and developed by the gold of the Reef, given muscle by black labor.

Soweto is both very near and very far from Hollard Street and the Johannesburg Stock Exchange where the gold stocks are traded. By road it is less than ten miles at its nearest point, about twenty-two at farthest, but there is an almost infinite gulf separating the whites who go about their business in downtown Johnnesburg and the Sowetonians who service them. It may perhaps be questioned whether it is greater than the gulf separating the inner cities of America from its affluent suburbs or, in English terms, Hampstead from Brixton. The answer is yes, incomparably so, for it cannot be bridged under the status quo. No Sowetonian can ever own property in Johannesburg, vote there, or hold public office in the city. No one born in Pimville can aspire to reside in Parktown.

It is not possible to say with any accuracy how many people live in Soweto. As of mid-1977, the total legal population was 646,233. There are rather more than a hundred thousand houses, which, taking into account those lodged in hostels, allows for approximately six to a house. But these official figures are meaningless. They fail to take into account the vast illegal population. Those who are not there legally do their best to avoid official notice, since on discovery they are likely to be "endorsed out,"—that is, sent to rot in one of the many rural resettlement areas up and down the country. Industry needs labor, but not labor's inevitable detritus: the old, the halt, the feebleminded, the maimed, the surplus. The elimination of social security by deportation is one of apartheid's substantial economies. Steve Biko explained to the court at the 1976 SASO-BPC trial how government head-counters got their figures wrong:

> Well of course, M'lord, when the census official comes around to my home as a black man, he never really says to me: "We are counting the people who are here in the country." It is a typical white approach again. He comes in and he says: "How many people live here?" Now the first thing you think about is registration. If I have got people squatting in my house I am going to be arrested, so if there are ten people but six are registered you say: "Six, baas," so he writes six and he goes next door. . . . If it was explained to people nicely that the officials were only counting, and would not prosecute, people would give the correct figures, but they never know, they are never told.

The actual population of Soweto has been quite credibly estimated at between a million and a half and two million. Obviously this makes for a lot more than six to a house, even taking into account construction over the past few years. Since most of the houses in question have four rooms or fewer, overcrowding reaches levels simply unthinkable in Western countries. Perhaps 20 percent of the houses in Soweto have electricity. Seven percent have a bath or shower. Only 3 percent have running hot water. The West Rand Administration Board, which technically owns all these houses, evidently does not think it vital that the black muscle that powers Johannesburg be washed. In the fiscal year 1976–77, the board spent only R750,000 on housing out of a total budget of R57,778,600.

But statistics of this sort cannot possibly give an American or European or white South African (few of whom ever visit such places) any real idea of what life in Soweto is like: of dark, smoky rooms, barren spaces between houses littered with trash in lieu of gardens, half-naked children in the icy highveld winter. Of a level of air pollution that may be the worst in the world. In 1975 South Africa produced seventy million metric tons of hard coal, ranking eighth in the world in this category. And without electricity or natural gas, coal is what the people of Soweto burn. They burn it to cook, to keep warm, to heat water. Like Los Angeles and Denver, the Witwatersrand suffers from cold-weather temperature inversions, which prevent smog from dispersing. As a consequence Soweto hunkers under a pall of smoke in winter.

The Johannesburg City Health Department regards readings of 20 or more on the "soiling scale," by which smoke pollution is measured (giving the concentration of sulphur dioxide per cubic meter of air), as unacceptable for the central city, but the average reading in Soweto in June (that is, midwinter) is at least 60. At peak pollution periods, concentrations of sulphur dioxide as high as 1,000 micrograms per cubic meter of air have been measured. By contrast, readings higher than 200 micrograms are unknown in the worst industrial areas. The pollution of Soweto's air may be getting worse, but there is no way of knowing. The health department's monitoring equipment there was destroyed during the 1976 rioting, and has reportedly not been replaced at the time of writing. The only answer is electrification, but it has been estimated that this would cost more than R90 million, and the minister of the environment has stated that Soweto's smoke pall is likely to be around for another twenty years at least. Near-epidemics of respiratory infections have been reported, while tuberculosis is endemic among blacks, with the number of cases in the Republic estimated at between 150,000 and half a million.

And there is fear—both of the police and of the *tsotsi* gangs that prey on location dwellers. During any twelve-month period there is at least one victim of robbery, assault, rape or theft in a quarter of all Soweto households. In a recent year the police were notified of 557 cases of murder—said to be the highest homicide rate in the world. Yet it has been estimated that no more than a quarter of the crimes committed in Soweto are reported at all. Bloke Modisane has vividly described the demoralization and helplessness of the location-dweller in the face of unchecked crime:

> Violence and death walk abroad in Sophiatown, striking out in revenge or for thrills or caprice; I have lived in my room trembling with fear, wondering when it would be my turn, sweating away the minutes whilst somebody was screaming for help, shouting against the violence which was claiming for death yet another victim. The screams would mount to a final resounding peal, then nothing but the calm of death.

Other writers tell similar stories. "It is agony for a family to see daybreak with one member not having slept at home," writes Joyce Sikakane.

Immediately one of them is assigned to go and look for the missing person. Should members of such a family reach their point of departure to work, without recognizing one of the dead bodies they saw lying in the streets, they sigh with relief.

Baragwanath Hospital, which services Soweto, is said to have one of the world's largest paraplegic units, handling stabbing and assault cases.*

Up at 4 A.M. to ride a packed third-class railway car to a day of demeaning work, half-starved, underpaid, harassed by racist bureaucrats and police demanding papers, on the lookout for the *tsotsi* who may at any moment claim your meager pay-packet. That's a Soweto life.

By descent, Selby is a Mosotho, with ancestral roots in what is now the northeastern Orange "Free" State, on the borders of the independent kingdom of Lesotho. This land, which is unusually rich agriculturally for southern Africa, was forcibly taken from the Basotho by the Boers more than a century ago. (Without it, Lesotho is one of the poorest countries in the world, with a per capita income of about fifty dollars a year.) On the Natal-OFS border a homeland, or bantustan, has been decreed for the southern Sotho people; called Qwa Qwa, it is the smallest of all the bantustans, consisting of a mere four hundred sixty kilometers, with a population of about twenty-six thousand—

But all this is academic, and has little to do with the subsequent realities of Selby's life. Though he can remember living in the "Free" State with his grandparents when he was a small boy, he grew up in the utterly different world of Pimville, near the sewage "farms" to which the muck of white Johannesburg was pumped for disposal. (The people of Pimville, wrote Noni Jabavu at just about the time of Selby's birth, waged "a ceaseless struggle against dirt and disease and depression of the spirit," amid the stink of raw sewage.) When Pimville was bulldozed some years later, Selby moved with his family to nearby Klipspruit. Soweto is, in fact, his homeland.

As a child, Selby lived with his mother, who went to work at eight every morning, leaving him five cents to feed himself for the day. Breakfast was usually black, sugarless tea, with perhaps a slice of bread. Lunch was mealie meal (cornmeal mush) or potatoes. In the evening, when his mother returned with leftovers from the

* Soweto gangsters are said to have been taught by some doctor how to permanently paralyze from the waist down with one thrust of a sharp instrument between two vertebrae, and enough of these cases were better than corpses at dissuading people from trying to interfere with them.

homes of her white employers, they would have the only decent meal of the day.

They lived in a three-room shack. There were a few sticks of furniture, but no facilities of any kind. Not even a tap. The nearest water source was about a mile away, and all the water used in the house—for drinking, cooking, bathing, laundry—had to be carried from there by hand.

Sometimes on a Saturday his mother would take him to town to the homes of the whites she worked for. Though the contrast between the way these suburbanites lived and life in Soweto was glaring, he did not even think to question it. "You are told not only at school but even by your parents that whites are our masters and our superiors," he says. "When you see a white man, you shiver. You couldn't afford to believe in equal rights. Whites were regarded as gods. To me it was something that was accepted, and I couldn't even question it." At home "white" meant "good," while "black" meant "bad." Children being praised for some small achievement might be told, "You are like a white man! You are a white!"

The first time Selby can remember hearing the social hierarchy of apartheid and *baasskap* called into question was when he was in Standard 3 (fourth grade). A schoolmate a few classes ahead of him asked him how he felt about whites. Did he like them? Did he like living in Soweto? "To me those were crazy questions. What was he getting at? 'Yes, I like whites,' I told him. 'I wish I was a white!'" *

In September 1505, Pedro D'Anaya, a captain in the service of King Manuel I of Portugal, commenced construction of a fort on the Mozambique coast at a place called Sofala. The Portuguese believed this to be the Ophir of the Bible and, among other things, planned to use it as a base from which to monopolize the gold trade of the interior. The fact that Portugal was able to maintain her bases in Mozambique during the seventeenth century, despite the efforts of the Dutch to wrest them away, was one reason why the latter established their own colony at the Cape of Good Hope. And thus, ultimately, modern Soweto came to be.

Though they were to rule here for almost half a millennium, Mozambique under the Portuguese remained weak and undeveloped, a mere source of labor for the powerful state that grew up to the south. From the 1890s on, first tens of thousands, then hundreds of thousands of so-called "Shangaans" from southern Mozambique came every year to labor in the gold mines of the Witwatersrand. By

---

* In *Blame Me on History* (p. 36), Bloke Modisane uses the identical words to describe how he felt as a child: "I wished I was white."

cozy arrangement, a proportion of their earnings was remitted directly in gold to the administration in Lourenço Marques (now Maputo). Toward the end of the long night of Portuguese rule, Eduardo Mondlane, a former professor of anthropology at Syracuse University in New York State, formed a movement that called itself the Frente de Libertação de Moçambique—"Frelimo" for short. Mondlane was assassinated by parcel bomb in Dar es Salaam in 1969, but his successor, Samora Machel, carried the insurrection to a conclusion. In September 1974, Machel and the Portuguese foreign minister signed an agreement, known as the Lusaka Accords, in the capital of neighboring Zambia. Formal independence came on June 25, 1975.

The signing of the Lusaka Accords sent a tremor through white-ruled southern Africa, and was to transform Selby Semela's life. Reading about the guerrilla war in Mozambique in the South African papers, Selby had been filled with horror and anger. The press had consistently portrayed Frelimo as an organization of terrorists given to bloody massacres of innocents. He was virtually ready to go to Mozambique and give battle to the guerrillas himself! Paradoxically, though, there seemed little cause to do so. Indeed, if the South African reports were to be believed, Frelimo would soon be wiped out. Headline after headline proclaimed their slaughter in droves, while an occasional Portuguese soldier or gendarme sustained minor injuries.

Then, at a stroke, the facade of official propaganda was torn away. With Frelimo on the point of forming a government, the carefully nurtured illusion of Portuguese power evaporated. Throughout southern Africa the myth of white omnipotence sustained a deadly blow. (Steve Biko would name his son Samora in honor of Machel.) In Durban the signing of the accords moved SASO and the BPC to call a pro-Frelimo rally at Curries Fountain Stadium on September 25, 1974. Predictably, it was banned. When demonstrators gathered regardless, they were violently attacked by the police. Among those arrested was Selby, not yet seventeen.

That was not in itself a novel experience for him. Unlike most schoolboys his age outside South Africa, Selby had been arrested several times before this, for "pass" offenses—infringements of the maze of laws and regulations pertaining to the documents certifying identity and right of residence. Few Africans can avoid trouble with the police on this score if they live in an urban area. In the cities of South Africa, the condition of being black is only marginally legal.

He had a little money on him at the time of his arrest, about R7, or ten dollars. This was taken from him, and would not be returned. No charges were brought. After being held in prison in

Durban for about three weeks, he and the others arrested were transferred to Johannesburg in police trucks, and taken to John Vorster
Square, the maximum-security prison which is the South African
equivalent of Moscow's Lubyanka. (Other leaders name bridges, sta-
diums, or hydroelectric projects after themselves—but not Vorster!)
The cell he was put into was empty but for a blocked toilet.
Tiny windows, painted over, were set high up in the walls. The
smell of the toilet, in that airless space, was appalling. South Africa's winter had not yet ended, and it was freezing cold. The two
blankets he was given were nothing but rags. None of this, as will
become apparent, was by neglect or oversight. Reports of what takes
place at John Vorster Square seem to indicate that prisoners are
treated according to some preconceived plan. Even the finest details
are calculated. Selby's experience follows the pattern, even in small
particulars.

The question of whether torturers are born or made is perhaps
an academic one.* But the totalitarian racism that functions under
the name of apartheid is undoubtedly a thorough school of persecution. As Noni Jabavu's old aunt explained to her on a visit to
Pimville almost a generation ago (employing the vernacular form),
"iApartheid opens up opportunities of that sort for those with pro-
pensities to goad, bait, provoke." With scant fear of reprisal or inter-
ruption, apartheid bureaucrats are able to "persecute to a fine art."
Apologists dismiss these little daily indignities, the spitefulness of
"petty" apartheid, as mere aberrations. They are, however, an essential part of the business of "keeping the kaffir in his place." On the
tenth floor of John Vorster Square, they are transformed into torture
and murder. (This is the place where, as they say, you "come in
through the door and go out through the window.") It is all one
system.

Selby lost all sense of time in prison. Unable to tell if it was
day or night, starved, systematically humiliated and brutalized, he
found himself plunged into a fog of unreality. Time telescoped. Or
expanded. "I couldn't tell you the difference between a day and a
week," he remembers.† By the "rules," prisoners had to be up at 6

---

* Evidently they can be made, however. Hannah Arendt quotes an SS guard at Buchenwald who told David Rousset, "Usually I keep on hitting until I ejaculate. I have
a wife and three children in Breslau. I used to be perfectly normal. That's what
they've made of me." See Arendt, *The Origins of Totalitarianism* (New York: Harcourt, Brace & World, 1951, new ed., 1966), p. 454.
† Research into the disruption of circadian rhythms by "jet lag" points up the logic
of systematically fostering a loss of time sense. The human body operates on various
biological cycles, some daily, some longer. Body temperature, digestion, liver func-

A.M., and were not to go to sleep until 11 P.M. He was told that even sitting or lying down during the "day" were forbidden—that is, he was supposed to stand for seventeen hours at a stretch! But since he had no way of knowing what time it was, he could not comply, even with the best will in the world. (Giving orders impossible to fulfill is a typical method of creating stress.) In reading the following reconstructed chronology of the events of the next three months, it is as well to keep in mind that all these things were being done to a slightly built sixteen-year-old schoolboy, who even as an adult stands only five feet, six and a half inches tall, and weighs perhaps 120 pounds.

For about a week nothing happened. Food was provided in the shape of *samp* (hominy grits), gravy and tea. On the ninth day, however, Selby was fetched from his cell, and taken up to BOSS interrogation headquarters on the ninth floor of the modern police building. Here he was put through a preliminary questioning by a policeman named Stroewig. Of course, since he possessed no secret information, there was nothing he could tell. But it is a profound mistake to think of the extraction of information as the primary object, or even an object at all, of interrogation and torture.

On the tenth day, questioning continued, and Selby was beaten up for the first time.

On the eleventh day, he and other prisoners were given paper and pens and ordered to write down everything they had done, or that had happened to them, since Standard 6 (eighth grade). Selby wrote about 56 pages. But this was not enough for the interrogators. "Mandela wrote 360 pages," he was told,* as though this were what was expected of him. He tried again, and managed to produce 78 pages, by dint of much padding. This writing of his autobiography continued through the twelfth day.

On the thirteenth and fourteenth days he was back in his cell again.

On the fifteenth day—it was a Sunday, he remembers—he and two other prisoners were made to stand barefoot on blocks of dry ice. A burning sensation gradually spread from his feet throughout his entire body. After about half an hour of this, he collapsed. When he recovered, he was back in his cell. At this point he was given food and water.

---

tion, and the secretion of hormones like adrenalin and cortisone—both of which have functions in handling stress—all have their own timetables, some triggered by external signals like the light-dark cycle, others cued internally.
* The reference is, of course, to Nelson Mandela, the ANC leader imprisoned on Robben Island since the early sixties.

The next week or so was spent in his cell. He had nothing to eat. The only water available was from the blocked toilet.

On about the twenty-third day (he had by now lost all reliable sense of time) he was taken up to the tenth floor of the building. "I knew what happened to people who are taken to the tenth floor," he says. "You get in there through the door and you get out through the window. So I thought they were going to throw me out of the window and tell my people that I committed suicide."

With Selby was an older man from Durban, a Zulu, with whom he had been interrogated before. On reaching the tenth floor they were first taken to an empty room. The white walls were splashed with blood, and there was the smell of blood everywhere. But the police escorting them indicated that a mistake had been made— they were not supposed to be taken to that room.

They were then taken to another room, this one on the ninth floor. It was empty but for a wooden table. Six security men, including Stroewig and a man called Spyker ("Nail") de Wet, accompanied them. This Spyker de Wet, they were told, had been flown in from Cape Town the night before especially to deal with them.

Selby was told to take a seat. He looked around the room, but there was no chair, so he said politely in Afrikaans, "*Meneer* [Sir], there is no chair here." "What's that, you damn kaffir?" was the response. "Who are you calling '*Meneer?*' I'm not your '*Meneer!*' '*Meneer*' is your kaffir *predikant* [preacher]. I'm your *baas* [boss]!" Selby, who had been trying to be polite, was taken aback. "*Baas,*" he said, "I don't see any chair in this room."

One of the SBs (security police) was told to show him where to sit, and demonstrated how one sat on an "imaginary" chair. The two prisoners were made to sit in imaginary chairs for thirty minutes or more without moving. They had to sit up straight. In that posture the interrogation continued. At the end of half an hour, Selby says, you felt as though your spine were breaking.

They were then told to strip. Selby's shock at an "old man" ("about forty-five years") like his companion being subjected to such indignity is only too obvious in his telling of the story. While he himself was left sitting in his imaginary chair in one corner, the older man was shoved against the wall, and the table was pushed up against his crotch.

"Get the tools," Spyker de Wet told Stroewig. The latter went out, and returned with a hammer and a six-inch nail. The prisoner's penis was laid on the table, and his foreskin pulled forward. "Kaffer, do you want to talk or not?" said De Wet, hammer and nail in hand.

"*Baas,*" the Zulu pleaded, "I know nothing. There is nothing I can tell you."

De Wet then drove the nail in through his foreskin. "I was shivering in my corner," Selby remembers. "I couldn't believe it. He was an old man and he screamed like a three-year-old baby. I can't forget that time. The man was really in terrible pain." "Do you want to talk or not?" De Wet repeated. The victim was unable to reply, and he drove the nail in for the second time. "There was blood all over the floor," Selby says. "I looked away because I didn't want to see. I was shivering like I never did before." The older man collapsed, and was carried away, presumably to the prison doctor. Selby was returned to his cell without being tormented further.

On the twenty-fourth day, he was again taken to the ninth floor. Again he watched as other prisoners were tortured. The middle-aged Zulu was one of them. Another was a younger man, an officer of the BPC organization. A pot of boiling water was brought in. The man was blindfolded. The boiling water was then replaced with a pot of iced water, and the prisoner's hand was plunged into it. So great was the power of suggestion that it came out burnt and blistered. This procedure too was supervised by Spyker de Wet.*

On the twenty-fifth day, Selby was questioned by Stroewig and by a "Coloured" SB, Lieutenant Sons, whose name figures in the statements of a number of prisoners who have undergone torture. They now put Selby through the classical "third degree" under bright spotlights in a darkened room. All he could see of his questioners were their burning cigarette ends. There seemed to be a whole roomful of them, perhaps as many as sixteen. Stroewig told him that if he didn't talk now, they'd all beat him up. In the end, Sons kicked him around the room.

He was then taken back to his cell. When he recovered, he found that his toilet had been fixed. After an interval of some days, he was brought cold, black tea to drink. A few days later food was brought to him. He spent another five or six weeks in solitary confinement, and was then released without explanation, after being warned that they were only letting him go "temporarily," and cautioned not to tell anyone what had happened to him. "It was the turning point of my life," he says of this experience. "When I got out of prison I really hated whites."

The year 1976, the time of the great rebellion of Soweto's students, has seemed to many to be a watershed in the history of the

---

* It should not, of course, be assumed that the names told to prisoners were genuine ones—other reports also speak of torturers nicknamed "Spyker," but with different surnames.

apartheid state. "In 1976, for the first time ever, the Republic's leaders began to acknowledge openly that the country would have to fight alone in the event of a violent conflict on its borders or inside the country," says Colin Legum, a veteran observer of South African affairs. "It would be hard to overestimate the traumatic effects that recognition of this reality—so long denied or repressed —will have in white SA thinking."

The Soweto student uprisings focused world attention on the plight of black South Africans, and for a while created a new climate of self-confidence among township dwellers themselves. Freedom, it again began to seem, could be a reality in the foreseeable future. The vision for which Steve Biko and his friends had worked and fought in SASO and its junior division, SASM, of which Selby now became one of the leaders, communicated itself to young blacks up and down the country.

But the state unfailingly reacted with arrests, bloodshed, terror. It was unlikely that it would prove otherwise. "The social, economic and political forces that have helped to shape SA's present inequitable society have also placed its ruling class in a straitjacket from which it appears to be unable to escape for so long as political power is held exclusively in white hands. . . . the inflexibility of the present political system . . . makes it difficult, if not impossible, to respond to the developing internal crisis," Legum observes. Police violence is an effective mark of governmental impotence. But it kills nonetheless. During 1976, at conservative estimates, 467 people died in Soweto as a consequence of the "disturbances." And this figure is almost certainly hopelessly inadequate.

The power psychosis sees *kragdadigheid* as a sign of strength, however. "If you had seen the way our police shot down these African school kids in Soweto, you would have realized that the white man still has a future in South Africa," one Afrikaner told British Labour party MP John Mackintosh.

By the second day of unrest (June 17), the police admitted to a death toll of 58, including two whites. But, Selby says, "we know that the figures given by the police were not correct, because we know that more than 200 people were killed on the first day of the demonstration. Many people were arrested at that time and some never returned. It was difficult to find out what had happened to them. At that time a lot of people were just disappearing. It was very difficult for us to know where the people were. We didn't know whether to start by going to a police station, or to a hospital, or to go to a mortuary. . . . There were people killed in scores in police custody, and their bodies were never given back to their families. One day a night watchman at one of the cemeteries in Soweto [Avalon cemetery] came to us and told us that people were being buried at night by the fifties. We couldn't believe it."

To check on this, Selby and some other students went out to the cemetery at about 11 one night and hid among some rocks. By 1:30 A.M. nothing had happened. Just as they were preparing to leave, however, a helicopter made several passes over the area, and a few minutes later they saw two police trucks pull up.

There was a full moon. They could see clearly and even count the bodies as they were unloaded. A total of fifty-eight were buried in two mass graves, thirty in one hole and twenty-eight in the other. The graves were then filled in and the trucks drove off. It was clear where people were disappearing to. The students told people what they had seen, but they didn't know what else to do about it. By now they were hunted men themselves. "It was a hard thing to swallow. Hard to accept, but it was happening," Selby says. Not long afterward, the night watchman who had alerted them to the mass burials disappeared—they didn't know where to.

To all these dead, admitted and unadmitted, we may reasonably add the 117 detainees who died in police custody during 1976 according to the minister of police himself, replying to a question in Parliament. Four of these are said to have died of "excessive use of alcohol" (giving a rather convivial picture of South Africa's prisons). During 1976, too, more than two hundred people were shot and killed by the police "in the execution of their duties," *excluding those shot during "civil unrest."* Of these, two were white, thirty-two were "Coloured," and one hundred and sixty-eight were African. Fully one hundred and sixty-four of the dead were allegedly shot "while attempting to escape."

Selby had been wounded by buckshot fire during the demonstrations, and he and the other leaders of the Soweto Students Representative Council (SSRC), Tsietsi Mashinini and Barney Makhatle, found themselves on the run. A reward of R500, a large sum for Soweto, was offered for their capture, announced in the press and on thousands of flyers distributed in the townships. Arrest could well mean death, but with an intensive search for them under way, the borders heavily patrolled, and roadblocks everywhere, the chances of their getting out of the country looked poor. Finally, however, the veteran BAWU leader Drake Koka hit upon the ruse of notifying the press that Barney, Tsietsi, and Selby had arrived safely in neighboring Botswana. News of their escape, which made headlines, convinced the police that they had slipped through the net. The manhunt was called off, thus giving the three a chance to flee across the frontier on August 23.

In Botswana they were by no means safe from "the System" (as blacks call the South African police state), and as soon as arrangements could be made, they went on to Europe to publicize the struggle of the Soweto students still continuing in the Republic. In England they found old guard politicals willing to provide them with money and help, but at a price. "At first we thought that they were being genuine, but we realized after some time that they did all these things just to buy us off," Selby says. "They tried to talk us into going about telling the world that they were behind what happened, and that's why we cut ourselves loose from them."

Moreover, they found that the long arm of BOSS reached to Europe too. In 1977 Selby was waylaid near the Baker Street underground station in London one night by two men with South African accents who beat him unconscious and stole his address book while ignoring more than thirty pounds in cash he was carrying.

Currently he is a student in the United States, waiting like so many others for the day when he will be able to return home.

7

BEYOND NATIONALISM?

We are witnessing right now a violently growing
planetarization of mankind.
MIHAJLO MIHAJLOV

ONE REASON FOR THE CONTINUED
vigor of the South African system is the covert esteem it enjoys
among many of its loudest critics. The traditional Left has always
had a pronounced respect for what it perceives as hardnosed efficiency, even in fascists, and apartheid has, after all, been called "the
theoretically most perfect system of labour exploitation yet devised." Whether or not this is true, numerous liberals and self-styled
radicals seem to take a perverse delight in expounding the power of
the state. "They are quick to quote statistics on how big the defence
budget is," Steve Biko wrote, and continued:

> They know exactly how effectively the police and the army can con-
> trol protesting black hordes—peaceful or otherwise. They know to
> what degree the black world is infiltrated by the security police.
> Hence they are completely convinced of the impotence of black peo-
> ple.

In historical perspective, the role of the "radical" orthodoxies has
been to create the illusion that something is being done, while looking to outside powers—chiefly the Soviet Union and its allies—to
provide a "solution." Power—not freedom—is what these politicos
ultimately believe in. And, as O'Brien says in George Orwell's *1984*,
"The object of power is power." They do not grasp that peoples, like
individuals, can be free only when they take their destiny into their
own hands, and think and act for themselves. A major aim of the

preceding pages has been to make a start at stripping away the masks behind which some of apartheid's secret allies shelter. Meanwhile the signs point to continuing insurrection and ultimately civil war. The defenders of Afrikanerdom have long thought in such terms. "In that new Blood River," Dr. D. F. Malan fulminated decades ago,

> black and white meet together in much closer contact and a much more binding struggle than when one hundred years ago the circle of white tented wagons protected the laager, and a muzzleloader clashed with an assegaai.

Romantic hysteria, left and right, is a more formidable obstacle to freedom than all the guns in the apartheid arsenal.

For the West, South Africa is a strategic nightmare that refuses to go away. Direct foreign investment in the country is measured in billions of dollars. More than 10 percent of Britain's total foreign investments are reportedly located in the Republic. The loss of these enormous holdings, and the disruption of trade with South Africa, it has been suggested, would cause a serious drop in the British standard of living and a significant rise in unemployment. The effects of such a dislocation on the capitalist world, already walking a fine line between depression and runaway inflation, would be hard to calculate.

Western involvement in South Africa is widely perceived as favoring the white minority's continued *baasskap.* "America's foreign policy seems to have been guided by a selfish desire to maintain an imperialistic stranglehold on this country irrespective of how the blacks were made to suffer," wrote Steve Biko in a memorandum to United States Senator Dick Clark. "Because of her bad record America is a poor second to Russia when it comes to choice of an ally in spite of black opposition to any form of domination by a foreign power."

A South Africa in orbit would give the Russian bloc a dominating position in the production of a whole range of vital strategic nonfuel minerals: 92 percent of the world's platinum reserves, 72 percent of the gold, 70 percent of the vanadium, 69 percent of the chromium (with Zimbabwe), and a very substantial percentage of the uranium and manganese besides. Moreover, it can be taken for granted that a South Africa under majority rule (or even, to use Henry Kissinger's phrase, "rule *in the name of* a majority") would dominate the entire subcontinent—if not all Africa—politically, industrially, militarily, and socioculturally. It is only apartheid that stands in the way of this.

Add to all this the fact that recent polling indicates that in the

United States, at least, the overwhelming majority of the public— 86 percent—find South African institutional racism distasteful. It should be apparent that the West's essential interests and sentiment (as opposed to a handful of international entrepreneurs and investors and the lunatic right) coincide with the longing of the great mass of the South African people for a speedy and conclusive end to apartheid and neo-apartheid in every shape and form—a revolution that will transform South African society from top to bottom.

Hannah Arendt has pointed out, however, that liberation and freedom are not the same thing, that "liberation may be the condition of freedom but by no means leads automatically to it; that the notion of liberty implied in liberation can only be negative, and hence, that even the intention of liberating is not identical with the desire for freedom." The modern history of Africa makes it apparent, in fact, that the intention to "liberate" can go hand in hand with indifference to freedom, even with hostility to it. The Algerian struggle for independence lasted almost eight years, may have cost as many as a million dead, and left terrible scars. Former Black Panther leader Eldridge Cleaver, still an acute observer nothwithstanding his newfound evangelism, writes of the postrevolutionary Algeria he saw in the early seventies:

> Bribery, payoffs, blackmail, and smuggling were identifiable national goals. A ruthless, frequently violent, male chauvinist brotherhood ruled the country, with savage skullduggery and unwritten rules that one could hardly fathom. Trust and loyalty were unknown words. Money, power, and influence were about all that worked. . . .

Why this terrible outcome to the heroic struggle of a people against a brutal and arrogant enemy? The reasons are probably to be found in the perspectives of its leadership—which at the core seem to have been revenge, nationalism, and personal aggrandizement. Following the sad, familiar pattern, moderates and mere "liberals" were systematically eliminated, frequently by murder. The groundwork for a new coercive state was laid during the course of the Algerian revolution itself.

Today Arabs have taken the place of the departed *pieds noirs* in the power structure. Kabyles and Berbers, whose ancestors occupied the country many thousands of years before the arrival of the Arabs, and who still constitute a very large proportion of the population, are reportedly denied the right even to learn their own languages at school, though they played a major part in the struggle against the French. The unfortunate Algerians may have to wage another revolution to attain freedom. South Africans might do well to study this example carefully, and to set their sights higher from the start—as indeed Robert Sobukwe and Steve Biko always seem to have done.

The Idea of the Nation

In the ANC Youth League's historic *Basic Policy*, the section headed "Historical Basis of African Nationalism" amounts to only six lines. Africans, it is noted, resisted the whites not as a united force but as isolated tribes; it was this, in conjunction with the superior weapons of the Europeans, which ensured their defeat.

What were African societies in South Africa like before the arrival of the Europeans in the mid-seventeenth century? How did they think of themselves? David Hammond-Tooke suggests a resemblance between the Sutu-nguni world and Capetian France or Anglo-Saxon England, with the important distinction that most traditional African polities conceived of sovereignty in broader terms than those of medieval Europe. "Constituent chiefs were in no way vassals of the paramount and no tribute was paid . . . nor, significantly, was there an obligation for chiefdoms in a cluster to unite in defense of one another," he writes. A closer comparison might be made to the German tribes described by Caesar and Tacitus. As with the ancient Germans, there was no centralized authority among the Sutu-nguni capable of mustering a general resistance to the invader—not even of the sort Vercingetorix raised against the Romans among the tribes of Gaul in 52 B.C. One might argue that it was their very freedom that made them vulnerable to conquest. Yet the Gauls were subjugated too, despite the much greater rigidity of their social hierarchies.

On closer examination, the familiar "tribal" divisions into Zulu, Xhosa, Sotho, Tswana and so on turn out to be imprecise innovations of relatively late date, more European misconceptions than reality. Nguni genealogies, for example, do name eponymous founders—an original leader named Zulu, Xhosa, Thembu, Mpondo, or Mpondomise—but in every case they also list even earlier chieftains of the lines. The very term "Nguni" was originally given currency by the missionary-historian A. T. Bryant to substitute for the anachronistic "Zulu" in describing the pre-Shakan inhabitants of Zululand.

Prior to the rise of Shaka in the early nineteenth century, the Zulus were a relatively unimportant clan, numbering about two thousand people, subject to the Mthethwa confederacy, whose overlord Dingiswayo would presumably have been astonished to know that they were destined to bestow their name on his whole people and more. The Ndebele (whose name derives from a Sotho term for Nguni) received historical definition as a result of Mzilikazi's break with Shaka in 1822. Shoshangane, whose followers established hegemony over the Tsonga in the vicinity of Delagoa Bay, was also a refugee from Shaka. So too were the Mfengu, or Fingoes, whose name seems to imply something on the order of "armed supplicants." The Swazi kingdom which was the basis for modern Swaziland developed parallel to and under the influence of the Zulu, taking its name from Mswazi, who ruled as recently as 1840–68. Shaka must therefore be viewed as the *accoucheur* of a series of new societies that were national at least in potential. As for the great southern branch of the Nguni, the Xhosa, they seem to have acquired their name by attribution from their Khoi neighbors, who called them //kosa—"angry ones," "the men who do damage." *

It was in the first half of the nineteenth century, too, that the Sotho emerged as a national entity in Lesotho under the great Moshweshwe. The word "Sotho" is apparently derived from a Nguni term implying "brownish black, light black, dark brown," though this was not necessarily applicable to the people. The tribal designation of the Tswana, a Sotho subgroup, likewise appears to originate in Cape Nguni usage, and the adoption of the name, D. M. Ramoshana has suggested, was in the nature of a witticism on the part of those who took it over—so little seriously did they regard such concerns.

All these groups were parts of a continuous tradition and culture, closely linked in innumerable ways, and comprising a social entity probably more homogeneous than the modern United States. But with the Mfecane (Difaqane) or "time of the marauders" in the years 1822–37, this society had begun to break up and reorganize itself, largely perhaps because of population pressures.

The Mfecane period is termed "precolonial" by historians. In the words of William Lye, it was "the last great event in the traditional history of the southern Bantu before white intrusion." Suggestions of European influence are dismissed as nineteenth-century reluctance, in the words of the *OHSA*, to "envisage a local provenance for significant achievements in Africa." But this can be regarded as just as patronizing as the point of view it seeks to combat.

---

* Other peoples have acquired their names in very similar ways. Tacitus tells us that "German" derived from *Wehr mann*, i.e., warrior, man of war, observing that "the title of Germans, first assumed . . . in order to excite terror, was afterwards adopted by the nation in general." (Strabo, however, asserts that *Germani* meant genuine, in the sense of original or authentic.) See also the origins of "Hebrew," traced to *khabiru*, a word signifying vagrants in Akkadian, the main language in use in ancient Babylon. Many have died over the centuries for these uncertain words.

All peoples are subject to foreign influences where channels of communication exist. While Dingiswayo may never have paid the youthful visit to the white-ruled Cape which Theophilus Shepstone believed had inspired his innovations, there is reason to think that he did go to Delagoa Bay, and that the "window on the sea" represented by the Portuguese trading establishment played a role both in his policies and in Shaka's.

But if the developments of the 1820s and 30s seemed to be leading to the coalescence of modernizing national entities in east-central South Africa, the whole process was short-circuited by the eruption onto the scene of violent and terrible enemies, whose technology and ideas willy-nilly reduced all blacks to a common mass of servitors in a matter of decades. And the foreign leaven henceforth worked on Africans in countless ways: to cite only one, traditional Nguni marriage customs were already succumbing to what a tribesman described as "a thing called love" as early as 1882. Nothing would ever be the same again.

The modern geopolitical essence of the *nation*, the concept of land as private property in macrocosm, is an un-African idea. It was introduced into southern Africa by the whites. Hannah Arendt called nationalism "the cheapest and the most dangerous disguise the absolute ever assumed in the political realm." It is secular religion and an almost unrivaled means of mobilizing men for violence. Europe and the rest of the world have paid the price in war upon war, and in the wholesale destruction of traditional values. During the colonial era, nationalism was perhaps the most potent of Europe's weapons, more important than the gun in subjugating its own and other peoples.

Those non-European peoples who exhibited appropriate national trappings—Japan and Siam are two examples—were able to retain their independence. Conversely, whites who lacked them, for whatever historical reason, found themselves colonized, and indeed treated much like non-Europeans. Lord Salisbury, the British prime minister, pronounced the Irish as unfit for self-government as Hottentots. And in the Balkans, the Turks called their European Christian subjects *râya* (singular, *raiyye*), herds at pasture, literally "cattle."

It is noteworthy that subject peoples around the world cast off alien tutelage in much the order in which they were able to establish the credibility of their national claims—as much to themselves as to their foreign overlords. That is to say, the order in which they surrendered their ancestral characteristics and succumbed to the demands of industrial society, and what Immanuel Wallerstein calls the "European World-Economy." Thus, form supplanted content.

"The technical advances which are common to all nations strip them more and more of their national characteristics," Franz Kafka observed. "Therefore they become nationalist. Modern nationalism is a defensive movement against the crude encroachments of civilization." Kafka was speaking primarily of prewar Europe, and modern realities are obviously more complex. In our time nationalism has also been the form necessarily taken by the struggle against colonialism.

Where it did not exist, the nation, therefore, had to be invented. "Had I discovered the Algerian nation, I would be a nationalist," declared Ferhat Abbas in 1936. "I will not die for the Algerian nation, because it does not exist. I have not found it. I have examined History, I questioned the living and the dead. . . . One cannot build on the wind." Nonetheless, Abbas went on to become the first prime minister of the Provisional Government of the Algerian Revolution. Today, a few decades later, no one could dream of doubting the existence of an Algerian nation.

In politics, one might add cynically, one can indeed build on the wind; what one builds is another matter. Still, there is no doubt that the creation of a nation is an achievement of a high order, not to be scoffed at whatever its shortcomings. It is a sad paradox that the very ancestral values underpinning nationalist struggles tend to be obliterated in the process of winning them. The physical expulsion of the colonialists has all too frequently been accompanied by expanded colonization of hearts and minds, so that newly independent nations end by imitating the worse vices of their former Western metropoles, or of the latter's "socialist" counterparts. Given perceived economic and technological dependence and skyrocketing numbers (the population of Africa has increased by almost 100 million in the past ten years, while food production has simultaneously declined by 10 percent), the stage is set for neo-colonialist exploitation, and a new and more insidious mode of enslavement.

If there is to be a chance of avoiding this, the nation-builders must strive constantly to live up to the spiritual values which are the essence of their historical tradition—in South Africa's case of *ubuntu.* Nationalism is by definition exclusive—that is precisely the source of its terrible, overweening power. It follows that a genuine democratic movement will be not merely international but supranational. As long as we exclude, we deny a part of ourselves. Alienation will end only when there are no more aliens. "We breathe, we dream, we live Africa; because Africa and humanity are inseparable," said Robert Sobukwe. "It is only by doing the same that the minorities in this land, the European, Coloured, and Indian, can secure mental and spiritual freedom. On the liberation of the African depends the liberation of the whole world."

This may sound like wild idealism. In fact, it is nothing but common sense.

The Next Step

It has been an underlying theme of this book that the South African predicament must be seen as in some sense an archetype of the destiny we are all living out or fated to live out—a summary of the problems confronting humankind at large. It is increasingly obvious that white South Africans will presently have to pay the price of evading the responsibilities of being human. What is not yet so apparent is the degree to which the rest of the affluent world confronts a similar, if less excruciating dilemma. While André Gunder Frank's famous "development of underdevelopment" thesis is no doubt an oversimplification, millions upon millions of people do literally die of malnutrition and starvation every year. The rich are getting richer and the poor are getting poorer, and this is only one aspect of the problem. As Gerard Chaliand puts it, we may anticipate a world increasingly "poorer and less white." By the end of the century, it is estimated, Asia, Africa, and Latin America will together account for roughly 80 percent of the human race, while disposing of less than 20 percent of its income. According to one source, the poorest 40 percent of humanity (entirely by virtue of accident of birth) currently enjoy a mere 5.2 percent of the planetary product. As the years go by, it may be that talk of "global apartheid" may come to seem less and less extravagant.

In the past decades Africa has witnessed numerous examples of the consequences of ideological and social polarization—colonists versus colonized, white versus black, minority versus majority.* And in this Africa is no more than typical. *Homo homini lupus*

---

* These stereotypes do not always fit the case, however. Witness the genocidal conflict between the Hutu and the Tutsi in the small Central African states of Rwanda and Burundi not so long ago, in which hundreds of thousands of people died. "Tutsi apartheid is established more ferociously than the apartheid of Vorster, more inhumanly than Portuguese colonialism," declared a Burundi students' organization in an appeal to the heads of African states. "Outside of Hitler's Nazi movement, there is nothing to compete with it in world history. . . . Sirs, heads of state, if you wish to help the African peoples of Namibia, Azania, Zimbabwe, Angola, Mozambique and Guinea-Bissau to liberate themselves from their white oppressors, you have no right to let Africans murder other Africans. . . . Are you waiting until the entire Hutu ethnic group of Burundi is exterminated before raising your voices?" See Leo Kuper, *The Pity of It All: Polarization of Racial and Ethnic Relations* (London: Duckworth, 1977), p. 100.

est holds true in every part of the world—and is, some might say, a gross injustice to wolves.

Responses to the problem of our seemingly murderous nature have been varied. Arthur Koestler, basing himself on the so-called Papez-MacLean theory of the emotions, argues that the explosive expansion of the hominid neocortex over the past half million years has produced a species that is literally mentally unbalanced, with defective connections between reason and feeling. In this view, the human mind is an evolutionary blunder, and Armageddon was in the cards the moment the technology of planetary suicide had been mastered.

Princeton psychologist Julian Jaynes, on the other hand, has offered a complex scenario for the evolution of human self-consciousness via alienation and identity crises caused by the disruption of communication between the left and right hemispheres of the brain. The two cerebral hemispheres have been experimentally shown to be capable of functioning independently of one another. The dominant one (in the case of right-handed people, the left) controls speech and hence ratiocination, while the nondominant hemisphere is the seat of intuitive powers which, in Jaynes' hypothesis, manifested themselves in the "unconscious" phase of human history as hallucinated divine or ancestral voices serving as an automatic system of social controls. "The right hemisphere . . . sees parts as having a meaning only within a context; it looks at wholes," Jaynes says. "While the left or dominant hemisphere . . . looks at parts themselves." Overloaded by the information explosion which followed the development of writing and the establishment of large urban societies, Jaynes argues, the ancient balance between intuition and reason broke down—perhaps for the first time in Mesopotamia in the second millennium B.C., where it promptly gave rise to the first totalitarians in the shape of the aggressive military rulers of the Assyrian middle period. "The very practice of cruelty as an attempt to rule by fear is, I suggest, at the brink of subjective consciousness," Jaynes says. In his view, schizophrenia is partly a relapse to the bicameral, preconscious phase of mental development he postulates. Jaynes comes to no very convincing conclusions, however, and he seems to miss the wider implications of his only personal experience of direct intervention by the nondominant hemisphere, a hallucinated voice which admonished him to "Include the knower in the known!" Still, even in rejecting much of his argument, there is much to stimulate speculation.

From the fleshpots of California to the frozen islands of the Gulag Archipelago, more optimistic eschatologies have in recent years looked to the development of a "higher" human consciousness as the only answer to mankind's problems. "In our time the most urgent need of the human race is not to solve the problem of war or peace, or the problem of the lack of food and energy, or even the ecological problem," writes Mihajlo Mihajlov (reportedly serving a seven-year sentence in a Yugoslav prison). "Its most vital need is a new consciousness, i.e., a new, all-embracing, profound ideology which would bring order to that unbelievable chaos in human minds which is virtually the basic difference between contemporary man and men of all other eras." Jaynes suggests the need for a "paleontology of consciousness," while Kenneth Pelletier has proposed that the study of human consciousness be treated as an independent branch of science, and perhaps the most important of them all.

While there can be little doubt about the "unbelievable chaos in human minds," the cause of this disorder remains obscure. Joseph Koekemoer roundly blames materialism, whether of the Marxist or the capitalist variety. Mihajlov would probably agree. "Freedom of men and society is not a scientific-technical problem, but an existential one," he asserts. "That means *first of all a religious problem.*" The answers we seek are likely to be metaphysical as well as political, historical, and psychological.

The concept of the universe as a battleground of Light and Dark, Good and Evil, Truth and Error appears to be roughly coeval with Jaynes's dating of the breakdown of bicameral thinking. Perhaps, then, dualism is to be traced to the rise to dominance of the left cerebral hemisphere and the suppression of the intuitive function, and should be viewed as only one phase—albeit an unavoidable one—in the continuing development of consciousness? Study of the origins and evolution of the dualist mode of thinking may shed light on this.

From the sixteenth century on, the world moved into an explosive phase of growth and development, of which dualist thinking can be perceived to be the necessary underpinning. The individual ego moved increasingly to the foreground. Nationalism is ultimately a species of generalized egotism. L. L. Whyte has drawn attention to the fact that "conscious" in the meaning of "inwardly sensible or aware" first appears in English in 1620, "self-consciousness" in 1690, and the German equivalents around the same time. It was no accident that the greatest single disquisition on the subject, Shakespeare's *Hamlet,* was written toward the end of the sixteenth century. The growth of self-consciousness was a rapid unfolding of mind, and proceeded by distinct stages. "In Europe from around 1750 onwards a shift of emphasis is evident in philosophical and scientific thought toward process concepts," says Whyte. One such concept that was of tremendous impact was the idea of organic evolution, which laid the basis for arranging the whole spectrum of living creatures, including humanity, into a hierarchy of superiors and inferiors—the so-called Great Chain of Being. Evolutionary thinking, Whyte points out, constituted

> one component, or expression, of a more general change: a shift toward greater power and generality in the structure of the basic concepts of the Western intellect, potentially affecting all realms of thought. Basically this change is from *symmetrical relations* (like *equal to*; if A is equal to B, then it follows that B is equal to A), toward *asymmetrical* relations (like *greater than*; if B is greater than A, then A cannot be greater than B). Change, in the fuller sense of transformation, implies that something apparently changes into a later something else, and involves the asymmetrical relation *later than*. The historical transformation of thought is thus from ideas based primarily on symmetrical to others based on asymmetrical relations.

This development provided the dualist mind with one of its most productive tools, but it was also in many ways the source of the "total obsession with partial ideas" which Whyte—following William Blake—identifies as one of the most characteristic menaces of our epoch. Blake's "single vision" is the viewpoint of the fanatic who reduces life's infinite complexity to a self-serving formula.

Human consciousness may today be observed to be moving back to a viewpoint stressing the equivalency rather than the asymmetry of relations. Contemporary science, especially physics, gives reason to think that the cosmos is a unity transcending in some profound sense the local distinctions we make between mind and body, past and present, self and other—and this is also suggested by the deepest human wisdom throughout the ages.

This is by no means, of course, to void the reality of such distinctions, as is proposed by the narrow and ignorant solipsism which all too often masquerades as "higher consciousness" in the affluent societies of the West. It can scarcely be stressed sufficiently that this kind of unreflecting repudiation of dualism is itself a prime example of dualist thinking—and particularly insidious in that it provides its complacent proponents with tacit justification for every kind of evil. It is, in fact, the quintessential mentality of totalitarianism, and if it goes unchecked could conceivably provide underpinnings for a fascist revival. At best it speaks for greed and quiescence.

A real basis nonetheless exists for a reintegration of humanity's powers in the face of the challenges of the period into which we are now entering. The truth, if we trust in it, really will make us free. The next step is therefore to learn this trust.

APPENDIX

ON AZANIA

THE IDEA OF RENAMING South Africa "Azania" is rumored to have originated with Peter 'Molotsi, secretary for pan-African affairs of the Pan Africanist Congress and, after 1960, one of the PAC's representatives outside South Africa. Historically, "Azania" is nowhere found applied to South Africa, and it is rarely to be met with prior to the latter half of the 1960s. Lately, however, it has become increasingly popular as a new name for the country, especially among the younger generation of blacks. In a grotesque twist, the National party's parliamentary caucus, perhaps the ultimate repository of *baasskap*, has also apparently debated its adoption. A proposal to abolish the name "South Africa" is reported to have been "widely discussed in senior Government circles," on the grounds that "once South Africa has divested itself of all the black homelands it will cease both politically and geographically to be 'South Africa.' " "Azania," it is said, was among the new names under consideration. "Such a move, it is argued with some seriousness, would take away the PAC and ANC 'copyright' on Azania," writes Fleur de Villiers.

In fact, however, far from having a stake in the "copyright" on the name "Azania," the African National Congress until quite recently unambiguously rejected it as "riddled with connotations of cultural aggression towards blacks, going back to ancient times, and of imperialism, colonialism and slavery," and hence "an unsuitable name for any part of Africa." Moreover, the ANC spokesman

215

points out, it anciently applied to an utterly different part of the continent:

> During the First Century AD the East African coast as far south as the mouth of the Rufiji River in Tanzania (site of the old city of Kilwa) was widely known as Azania. The Greek meaning of the word Azania is "dried-up country," probably from the long stretches of arid coastline and semi-desert hinterland in what is now Somalia and northeast Kenya. . . . After AD 900 some Persians migrated to East Africa and established settlements at such places as Kilwa, Lamu and Zanzibar. They named this part of the coast Zanj (Zinj/Zenj), the Persian root from which "Azania" is derived. It means "black"—and was used by the Persians to distinguish themselves from those they colonised.

It will be convenient to consider the two mutually contradictory etymologies for the name "Azania" which are asserted here in reverse order. They are worth going into in some detail, inasmuch as they constitute a fascinating study in racial and cultural stereotyping and its evolution over a period of millennia.

In the first place, it is true that "Zanzibar" derives from an Arabized form of the Persian zangbār, of which the constituent elements are zang, denoting "rust," and bār, a suffix of place designating a shore or littoral. The pre-Islamic Middle Persian use of zangīg similarly has the connotation of "rusty-colored." Conceivably the ancient Persians perceived Africans as more reddish brown than black. In Neo-Persian the term zangi has also variously been used to mean Egyptians and Ethiopians. It may be worth recalling here that the ancient Egyptians as a matter of artistic convention depicted themselves as redskinned in their paintings (as opposed to Nubian blacks, Libyan Berbers with white skins, and tan-colored Levantines).* With the passage of time, though, zang, and its Arabized forms zanj or zinj, plural zunūj, specifically came to mean "Negro," and Arab historians apply the name Zandj to the mostly black slaves from East Africa who rebelled against the 'Abbāsid caliphate of Baghdad in the seventh and ninth centuries, and who for some fifteen years on the latter occasion (A.D. 868–83) successfully fought off the overlords of Mesopotamia.† As it happened, a

---

* See, for example, the wall paintings in the tomb of Seti I at Thebes in the Valley of the Kings, dating to circa 1300 B.C., which clearly depict the various human types known to the Egyptians at that period; while by convention Egyptian men were colored red, women were shown as yellow.

† "This rising is very important for it is a war of a classical type, a regular 'social' war directed against Baghdad like those of Eunus (140 B.C.) and Spartacus (73–71 B.C.) against Rome, like that of Toussaint L'Ouverture of Haiti (1794–1801), like the strikes of the Natal coolies led by Gandhi," says the Encyclopaedia of Islam (London: Luzac & Co., 1934), vol. 4, p. 1213. The Zandj rebels found a leader in one "al-

very similar process of synecdoche had taken place in Egypt many centuries earlier. Prior to the nineteenth dynasty, the ancient Egyptians used the name *"nhsj"* ("Nehsy"), which is linguistically connected with Hebrew and Arabic words meaning "blackish brown" and "copper," to describe all the varied peoples to the south;* subsequently, however, it is gradually transferred in the inscriptions to Negroes in particular. Other examples of this would probably not be very hard to find.

There is, however, not the slightest reason to think that the name "Azania" is of Persian origin, or has anything to do with the subsequent Perso-Arabic uses of *zanj*. In fact the use of "Azania" in connection with East Africa is first met with in an anonymous work, the *Periplus of the Erythraean Sea*, supposedly written by an Egyptian-Greek merchant of the Red Sea port of Berenice around A.D. 60, and much predates Persian influence in the area. Describing the coast south of the Horn of Africa, the *Periplus* writer says:

> Beyond Opone ... there are the small and great bluffs of Azania ... this course is of six days, the direction being south-west. Then come the small and great beach for another six days' course and after that in order, the Courses of Azania, the first being called Sarapion and the next Nicon; and after that several rivers and other anchorages, one after the other, separately a rest and a run for each day, seven in all, until the Pyralaæ islands and what is called the channel; beyond which, a little to the south of south-west, after two courses of a day and night along the Ausanitic coast, is the island of Menuthias. ... Two days' sail beyond, there lies the very last market-town of the continent of Azania, which is called Rhapta. ... The Mapharitic chief governs it under some ancient right that subjects it to the sovereignty of the state that is become first in Arabia. And the people of Muza now hold it under his authority, and send thither many large ships; using Arab captains and agents, who are familiar with the natives and intermarry with them, and who know the whole coast and understand the language. ... And these markets of Azania are the very last of the continent that stretches down on the right hand from Berenice; for beyond these places the unexplored ocean curves around toward the west, and running along by regions to the south of Aethiopia and Libya and Africa, it mingles with the western sea.

Elsewhere the *Periplus* author states that "Azania is subject to Charibael and the Chief of Mapharitis," that is, of the Himyarites of southern Arabia. According to Wilfred Schoff, the translator and

---

Burkui" ("the Veiled"), whose "system of government was of a communistic type." Though supported by at least one Arab tribe, they were eventually defeated by the 'Abbāsid regent Muwaffak, who waged war on them mercilessly, and slavery was restored.

* "To the south of Egypt are four great races of mankind," wrote the grammarian Agatharchides of Cnidus in the second century B.C.

annotator of the *Periplus,* the "Ausanitic Coast" referred to was probably so called because it was a possession of Ausan, which can be identified with modern Sanaa in the Yemen. When the Himyarites conquered Ausan, sovereignty over the coast passed to them. Later the franchise to exploit the coast trade passed to the Himyarite port of Muza (broadly identifiable with our Mocha). According to Cosmas Indicopleustes and other sources, the East African coast was Abyssinian territory between the third and sixth centuries; subsequently it passed to the Sultan of Muscat, who eventually surrendered his remaining authority over it to the British in the nineteenth century. Here, then, we have another potential etymology for "Azania," dating back to at least the seventh century B.C.—the latest period of Ausanian hegemony.

Probably not very long after the *Periplus* was written, Claudius Ptolemaeus produced an even more detailed account of the geography of eastern equatorial Africa. Ptolemy had access to the considerable resources of the great library at Alexandria. He also, he tells us, consulted "merchants who traveled from Arabia Felix to Aromata [Cape Gardafui?], Azania, and Rhapta, to which whole district they give the characteristic name of Barbaria." It is, he tells us, the coast which "is called Barbaria, but the country which is more inland is called Azania." In 1891 Henry Schlichter went over Ptolemy's topography of East Africa in a paper read to the Royal Geographical Society, and Schlichter's reconstruction (see map) places "Azania" clearly in the hinterland. Barbaria, incidentally, refers presumably to the Berbers, who at that date still spread right across North Africa. The name survives in the modern Somali port of Berbera, and the *Periplus* writer states that "On the right-hand coast next below Berenice is the country of the Berbers," also locating them farther down the coast—this whole region being subject to one "Zoscales; who is miserly in his ways and always striving for more, but otherwise upright and acquainted with Greek literature." This "Zoscales" has been identified with Za Hakale, an Abyssinian monarch of the first century A.D. The prefix *Za* here is the honorific appropriate to Abyssinian kings, giving way in the third century to *El,* "indicating perhaps a change of dynasty from the Habash stock to the Sabæan," says Schoff.

The region as a whole was racially very mixed—indeed, the word "Ḥabaš," of which "Abyssinia" is a Latinized derivative, has been translated as "mixture." The Berbers, ancient Caucasoid inhabitants of North Africa, are not infrequently blond- or reddish-bearded; among some tribes in the Rif the incidence of pinkish-white unexposed skin color is reportedly as high as 86 percent. Millennia before Christ the so-called Cushites had moved south and west into Arabia and northeast Africa from a homeland located in Mesopotamia and the Persian Gulf region, making their appearance in the Egyptian records during the twelfth dynasty. The Cushites were followed by the Semitic "Joktanites," who conquered South Arabia early in the second millennium B.C. The languages of Ethiopia, Eritrea and Somalia are for the most part either Cushitic—like Galla, Sidamo, Beja, Afar, Saho, and Somali—or Semitic—like Amharic and its ancestral form, Ge'ez. It may perhaps be surmised that the hybrid society which came into being on either side of the Bab el Mandeb was the mysterious "Land of Punt," known to the Egyptians, which may have left its name in the "Opone" of the *Periplus* (identified with Ras Hafun, about ninety miles below Cape Gardafui), the last point recorded before the seafarer reached "the small and great bluffs of Azania."

Modern writers have applied the name "Azanian" to archaeological findings in East Africa, but they have simply plucked it out of Ptolemy and the *Periplus*. With reference to the supposed "Azanian" culture of Kenya, G. W. B. Huntingford writes that

> Tradition and the use of stone for building suggest a northern origin, and from the traditional evidence current in the first quarter of this century we gain a picture of these "Azanians" as tall, bearded, long-haired, and "red" in colour. . . . Taken as a whole, these accounts suggest a people of Hamitic rather than Negro affinities.

But propositions of this sort, with their heavy freight of political implications, must necessarily be subjected to the most careful scrutiny—and the application of the term "Azanian" to the culture Huntingford is describing (which he himself hesitates to locate earlier than the sixth century) is most probably anachronistic.

To add to the confusion—or perhaps to clarify it—there is a completely different historical "Azania" to be considered, situated in northwestern Arcadia, in the Peloponnesus, in Greece itself. Mentioned by Herodotus (writing in the fifth century B.C.) and other writers, the Peloponnesian Azania was proverbially inhospitable country, and its name may very likely derive from the verb ἀζαίνω, signifying "to dry up" or "to become parched" (ἄζα, ἀζαλέος, ἀζατά —"heat," "parched," "drought"—are cognate). But not necessarily. In the fourth century A.D., Stephanus Byzantius called the Greek Azania "the land of Ζᾶν," that is, of Zeus. Peter Green comments that "though this won't work it *is* just possible that the A- is privative, and that what 'Αζανία really means is 'the land *without* Zeus,' i.e., 'that Godforsaken hole.' . . . In any case Steph. Byz. is referring to Arcadia." It remains conceivable though that the name "Azania" was simply transferred by the Greek geographers to the desert regions of East Africa by a process of assimilation to a local name that sounded similar to their ears.

What this was unfortunately remains obscure; it seems not unreasonable, however, to suppose that it originated either in Berber or in the Great Hamito-Semitic or "Afro-Asiatic" language group of northeast Africa. It is curious, then, to find that in a number of languages of the so-called "Afro-Asiatic" group the following words mean "brother":

(Northern Cushitic)	Beja: *san*
(Central Cushitic)	Demba: *zan, zin*
(Chad)	Bachama: *zino—zinogi,* "my brothers"
(Chad)	Modgel: *sen*
(Chad)	Somrai: *sen*

Cognate is the ancient Egyptian *sn.* Here, of course, we tread the slippery path of sheer speculation. But since we are doing so (and have no philological reputation to lose anyway) it may be worth recalling that *san* was the name applied in South Africa to the so-called Bushmen, there said to mean either "natives" or "hunter-gatherers." And, Huntingford tells us, "at the end of the Stone Age most of the area of what is now called East Africa was shared by Bushmen and Proto-Hamites." The surviving Bushmen of East Africa are the Hadzapi of Lake Eyasi in Tanzania, whose language contains clicks and may be related to that of the Central Bushmen of South Africa. Seventy miles to the south of them are the San-dawe, who speak a click language akin to South African Khoikhoi. "There is no doubt that both physically and linguistically they are related to the Hottentots, and are not merely analogous to them," writes Huntingford of the Sandawe. "The establishment of this re-lationship suggests at first sight that they might be a later northern extension of the Hottentots, just as the Hadzapi seem to be a later northern extension of the Bushmen of South Africa."

Brothers, natives, hunters? The correlation may seem an odd one, but it should be remembered that if there is anything in this at all, we are certainly dealing with a complex idea not readily trans-latable into modern language or Western concepts—and doubtless already distorted by attempts to cram it into these molds. For peo-ples minuscule by modern standards, one's brothers *are* the nation, and by extension the natives of its territory; needless to say they are also its hunters and warriors.

Since the San are indisputably the archetypal people of South Africa, it seems highly appropriate that the country's new name should honor them—the more so if it means what the preceding paragraphs seem to suggest. And the alternate meaning of "Zandj" can be viewed as accruing even if linguistically unrelated; this was, after all, the name of one of the greatest slave rebellions in human history, which bears comparison with that of Spartacus.

It would be dishonest, though, not to record two caveats. Just as similarity to its central element does not mean that the Persian *zang* is etymologically connected with "Azania," so the resemblances to the Afro-Asiatic *san* may likewise be chance ones. Other specious etymologies based on apparent congruence could be turned up without much trouble. There are, for example, Somali *ajanabi* and Arabic *ajnabi*, meaning "foreigner" or "alien" (as in *al-bilād al-ajnabīyah*, the outside world, foreign countries). *'Ajam* is a collective noun in Arabic denoting "barbarians," "non-Arabs," and "Persians." Or one might note that Persian *Zandīk* (Arabized as *Zindīq*) was, according to the historian Mas'ūdī, used to denote heretics—particularly atheists and Manichees. And there remains the possibility that even if the root of "Azania" is to be found in the Afro-Asiatic *san*, the *A-* may be privative, tacked on together with the suffix by the Greek geographers from whom we have it. In that case "Azania" would presumably mean "the land *not* of our brothers." Renaming one's country is not something to be undertaken without reflection, and the question can scarcely be regarded as closed.

This appendix owes much to Professors Peter Green, Michael Hillmann, and Edgar Polomé, respectively of the Department of Classics, the Center for Middle Eastern Studies, and the Department of Oriental and African Languages and Literatures of the University of Texas at Austin, and to Professors Martin Schwartz and Leonard Lesko of the Department of Near Eastern Studies of the University of California at Berkeley. It goes without saying that none of these gentlemen are in any way responsible for the statements and speculations here offered.

NOTES AND SOURCES

Introduction

See Sobukwe's address on behalf of the graduating class at Fort Hare College, October 21, 1949, reproduced in Thomas Karis, ed., "Hope and Challenge, 1935–1952," pp. 331–336, vol. 2 of Thomas Karis and Gwendolen M. Carter, eds., *From Protest to Challenge: A Documentary History of African Politics in South Africa, 1882–1964*, (Stanford: Hoover Institution Press, 1972–77).

E. H. Damce, *The Victorian Illusion* (London, 1928), is quoted by Hannah Arendt in *The Origins of Totalitarianism* (New York: Harcourt, Brace & World, 1951, new ed., 1966), p. 151.

Notwithstanding the criticisms leveled at it by radical historians, *The Oxford History of South Africa*, edited by Monica Wilson and Leonard Thompson, 2 vols. (Oxford: Clarendon Press, 1969 and 1971), remains a monumental contribution to the subject.

For a transcription of the 1976 SASO-BPC trial see Millard Arnold, ed., *Steve Biko: Black Consciousness in South Africa* (New York: Random House, 1978), excerpt on p. 22.

Chapter 1: Breyten and the Price of Illusions

See "Breyten bid vir homself," pp. 14–15, "Voorlopige vervulling," p. 25, and "Kopreis van vrees tot saad," p. 33 in *Die ysterkoei moet sweet* (Johannesburg: Afrikaanse Pers-Boekhandel). Unless otherwise stated, translations are my own.

For Garbus see "South Africa: The Death of Justice," *New York Review of Books*, August 4, 1977.

See Jack Viviers, *Breyten: 'n verslag oor Breyten Breytenbach* (Cape Town: Tafelberg, 1978), introductory remarks. In a letter smuggled out of prison to André Brink, Breytenbach asserted that Viviers (currently a news editor for the Afrikaans Sunday paper *Die Beeld*) was one of several journalists being used by the "Grayshit," that is, the security police.

See *Breyten Breytenbach on Trial* (Amsterdam: Friends of Breyten Breytenbach, n.d.), p. 3.

In *Breyten en die bewaarder* (Johannesburg: McGraw-Hill, 1977), Martin Welz reproduces transcriptions of the conversations with Breytenbach secretly taped by Groenewald.

Hugh Lewin's account of life in a South African prison, *Bandiet,* is quoted by Greg Wallance, "South Africa: Racism and the Death Penalty," a paper prepared for the Amnesty International Conference on the Abolition of the Death Penalty, Stockholm, 1977, reproduced in *Race & Class* 19 (Spring 1978): p. 404.

The comments of the Commissioner of Prisons on Breytenbach's allegations were solicited by the publishers of Viviers' *Breyten;* see p. 218.

The deaths of Mdluli and others in custody are reported in *A Survey of Race Relations in South Africa, 1977* (Johannesburg: South African Institute of Race Relations, 1978), pp. 150–164.

Arrest statistics quoted are in *A Survey of Race Relations in South Africa, 1971* (Johannesburg: South African Institute of Race Relations, 1972), p. 73, and *A Survey of Race Relations in South Africa, 1977,* same publisher, 1978, p. 92.

See André Brink's monograph *Die poësie van Breyten Breytenbach* (Pretoria and Cape Town: Academic, 1971), p. 11.

See *inter alia* Breyten Breytenbach, *Om te vlieg: 'n opstel in vyf ledemate en 'n ode* (Cape Town: Buren, 1971), p. 35, *passim,* and "Vulture Culture: The Alienation of White South Africa," in *Apartheid,* ed. A. La Guma (London: Lawrence and Wishart, 1972), p. 145, for biographical details and comments on Afrikanerdom respectively.

Ingrid Jonker, "Ek wil nie meer besoek ontvang nie," in *Rook en oker* (Johannesburg: Afrikaanse Pers-Boekhandel, 1963); "I drift in the wind," in *Selected Poems,* trans. Jack Cope and William Plomer (London: Jonathan Cape, 1968), originally published in *Kantelson* (Johannesburg: Afrikaanse Pers-Boekhandel, 1966); and "Die kind" in *Rook en oker.* For Zulu translation of "Die kind" see Jan Rabie, ed., *In memoriam Ingrid Jonker* (Cape Town and Pretoria: Human & Rousseau, 1966), p. 50.

Breytenbach's reminiscences of Grassy Corners are in "Ek het amper vergeet, maar met die sigaar," in *Ysterkoei,* pp. 26–27.

See *Skryt: Om 'n sinkende skip blou te verf* (Amsterdam: Meulenhoff Nederland, 1972), pp. 27, 57, 56–57.

Saayman is quoted by Jaap Boekkooi in *The Star* (Johannesburg), November 25, 1975.

Comment on BOSS's overtures to Breytenbach is from *Breyten Breytenbach On Trial,* p. 4. The stories of the meeting at the Mount Nelson and the encounter with Van den Bergh at the airport were told me by former Okhela member Don Morton.

See Barbara Rogers and Zdenek Červenka, *The Nuclear Axis: The Secret Collaboration Between West Germany and South Africa* (New York: Times Books, 1978), pp. 180, 39, 174, 196, *passim*. See also *The Nuclear Conspiracy—FRG Collaborates to Strengthen Apartheid* (Bonn: African National Congress of South Africa, 1975). Response to these allegations is to be found in *Fact v. Fiction: Rebuttal of the Charges of Alleged Co-operation Between the Federal Republic of Germany and South Africa in the Nuclear and Military Fields* (Bonn: Press and Information Office of the Federal Government, n.d.). It must be conceded that the whole question remains extremely murky. If the federal government is less than ingenuous, neither are the accusers to be trusted. Rogers and Červenka assert, for example, that "In order to appease disturbed white opinion in South Africa, in 1976 BOSS arrested Breyten Breytenbach, a South African writer, who had left his Paris exile to pay a visit to his home country" (*The Nuclear Axis*, p. 6). Quite apart from the fact that they get the date wrong, which indicates sheer carelessness, it will be obvious to any reader of this book that this is a blatant misreading of what transpired. *Der Spiegel* (June 28, 1976) is quoted by Rogers and Červenka, p. 412.

On treatment of Breytenbach's arrested "co-conspirators," and attempts to discredit Okhela members in the press, see *Breyten Breytenbach on Trial*, pp. 2, 1.

The Celliers poem quoted by Yutar is "Trou," to be found in the collection *Die vlakte en ander gedigte*, published by Tafelberg in Cape Town.

On events in Angola see, *inter alia*, John Stockwell, *In Search Of Enemies: A CIA Story* (New York: Norton, 1978), and R. W. Johnson, *How Long Will South Africa Survive?* (New York: Oxford University Press, 1977). The latter book has since been withdrawn from circulation by its publishers, evidently in response to threats of legal action by an unnamed African leader.

See Colin Legum and Tony Hodges, *After Angola: The War Over Southern Africa* (New York: Africana Publishing Co., 1976), p. 37.

For comment on appointment of Judge Cillié, see "Cillié Commission," *South African News Agency Bulletin*, July 1977.

Morand's comments are reproduced in *Breyten Breytenbach on Trial*, pp. 2–3.

Comment on the trial of the SASO nine is from Gail M. Gerhart, *Black Power in South Africa: The Evolution of an Ideology* (Berkeley and Los Angeles: University of California Press, 1978), p. 298.

For Biko quotation see "I Write What I Like: Fear—An Important Determinant in South African Politics," reproduced in Arnold, ed., *Steve Biko*, p. 274.

See Hannah Arendt, *Men in Dark Times* (New York: Harcourt, Brace & World, 1968), p. 210, for her observations on Brecht.

Chapter 2: Cultures in Collision

The epigraph to the chapter may be found in Donald Moodie, ed. and trans., *The Record, or a Series of Official Papers Relative to the Condition*

and Treatment of the Native Tribes of South Africa (1838–1842; photo.
rep. ed., Amsterdam and Cape Town: A. A. Balkema, 1960), pt. 1, p. 287.
These lines—"the spirit of which will ill endure the fetters of *sworn* translation," declared Moodie, a sworn translator himself—were copied down by
Commander Wagenaar, but who composed them is unclear. The original of
the couplet is as follows:

> Voor Hottentoos waren't eerteyts aerde wallen,
> Nu comt men hier met steen voor anderen oock brallen,
> Dus maekt men dan een schricq soo wel d'Europeaen
> Als voor den Aes. Amer. en wilden Africaen.

The translation here (by no means sworn to) is my own. "Hottentoos" was
the form in early use at the Cape.

On the "main problem," see Leo Marquard, *The Story of South Africa*
(rev. ed., New York: Praeger, 1968), p. 16. The assertion was drawn to my
attention by Harrison M. Wright's *The Burden of the Present: Liberal-
Radical Controversy over Southern African History* (Cape Town and London: David Philip and Rex Collings, 1977), also quoted here on the *OHSA*.
See OHSA, vol. 1, p. *v.*

See Richard Elphick, *Kraal and Castle: Khoikhoi and the Founding
of White South Africa* (New Haven and London: Yale University Press,
1977), p. 237, on destruction of the Khoikhoi in the Western Cape. Elphick's
book gives what is probably the best single account of his subject to date.

Van Plettenberg's instructions concerning the San are quoted in
M. Whiting Spilhaus, *South Africa in the Making, 1652–1806* (Cape Town:
Juta, 1966), pp. 115–116.

On Germans in the company's service see *OHSA*, vol. 1, p. 186. See
also Spilhaus, *South Africa in the Making*, p. 107, on ancestry of the Afrikaners. The early immigrants from France are discussed by Manfred Na-
than, *The Huguenots in South Africa* (South Africa, n.p.: Central News
Agency, 1939). M. F. Katzen quotation is in *OHSA*, vol. 1, p. 197. See also
Cornelius de Jong, *Reizen naar de Kaap de Goede Hoop, Ierland en Noor-
wegen in de jaren 1791* (Haarlem: 1802–3), vol. 1, p. 134, on Cape burgers,
and P. J. Idenburg, *The Cape of Good Hope at the Turn of the Eighteenth
Century* (Leiden: Universitaire Pers, 1963).

Proclamation of the Swellendam Jacobins regarding the Khoisan is in
Spilhaus, *South Africa in the Making*, p. 182.

On the Thirty Years' War see Hans Jacob Grimmelshausen, *Simplicis-
simus* (1669), ed. and trans. Goodrick, quotation on pp. 33–34, and C. V.
Wedgewood, *The Thirty Years' War* (London: Jonathan Cape, 1938), pp. 256,
381, 526, *passim.*

Marx's observations on the Dutch Republic are in *Capital: A Critique
of Political Economy*, (1867; London: Everyman's Library, 1930), p. 835. On
the powers of the *VOC* see C. Louis Leipoldt, *Jan van Riebeeck: A Biographical Study* (London: Longmans, Green and Co., 1936), p. 9. Geyl quotation is to be found in his *The Netherlands in the Seventeenth Century*
(London: Ernest Benn, 1961), vol. 1, p. 209.

On Portuguese visitors in the fifteenth and sixteenth centuries see

G. M. Theal, *History of South Africa* (1892–1919, facsimile ed. Cape Town: C. Struik, 1964), vol. 2. See also R. Raven-Hart, *Before Van Riebeeck: Callers at South Africa from 1488 to 1652* (Cape Town: C. Struik, 1967).

Monica Wilson is quoted from her *Religion and the Transformation of Society: A Study of Social Change in Africa* (Cambridge: At the University Press), p. 8.

See Edward Terry, *A Voyage to East-India* (1655; reprint. ed. London: J. Wilkie *et al.*, 1777), pp. 13–26. Comment on Khoikhoi eating habits is from John Cope, *King of the Hottentots* (Cape Town: Howard Timmins, 1967), p. 33, a popular account of Xhoré's life and times.

On Khoikhoi language and the origin of the term "Hottentot," see in particular G. S. Neinaber, *Hottentots* (Pretoria: J. L. Van Schaik, 1963), pp. 17–18, 43, *passim.* "Honquequa," sing. "onkey," as a term descriptive of whites is to be found in *ibid.*, pp. 305–6. This etymology for "honky" is submitted entirely without prejudice. Nienaber himself appears to be quite unaware of the American usage.

On Khoikhoi religion see Theophilus Hahn, *Tsuni-ǁ Goam: The Supreme Being of the Khoi-Khoi* (London: Trubner & Co., 1881), quotation from p. 61.

Xhoré's death is recorded in the British Historical Manuscripts Commissions' *Report on Manuscripts in the Welsh Language* (London: Eyre & Spottiswoode, 1905), vol. 1, pt. 3, p. 1012, quoted by Theal, *History of South Africa*, pp. 375–376.

See E. C. Godée Molsbergen, *Jan van Riebeeck en sy tyd* (Dutch ed., 1937; Afrikaans trans., Pretoria: Van Schaik, 1968), quotations at pp. 34, 43, on Van Riebeeck's life and times. Quotations from Van Riebeeck's diaries are from Moodie, ed. and trans., *The Record,* but see also H. B. Thom, ed., *Journal of Jan van Riebeeck,* 3 vols. (Cape Town: Van Riebeeck Society, 1958).

On the Angola slave trade see Henry W. Nevinson, *A Modern Slavery* (1906; New York: Schocken Books, 1968), p. 150, *passim.* The quotation from C. R. Boxer on the Dutch attempt to take over the Angolan slave marts is to be found in *Four Centuries of Portuguese Expansion, 1415–1825* (1961; Berkeley and Los Angeles: University of California Press, 1969), pp. 50–51.

See I. Schapera and B. Farrington, eds. and trans., *The Early Cape Hottentots Described in the Writings of Dapper, Ten Rhyne and J. G. Grevenbroek* (Cape Town: Van Riebeeck Society, 1933), quotations at pp. 12–17.

On the history of Robben Island (prior to its modern transformation into a political prison) see Simon de Villiers, *Robben Island: Out of Reach, Out of Mind* (Cape Town: C. Struik, 1971), quotation at p. 22.

The story of the Indonesian slaves and political exiles at the Cape is told by I. D. du Plessis in *The Cape Malays* (Cape Town: Maskew Miller, 1944), quotation at p. 3. On the evolution of the "Khoi-Coloured" population see J. S. Marais' invaluable study, *The Cape Coloured People, 1652–1937* (London: Longmans, Green, 1939), quotations at pp. 2, 7, 10, 12, 131, 179, 50. On the extermination of the Bushmen see also George Thompson,

Travels and Adventures in Southern Africa, 2 vols. (London, 1827), quoted by Marais, *The Cape Coloured People,* p. 18.

On genocide in nineteenth-century California, see Sherburne F. Cook, *The Conflict Between the California Indian and White Civilization* (1940–43; rep. ed. Berkeley and Los Angeles: University of California Press, 1976); Dole's remarks quoted at pp. 312–13.

On Cape Town in 1800 see William M. Freund, "Thoughts on the Study of the Cape Eastern Frontier Zone," in Christopher Saunders and Robin Derricourt, eds., *Beyond the Cape Frontier: Studies in the History of the Transkei and Ciskei* (London: Longmans, 1974), p. 90. See, too, Robert Ross, "The Griqua in the Politics of the Eastern Transkei," pp. 134–135, 140, in the same volume, on nonracial leadership in Griqualand.

The observations of Senator Dawes on land tenure among the Five Civilized Tribes are to be found in D. S. Otis, *The Dawes Act and the Allotment of Indian Lands* (Norman, Okla.: University of Oklahoma Press, 1972), p. 10.

Chapter 3: Sol Plaatje and the Dream of Deliverance

For originals of the epigraph to this chapter and other Zulu songs quoted subsequently, see Hugh Tracey, *"Lalela Zulu": 100 Zulu Lyrics* (Johannesburg: African Music Society, 1948); translations are by a friend of the author's who wishes to remain unnamed, and are published here for the first time.

On Sol T. Plaatje see, in particular, his *Native Life in South Africa, Before and Since the European War and the Boer Rebellion* (London: P. S. King and Son, n.d.), *passim,* and John L. Comaroff, ed., *The Boer War Diary of Sol T. Plaatje: An African at Mafeking,* (Johannesburg: Macmillan, 1973).

See Nirad C. Chaudhuri, *The Autobiography of an Unknown Indian* (Berkeley and Los Angeles: University of California Press, 1968).

On Gandhi, see Geoffrey Ashe, *Gandhi: A Study in Revolution* (London: Heinemann, 1968), quotations at pp. 73, 117, 96.

On the role of the Korana and Bergenaars in the struggle against the Ndebele, see J. A. Engelbrecht, *The Korana* (Cape Town: Maskew Miller, 1936), pp. 36, 58, 60. On Mzilikazi's persisting fear of the Zulus, see Richard Brown, "The External Relations of the Ndebele Kingdom in the Pre-Partition Era," in Leonard Thompson, ed., *African Societies in Southern Africa,* (New York: Praeger, 1969), p. 267. Comment on Moshweshwe's kingdom is in *OHSA,* vol. 1, p. 443. Moshweshwe's letter to Shepstone is cited in Anthony Atmore, "The Passing of Sotho Independence 1865–70," in Thompson, ed., *African Societies.* For Tswana on blacks and whites see Solomon T. Plaatje, *Sechuana Proverbs with Literal Translations and Their European Equivalents* (London: Kegan Paul, Trench, Trubner & Co., 1916), p. 26. Quotation on consequence of German annexation of Namibia is from Ronald Robinson and John Gallagher with Alice Denny, *Africa and the Victorians: The Climax of Imperialism* (1961; Garden City, N.Y.: Anchor Books, 1968), p. 205. On the Fingoes see, in particular, Richard A. Moyer, "The Mfengu, Self-Defence and the Cape Frontier Wars," in Christopher

Saunders and Robin Derricourt, eds., *Beyond the Cape Frontier: Studies in the History of the Transkei and Ciskei* (London: Longmans, 1974), pp. 101–126. On British rule in Natal see Shula Marks, *Reluctant Rebellion: The 1906–8 Disturbances in Natal* (Oxford: Clarendon Press, 1970), quotation here from p. 33; see also Frank Emery, *The Red Soldier: Letters from the Zulu War, 1879* (London: Hodder and Stoughton, 1977).

On Baden-Powell, see William Hillcourt, *Baden-Powell: The Two Lives of a Hero* (London: Heinemann, 1964), quotation from pp. 139–42; also Brian Gardner, *Mafeking: A Victorian Legend* (London: Cassell, 1966), quotations at pp. 40, 80, 116, 110, 73, 129.

On Boer perceptions of the war, see Smut's anonymously published pamphlet *En Eeuw van Onrecht* [*A Century of Wrong*], quoted in Sarah Gertrude Millin, *General Smuts* (London: Faber & Faber, 1936), vol. 1, p. 117. On the antiwar movement in England see Stephen Koss, ed., *The Pro-Boers: The Anatomy of an Antiwar Movement* (Chicago: University of Chicago Press, 1973).

For Jabavu's remarks, see "Bantu Grievances," in I. Schapera, ed., *Western Civilization and the Natives of South Africa*, (London: Routledge and Kegan Paul, 1934; rep. 1967); S. M. Molema is quoted from his *The Bantu Past and Present* (Edinburgh: W. Green and Son, 1920), pp. 319, 321, 303–304.

On Lord Selborne, see W. K. Hancock, *Smuts: The Sanguine Years, 1870–1919* (Cambridge: At the University Press, 1962), pp. 317–18. On the program of *Het Volk* see D. J. N. Denoon, " 'Capitalist Influence' and the Transvaal Government During the Crown Colony Period, 1900–1906," *The Historical Journal* 11 (1968): 301.

For Merriman and Duncan on Smuts, see Hancock, *Smuts: The Sanguine Years*, pp. 274–77. On the Bulhoek and Bondelzwarts massacres see W. K. Hancock, *Smuts: The Fields of Force, 1919–1950* (Cambridge: At the University Press, 1968), pp. 91–100.

On African reactions to the Italian conquest of Abyssinia, see E. Roux, *Time Longer Than Rope: A History of the Black Man's Struggle for Freedom in South Africa* (1948; Madison: University of Wisconsin Press, rev. ed. 1964), p. 302.

On Sol Plaatje's writings, see also Ezekiel Mphahlele, *The African Image* (New York: Praeger, 1962). Plaatje's activities in Kimberley are discussed in Brian Willan, "Sol Plaatje, De Beers and an Old Tram Shed; Class Relations and Social Control in a South African Town, 1918–1919," *Journal of Southern African Studies* 4 (April 1978): 195–215.

On the history of rural African communities in South Africa under white rule, see in general Robin Palmer and Neil Parsons, eds., *The Roots of Rural Poverty in Central and Southern Africa* (Berkeley and Los Angeles: University of California Press, 1977), and Colin Bundy, *The Rise and Fall of the South African Peasantry* (Berkeley and Los Angeles: University of California Press, 1979).

Chapter 4: Hopes and Enemies

The epigraph to this chapter aims at a meaningful as opposed to a merely literal translation of the theme of the famous anthem "Nkosi Sikelel' iAfrika" [God Bless Africa], originally composed for the South African Native National Congress by Enoch Sontonga and an unidentified Lovedale missionary in 1912.

The most crucial discussion of the early history of the CPSA is to be found in E. Roux, *Time Longer Than Rope: A History of the Black Man's Struggle for Freedom in South Africa* (1948; Madison: University of Wisconsin Press, rev. ed. 1964), and Eddie and Win Roux, *Rebel Pity: The Life of Eddie Roux* (London: Rex Collings, 1970); but see also A. Lerumo [Michael Harmel], *Fifty Fighting Years: The Communist Party of South Africa, 1921–1971* (London: Inkululeko Publications, 1971), and Martin Legassick, *Class and Nationalism in South African Protest: The South African Communist Party and the "Native Republic," 1928–34* (Syracuse, N.Y.: Syracuse University Program in Eastern African Studies, 1973).

The attempt to justify the "White South Africa" slogan appears in R. K. Cope's *Comrade Bill: The Life and Times of W. H. Andrews, Workers' Leader* (Cape Town: Stewart Printing Co., 1944), p. 231. The joint statement of the ministers of justice and defense is quoted in W. K. Hancock, *Smuts: The Fields of Force, 1919–1950* (Cambridge: At the University Press, 1968), p. 83.

Hertzog's praise for the Bolsheviks is quoted in B. Bunting, *The Rise of the South African Reich* (Harmondsworth, Middlesex: Penguin Books, 1969), pp. 34–35.

On Bukharin see Roy A. Medvedev, *Let History Judge: The Origins and Consequences of Stalinism* (New York: Alfred A. Knopf, 1971), p. 64.

See Selby Msimang, *The Crisis*, quoted in Thomas Karis and Gwendolen M. Carter, eds., *From Protest to Challenge: A Documentary History of African Politics in South Africa, 1882–1964* (Stanford: Hoover Institution Press, 1972–1977), vol. 2, p. 61.

For Smuts's agonizing over the "native question" see W. K. Hancock, *Smuts: The Sanguine Years, 1870–1919* (Cambridge: At the University Press, 1962), pp. 30–31, 149; letter to Merriman, p. 221.

Hertzog's reply to the AAC delegation is quoted in Mary Benson, *The African Patriots: The Story of the African National Congress of South Africa* (London: Faber and Faber, 1963), p. 82.

Tabata's letter to Mandela is reproduced in Karis and Carter, eds., *From Protest to Challenge*, vol. 2, quotation on p. 365.

Quotation on the origins of the NEUM is from *The Citizen* 1, no. 7, June 25, 1956. This Cape Town fortnightly, published by the Western Province Press Association between March 1956 and May 1958, should not be confused with the government-subsidized newspaper that appeared in Johannesburg in the 1970s under the same name.

Hosea Jaffe is quoted in Peter Dreyer, *The Death Agony of Non-Europeanism* (Cape Town: Western Province Press Association, 1959), p. 3, from an article entitled "Pondokkie Politics" which appeared in the *Workers' Voice*, a paper published by the Fourth International Organization of South Africa, in 1946. The FI organization originated in about 1933, after the expulsion of the Trotskyist Left Opposition from the CPSA in Cape Town. Neither it nor the rival organization on the Witwatersrand were ever, to the best of my knowledge, admitted to full-fledged membership in the Fourth International. On the covert racism of South African Trotskyists and Stalinists alike, see also my pamphlet *Against Racial Status and Social Segregation: Towards the Liquidation of Multi-Racialism and Non-Europeanism* (Cape Town: Western Province Press Association, 1959). Though gauche in more ways than one (they were written before I was twenty) and only broadly coinciding with my present sentiments, these early diatribes nonetheless made a start at exposing the inhibitive orthodoxies of the Left. The pity is that they were never followed up at the time.

Xuma's remarks in his presidential address to the ANC Annual Conference, 14–16 December 1941, are reproduced in Karis and Carter, eds., *From Protest to Challenge*, vol. 2, pp. 182–183.

For Smuts's postwar plaint ("Colour queers my poor pitch everywhere") see Hancock, *Smuts: The Fields of Force*, p. 473. His speech to the 1947 NRC deputation is in Karis and Carter, eds., *From Protest to Challenge*, vol. 2, quotation at p. 241; Thema's response is at pp. 243–244.

On the Youth League platform, see the manifesto issued by the Provisional Committee of the Congress Youth League, March 1944, in Karis and Carter, eds., *From Protest to Challenge*, vol. 2, quotation at p. 301.

On *ubuntu* and African traditional ethics, see in particular Jordan K. Ngubane, *An African Explains Apartheid* (New York: Praeger, 1963), pp. 75–77, and his *Conflict of Minds* (New York: Books in Focus, 1979).

The Youth League's response to Ruth First is reproduced in Karis and Carter, eds., *From Protest to Challenge*, vol. 2, p. 316.

"Basic Policy of Congress Youth League," a manifesto issued by the National Executive Committee of the ANC Youth League, 1948, is in Karis and Carter, eds., *From Protest to Challenge*, vol. 2, quotation at pp. 328–330.

On Communist strategy after dissolution of the CPSA, see Lerumo, *Fifty Fighting Years*, p. 97.

On the "Resist Apartheid Committee" of 1955 see Edward Feit, *African Opposition in South Africa: The Failure of Passive Resistance* (Stanford: Hoover Institution, 1967), quotations at pp. 113, 189.

On the drafting of the "Freedom Charter," see Ngubane, *An African Explains Apartheid*, p. 164.

Sobukwe's statement on human rights in a nonracial South Africa is from *The Star* (Johannesburg), April 7, 1959, quoted in Karis and Carter, eds., *From Protest to Challenge*, vol. 3, *Challenge and Violence, 1953–1964*, p. 317. Leballo's comment on the Kliptown declaration is in Gerhart, *Black Power in South Africa*, p. 158.

See Anthony Sampson, *The Treason Cage: The Opposition on Trial in South Africa* (London: Heinemann, 1958), p. 5, for quoted comment on the so-called Treason Trial.

On the role of the Jacobins and Bolsheviks respectively in crushing the *sociétés populaires* and soviets, see Hannah Arendt's indispensable *On Revolution* (1963; Harmondsworth, Middlesex; Penguin Books, 1973), pp. 239–248, 273. The Kronstadt uprising, Arendt points out, was a rebellion of the soviets against the party dictatorship; the name "Soviet Union" as applied to postrevolutionary Russia since that time therefore embodies a lie (p. 258). "Seen from the vanguard point of a true Soviet Republic, the Bolshevik party was merely more dangerous but no less reactionary than all the other parties of the defunct regime" (p. 265).

On the bus boycott, see Dan Mokonyane, *Lessons of Azikhwelwa: The Bus Boycott in South Africa* (London: Nakong Ya Rena, 1979). Some of the quotations here are drawn from earlier drafts of this document, circulated privately. See also Ruth First, "The Bus Boycott," *Africa South* 1 (July–Sept. 1957): p. 57. Quotations from Anthony Sampson on the boycott are in his *The Treason Cage*, at pp. 212–13. Quotation from Eddie Roux on the subject is in *Time Longer Than Rope*, pp. 397–398. Lutuli's comment is in his *Let My People Go* (London: Collins, 1962), p. 176.

Chapter 5: The Shapes of the Lie

On the Africanist breakaway, see Gerhart, *Black Power in South Africa: The Evolution of an Ideology* (Berkeley and Los Angeles: University of California Press, 1978), quotation at pp. 174–175. The letter notifying the conference of the Africanists' resolution to launch out on their own, dated November 2, 1958, is quoted in Thomas Karis and Gwendolen M. Carter, eds., *From Protest to Challenge: A Documentary History of African Politics in South Africa, 1882–1964* (Stanford: Hoover Institution Press, 1972–1977), vol. 3, pp. 505–506. Mokonyane's comments on the split and the April 1959 conference are in his *Lessons of Azikhwelwa: The Bus Boycott in South Africa* (London: Nakong Ya Rena, 1979), pp. 69–73; as before, some of the quotations here are from earlier unpublished drafts. Gerhart's description of Madzunya is in *Black Power in South Africa*, p. 176. On the ANC and PAC leadership, see *ibid.*, p. 319; 'Molotsi quotation is at p. 216.

Lee-Warden's plea in the House of Assembly (March 30, 1960) is quoted in Karis and Carter, eds., *From Protest to Challenge*, vol. 3, p. 375.

Patrick Duncan's diary, part of a collection of materials on South African political history assembled by Benjamin Pogrund, is preserved on microfilm at the Hoover Institution, Stanford, California. It unfortunately covers only a brief period, and is fragmentary even for that. See also Tom Lodge's important article, "The Cape Town Troubles, March–April 1960," *Journal of Southern African Studies* 4 (April 1978): 216–239.

Mandela's remarks about the circumstances of his arrest are in Karis and Carter, eds., *From Protest to Challenge*, vol. 3, p. 744. Tabata's charges are made in "Who are the Wreckers of Unity?" in *Imperialist Conspiracy in Africa* (Lusaka, Zambia: Prometheus Publishing Co., 1974), p. 128.

For "Operation Mayibuye," see Karis and Carter, eds., *From Protest to Challenge*, vol. 3, pp. 760–768; Fisher's comments at his trial are in ibid., pp. 767–777.

J. B. Marks's speech is in A. Lerumo, *Fifty Fighting Years: The Communist Party of South Africa, 1921–1971* (London: Inkululeko Publications, 1971), Appendix 13, pp. 175–182.

On the Algerian war of independence see Alistair Horne, *A Savage War of Peace: Algeria 1954–1962* (New York: Viking Press, 1977), p. 538, *passim.*

Venter's claims are cited in *A Survey of Race Relations in South Africa, 1971* (Johannesburg: South African Institute of Race Relations, 1972), p. 95, from the *Sunday Express* (Johannesburg), January 24, 1971, and the *Sunday Times* (Johannesburg), April 11, 1971.

Quotation from *New Age* (Cape Town), March 5, 1956.

On Roman law see Rudolf Ihering, *Geist des römischen Rechts* (Leipzig, 1873), vol. 1, p. 118.

On the "Clique of non-Africans" dominating the ANC's Revolutionary Council see "Surely a Terrible Nemesis Will Overtake the White-led SACP and Its Hangers-on," *Ikwezi: A Journal of South African and Southern African Political Analysis*, April 1977, pp. 18–33, quotation at p. 20.

Quotation from Mihajlov is from his *Underground Notes* (Kansas City: Sheed Andrews and McMeel, 1976), pp. 123–124.

Chapter 6: The Human Dimension

Biko quotation is from "White Racism and Black Consciousness," in H. W. van der Merwe and David Welsh, eds., *Student Perspectives on South Africa* (Cape Town: David Philip, 1972; banned in South Africa); see Donald Woods, *Biko* (New York and London: Paddington Press, 1978), pp. 50–51. On Biko see also Millard Arnold, ed., *Steve Biko: Black Consciousness in South Africa* (New York: Random House, 1978), and Aelred Stubbs, C. R., ed., *Steve Biko—I Write What I Like* (London: Bowerdean Press, 1978); Norman Fenton and Jon Blair have adapted *The Biko Inquest* for the stage. Biko's posthumous fame spread so suddenly that when a manuscript of his was submitted to a leading American publisher not long after his death, hardly anyone on the editorial staff even knew who he was, and in an in-house memorandum he was confused with Stephen Bilko, a first baseman for the St. Louis Cardinals during the 1950s who was then recently deceased!

For O'Brien quotation see "Why They Made Biko a Martyr," *The Observer* (London), April 30, 1978.

On the effects of infant malnutrition on the brain see Elie Shneour, *The Malnourished Mind* (Garden City, N. Y.: Anchor/Doubleday, 1974), pp. 1, 43, *passim.*

On the mining finance companies of the Witwatersrand, see Ann & Neva Seidman, *South Africa and U.S. Multinational Corporations* (1977; Westport, Conn.: Lawrence Hill, 1978 [ed. consulted]), p. 23. On manufacturing industry in S.A., see *ibid.*, pp. 17–18. On South Africa's ranking among world nations in economic capability, see Ray S. Cline, *World Power Assessment 1977: A Calculus of Strategic Drift* (Boulder, Colo: Westview

Press, 1977), pp. 59, 76. Cline (a former deputy director of the CIA) is published under the auspices of the Center for Strategic and International Studies in Washington, D.C. It is worth noting that while South Africa ranked 27th in GNP in 1977, after Saudi Arabia (26th) and before Austria (28th), Cline's assessment of the country's overall economic capacity places it much higher up on the scale, after Poland (17th) and before Brazil (19th). This is probably indicative of the degree to which apartheid is holding back South Africa's economic growth. By contrast the GNPs of Poland and Brazil are much higher than their assessed economic capability, ranking 13th and 11th respectively on the scale in 1977.

On housing in Soweto see *A Survey of Race Relations in South Africa, 1977* (Johannesburg: South African Institute of Race Relations, 1978), p. 405; on tuberculosis statistics in the Republic see *ibid.*, pp. 547–548. Air pollution in Soweto is discussed in Kevin Stocks, "People Are Living Down There: The World's Dirtiest City," *The Star International Airmail Weekly* (Johannesburg), July 8, 1978, pp. 12–13. Quotation from Modisane is in his *Blame Me On History* (London: Thames and Hudson, 1963), p. 59. Joyce Sikakane is quoted from *A Window on Soweto* (London: International Defence & Aid Fund, 1977), p. 6. See also Noni Jabavu, *The Ochre People: Scenes From a South African Life* (London: John Murray, 1963) for a vivid description of Soweto in the 1950s, quotation from p. 227.

Quotation from Colin Legum on the events of 1976 is from his *Southern Africa: The Year of the Whirlwind* (London: Rex Collings, 1977), pp. 5–6. See also the excellent report put together by Counter Information Services, *Black South Africa Explodes* (Washington, D.C.: Transnational Institute, 1977). John Mackintosh's report was published in *The Times* (London), June 19, 1978. On police killings see *A Survey of Race Relations in South Africa, 1977*, pp. 108–109.

Chapter 7: Beyond Nationalism?

On apartheid as a system of labor exploitation see John Rex, "The Plural Society: The South African Case," in *South Africa: Economic Growth and Political Change*, edited by Adrian Leftwich (London: Allison and Busby, 1974), p. 157.

The Biko quotation is from "White Racism and Black Consciousness," in H. W. van der Merwe and David Welsh, eds., *Student Perspectives on South Africa* (Cape Town: David Philip, 1972), reproduced in Donald Woods, *Biko* (New York and London: Paddington Press, 1978), pp. 50–51.

Dr. Malan is quoted in T. Dunbar Moodie, *The Rise of Afrikanerdom* (Berkeley and Los Angeles: University of California Press, 1975), p. 199.

For Biko's memorandum to Senator Clark see Aelred Stubbs, C. R., ed., *Steve Biko—I Write What I Like* (London: Bowerdean Press, 1978), p. 140.

On Russian and South African shares of world strategic nonfuel mineral reserves, see "Minerals—Key to S. Africa's Strategic Position," *The Times* (London), August 8, 1977. Percentages given are obtained by adding together current Russian and South African figures.

Polling on American attitudes to apartheid was conducted by the Carnegie Endowment, and is reported in the *San Francisco Sunday Examiner and Chronicle*, May 13, 1979.

On distinctions between liberation and freedom, see Hannah Arendt, *On Revolution* (1963; Harmondsworth, Middlesex: Penguin Books, 1973), p. 22.

Quotation from Cleaver is from his *Soul On Fire* (Waco, Texas: Word Books, 1978), pp. 145–46. On denial of rights to Berbers and Kabyles in Algeria, see Gérard Chaliand, *Revolution in the Third World* (New York: Viking, 1977), p. 110.

For David Hammond-Tooke, see "The 'Other Side' of Frontier History," in Leonard Thompson, ed., *African Societies in Southern Africa* (New York: Praeger, 1969), p. 240. On the etymology of "Xhosa," see Gerrit Harinck, "Interaction Between Xhosa and Khoi: Emphasis on the Period 1620–1750," in *ibid.*, p. 152n, citing L. F. Maingard, "The Linguistic Approach to South African Prehistory and Ethnology," *South African Journal of Science* 31 (1934): 132–34; see also Martin Legassick, "The Sotho-Tswana Peoples Before 1800," citing D. M. Ramoshana, "The Origin of Secwana," *Bantu Studies* 3 (1927–29): 197–98; William Lye, "The Distribution of the Sotho Peoples After the Difaqane," p. 191; and Monica Wilson, "Changes in Social Structure in Southern Africa: The Relevance of Kinship Studies to the Historian," p. 77.

Abbas is quoted in Alistair Horne, *A Savage War of Peace: Algeria 1954–1962* (New York: Viking Press, 1977), p. 40.

On the distribution of global wealth, see Chaliand, *Revolution in the Third World*, p. 10, and Gernot Köhler, *Global Apartheid* (New York: World Order Models Project, 1978), p. 2.

For Koestler's views, see his *Janus: A Summing Up* (London: Hutchinson, 1978), especially pp. 8–11. Quotations from Julian Jaynes are from his *The Origin of Consciousness in the Breakdown of the Bicameral Mind* (Boston: Houghton Mifflin, 1976), pp. 119, 214, 86, *passim*. Mihajlov's quotation on the need for a new consciousness is from his *Underground Notes* (Kansas City: Sheed Andrews and McMeel, 1976), p. 80. See also his "Mystical Experiences of the Labor Camps," *Kontinent* 2 (Garden City, New York: Anchor, 1977) pp. 103–31; Solzhenitsyn's *Gulag Archipelago*; A Shifrin, *In the Fourth Dimension* (Frankfurt-on-Main: Possev, 1973); D. Panin, *The Notebooks of Sologdin* (Frankfurt-on-Main: Possev, 1973); and A. Sinyavsky-Tertz, *A Voice From The Chorus* (London: Stenvalley, 1973) for metaphysical thinking in the contemporary Russian bloc. For Pelletier's survey of developments in the field, see his *Toward a Science of Consciousness* (New York: Delacorte, 1978). For Koekemoer see "Let It Come Back!" *San Francisco Review of Books* 4, no. 4, pp. 7–9. For Mihajlov on freedom's being essentially a religious problem, see *Underground Notes*, pp. 2–3.

Quotations from Whyte are from his *The Unconscious Before Freud* (London: Tavistock Publications, 1962), pp. 49, 52.

236

Appendix: On Azania

For de Villiers, see the *Sunday Times* (Johannesburg), March 5, 1978. The African National Congress position on the subject of "Azania" is stated in "Time for an End to the Myth," *Sechaba* 11 (3rd quarter 1977): 64.

On ancient Egyptian perceptions of African peoples, see Rosemarie Drenkhahn, *Darstellungen von Negern in Ägypten*, dissertation, Hamburg University, 1967, pp. 13–15; also Karola Zibelius, *Afrikanische Orts- und Völkernamen in hieroglyphischen und hieratischen Texten* (Wiesbaden: Dr. Ludwig Reichert, 1972), pp. 140–42.

See *The Periplus of the Erythraean Sea: Travels and Trade in the Indian Ocean by a Merchant of the First Century*, translated and annotated by Wilfred H. Schoff (New York and London: Longmans, Green, 1912), quotations at pp. 27–29, 66–68. In Roland Oliver and Gervase Mathew, eds., *History of East Africa*, (Oxford: Clarendon Press, 1963), vol. 1, p. 94, Mathew gives the most likely date of the *Periplus* as being circa A.D. 110 rather than Schoff's *circa* A.D. 60, and asserts of Schoff's version that it "should be used with caution; it is a free translation of an imaginatively emended text." A new translation of this important source of information about ancient East Africa would seem to be overdue.

For Schlichter, see *Proceedings of the Royal Geographical Society* (London: Edward Stanford, 1891), n.s., vol. 13, pp. 513–53, map at p. 576.

On the Berbers, see Carleton S. Coon, *The Living Races of Man* (New York: Knopf, 1965), pp. 116–17.

A concise summary of information about the Peloponnesian Azania may be found in *Paulys Real-Encyclopädie Der Classischen Altertumswissenschaft, Herausgegeben von Georg Wissowa* (Stuttgart: J. B. Metzlerscher Verlag, 1896), vol. 2, cols. 2639–40.

Peter Green's observations are in a letter to me, May 25, 1979.

On words meaning "brother" in the "Afro-Asiatic" languages, see J. H. Greenberg, *The Languages of Africa* (Bloomington, Ind.: Indiana University, 1966), p. 53.

For Huntingford see Oliver and Mathew, eds., *History of East Africa*, vol. 1, pp. 92, 61–62.

On the discussion of the *Zandīk* in Mas'ūdī, see R. S. Zaehner, *The Dawn and Twilight of Zoroastrianism* (London: Weidenfeld and Nicholson, 1961), p. 196.

INDEX

Abbas, Ferhat, 209
Abdurahman, Dr. Abdul, 122, 124
Abyssinia, see Ethiopia
Adenauer, Konrad, 37
Affluent Society, The (Galbraith),
    189
Africa, 209
  polarization in, 210
  slaves from, 87, 96
  see also East Africa, West Africa
African National Congress (ANC),
    17, 29, 45, 52, 57, 138–44, 148,
    149, 156–60, 167, 172, 174,
    175, 215
  and Alexandra bus boycott, 168–
    170
  membership in, 178, 185–86
  and Sino-Soviet dispute, 182–83
  1957 Transvaal provincial
    conference, 171
  Umkhonto we Sizwe, 43, 177,
    179, 182
  see also Youth League, South
    African Native National
    Congress

African People's Organization
    (APO), 122, 124, 132
African philosophy, vs. white
    philosophy, 154
Africanists, 162
  and Alexandra bus boycott,
    163
  and ANC, 185–86
  and CPSA, 156–57
  and "Freedom Charter," 159
  movement, 171–74, 181
Africans, 170
  as nationality, 155, 206–10
  strike at Cape Town, 175–76
  see also Blacks
Afrikaans language, 100
Afrikaans literature, 30–33
Afrikander, Jager, 99
Afrikaners, 29, 63, 107–8, 126–31,
    137, 147–48, 189
  and Black Consciousness, 59
  ancestral nationalities, 64–66
  psychology, 67
  skin color, 99–102
  see also Boers

"Afro-Asiatic" (Hamito-Semitic)
language group, 220–21
Agatharchides of Cnidus, 217
Akkadian language, 207
Alexandra bus boycott, 150, 162–70
Alexandra People's Transport
Action Committee (APTAC),
163–66, 168
Algeria, 209
and France, 179–80, 189, 205
Ali, Tariq, 181
All African Convention (AAC),
144–50
Almeida, Dom Francisco de, 69–70,
71
Andrews, W. H., 137, 142, 143
Anglo-American (mining finance
house), 190
Angola, 49–50, 59, 87
Angra Pequena, 108
Anthing, L., 98
Anti-Coloured Affairs Department
movement (Anti-CAD), 149,
150
Anti-Slavery and Aborigines
Protection Society, 125
Apartheid, 33, 126, 159, 194, 196,
234
and dualism, 154–55
foundations of, 99–102
and mixed marriages, 28–29
and power structure, 203–5
Arabia, 217–19
Arabic language, 221
Arabs, in Algeria, 205
Arcadia, 219
Areilza, José María de, 49
Arendt, Hannah, 60, 185, 196, 205,
208
Ashe, Geoffrey, 121
Asia, 210
slaves from, 96
Asiatic Land Tenure Act, 149
Assyrians, the, 211

Astor, Lord and Lady, 129
"Atoms for Peace" program, 38
Attaqua, the, 81
Ausan, 218
Australia, 161
Autshumao, see Harry
"Azania," 215–21

Baasskap, see Apartheid
Bach, Lazar, 142, 143, 185
Baden-Powell, Robert Stephenson
Smyth, 110, 112–14, 116
Bafebagiya, 158
Baghdad ('Abbāsid caliphate), 216–
217
Balfour Declaration, 130
Ballinger, Margaret, 147
Ballinger, W. G., 138
Bambata (Zondi chief), 120, 121,
139
Bantu, the, 128, 158
see also Sutu-nguni, the
Baragwanath Hospital (Soweto), 193
Barbaria, 218
Barber, Pieter, 90
Barnard, Chris, 28, 50
Barolong, the, 106, 107, 108, 112
see also Mafeking
Basner, Hyman, 147
Basotho, the, 108
Basters, the, 97, 98, 101, 102
Basutoland (Lesotho), 151, 177, 193
Bechuanaland (Botswana), 99, 105,
108, 124, 151
Becker, Erwin, 38
Bell, C. G. H., 111, 112, 113
Benguela slave route, 87
Benjamin, Victor, 25
Berbers, the, 205, 218
Bergenaars, the, 106
Bergh, H. J. van den, 34–35, 42
Bernstein, Lionel, 160
Beyleveld, Piet, 52, 160

Biko, Stephen Bantu, 12–13, 14, 23, 59, 187–88, 191, 195, 200, 203, 204, 206, 233
Bilko, Stephen, 233
Bismarck, Otto von, 108
Black Allied Workers Union (BAWU), 43
Black Consciousness, 12–13, 59, 187–88
Black Dwarf, The (underground paper), 181
Black People's Convention (BPC), 188, 195
"Black Republic" thesis, 140–41
Blacks, 117–18, 125–26, 134
  and CPSA, 138
  and land ownership, 103–5
  at Mafeking, 111–14
  in military, 151
  and Soviet Union, 140
  see also Africans
Blair, Jon, 233
Blake, William, 213
Blank, Jan, 79–80
Bloem, Jan, 106, 107
Boers, the, 63, 64, 99–100, 106, 122–23, 128, 130, 193
  vs. Britain, 107–15, 118–19, 127
  see also Afrikaners
Bolsheviks, in Russian Revolution, 66, 137, 161, 232
"Bondelzwarts affair," 130–31
Born, Jacob, 90
Boshoff, Judge W. G., 12–13, 18, 60
Botha, George, 21–22
Botha, Gideon, 136
Botha, Louis, 118, 119, 123, 124–125, 128, 130, 131, 133, 145
Boumedienne, Houari, 186
Boxer, C. R., 87
Brand, Robert, 129
Braudel, Fernand, 161
Brazil, 234
Brecht, Bertolt, 24, 60

Breuil, Abbé, 152
Breytenbach, Breyten, 13, 15, 23–24, 224
  on apartheid, 33
  birth of, 25
  book banned, 31–32
  and Groenewald, 53–58
  marriage and apartheid, 28–29
  political trials, 16–17, 45–51, 58–60
  as prisoner, 18–19, 51–53
  student days, 25–27
Breytenbach, Cloete, 33, 34, 55
Breytenbach, Jan, 33
Brietenbach, Conrad von, 64
Brink, André, 24, 56, 57, 58, 224
Britain, 38, 40, 43, 96, 99, 101, 105–106, 161, 181, 189, 218
  vs. Boers, 107–15, 118–19, 127
  imperialism in Africa, 63–67
  influence in South Africa, 120–30
  investments in South Africa, 204
  seafarers from, 71–77
Broederbond, 50
Broodryk, Colonel Kalfie, 46–47, 50, 51, 52
Broom, Robert, 152
Brotherhood Movement, 133–34
Bryant, A. T., 206
Buchan, John (Lord Tweedsmuir), 129
Bukharin, N. I., 140, 141, 142
Bunting, Brian, 160
Bunting, Sidney P., 135–36, 137, 138, 140, 142, 143
Burundi, 210
Bushmen, *see* San, the
Buthelezi, Gatsha, 34
Butler, Sir William, 111
Buys, Coenraad de, 99, 100
Byzantius, Stephanus, 219

Caesar, Julius, 155, 206
California Indians, 98

Calvinism, in Holland, 67
Camões, Luiz Vaz de, 69
Campbell, John, 101
Campbell, Roy, 131
Campbell-Bannerman, Henry, 127
Canada, 128
Cape African Teachers'
    Association, 150
"Cape Boy Contingent," 112
Cape Town "Troubles" of March-
    April 1960, 175–76
Cape Town, University of, 25–26
Capital (Marx), 67
Carabinga (Khoikhoi warrior), 89
Carnegie Commission on the Poor
    White Problem, 142
Carneson, Fred, 157, 160, 186
Carter, Gwendolen M., 174
Carter, Jimmy, 49
Catherine of Bengal, 96
Cavendish-Bentinck, Charles, 113
Cecil, Lord Edward, 111, 113, 114,
    116
Celliers, Jan, 47
Červenka, Zdenek, 37–41, 225
Cetshwayo (Zulu king), 64, 107,
    110, 120
Chad language, 220
Chainouqua, the, 81, 95, 97
Chaliand, Gérard, 210
Chamberlain, Joseph, 110–11, 115,
    126
Charles I, King of England, 66
Chaudhuri, Nirad, 105, 118, 132
Chesterton, G. K., 115
Chile, 40
China, and Soviet Union, 49, 179,
    182–83
Chobona (Choboqua), 81
    see also Xhosa, the
Choro (Gorachouqua chief), 80
Churchill, Winston, 13, 114–15,
    127, 129
Cillié, Judge P. M., 16, 48, 50, 51, 59

Cilliers, Mrs. Cecile, 50
Claas, Captain, 97
Clark, Senator Dick, 204
Clarke, Arthur C., 90
Class struggle, Marxist view of, 161
Cleaver, Eldridge, 205
Cline, Ray S., 234
Coal, production of, 191–92
Cochoqua, the, 81, 97
    and early Dutch settlers, 91–95
Coetzee, Ampie, 50
Colonization, with criminals, 75
Coloured Affairs Department, 149
"Coloureds," 86, 102, 117, 124,
    149–50, 155, 175
Communism, and dualism, 155
Communist Manifesto, The, 161
Communist party, in France, 29,
    179
Communist Party of South Africa
    (CPSA), 52, 131, 152, 161–62,
    167, 174, 181
    and ANC, 156–60
    founded, 135
    and racism, 136–40, 184–85
    and Soviet Union, 140–43, 153
Conco, Dr. Wilson, 155, 159, 160
Condorcet, Marie de, 184
Congress of Democrats (COD),
    157–59, 167, 174, 175, 181
Congress Movement, 158–59, 170,
    174, 181
    and mass arrests, 160
Conquest, Robert, 183
Consciousness, 162
    and dualism, 211–13
    see also Black Consciousness
Cope, Jack, 26
Council of Action (mineworkers),
    137
Crime, in Soweto, 192–93
Criminal Law Amendment Act,
    157
Cronjé, General Piet, 113, 118

Cross, Captain, 75, 76
Cuba, 17, 49, 178
Curtis, Jenny, 44
Curtis, Lionel, 118, 121, 129
Cushites, the, 218–19
Cushitic language, 219–20
Czechoslovakia, 39, 179

Dadoo, Yusuf, 160, 185, 186
Dagga (Cannabis sativa), 81
Dalindyebo, (Tembu chief), 124
Damce, E. H., 11
D'Anaya, Pedro, 194
Dart, Raymond A., 152
Dawes, Senator H. L., 101
Dawson, Geoffrey, 128, 129
de Beaulieu, Augustin, 73
De Beers Company, 133
Defiance Campaign (1952), 157
De Gaulle, Charles, 29, 189
Descartes, René, 153
De Villiers, Fleur, 215
De Villiers, Simon, 94
De Wet, "Spyker," 148, 198, 199
Diamond fields, value of, 126
Dias, Bartholomeu, 68, 69
Die huis van die dowe (The House of the Deaf Man) (Breytenbach), 30
Dingane (Zulu kingdom), 107, 109
Dingiswayo (Nguni chief), 206, 208
Dinuzulu (Zulu prince), 120
Dirk, Gerrit, 90
Diseases, and native tribes, 97
Dodsworth, Edward, 75, 76
Doke, C. M., 43
Dole, W. P., 98–99
Doman (Dominie, Anthony) (Goringhaiqua leader), 86, 88–89, 91, 92
Dout, Pieter (Griqua captain), 106
Drake, Francis, 71

Dualism
and consciousness, 211–13
vs. holism, 153–55
Dube, John ("Mafukuzela"), 103, 105, 117, 119–20, 121, 122, 123, 124, 148
Du Bois, Dr. W. E. B., 133
Dulles, John Foster, 189
Duncan, Sir Patrick (father), 129
Duncan, Patrick (son), 129, 157, 167–68, 173, 174, 175, 176
Dutch East India Company, 64
Dutch settlers (early), 64–67
and the Cochoqua, 91–95
and the Khoikhoi in general, 80–91, 95
see also Holland
Dworkin, Lawrence, 44, 45
Dyer, Dr. John E., 113

East Africa, 124, 125, 216–20
East Germany, 39
eGabeni, battle of, 107
Egyptians, ancient, 216–17, 219
Eisenhower, Dwight D., 38, 189
Eliot, T. S., 171
Elphick, Richard, 63, 71, 80–81, 89, 91, 92
Elphinstone, Sir George, 65
Engels, Friedrich, 161
England, *see* Britain
English East India Company, 71, 74, 77
Erasmus, Minister of Justice F. C., 175, 176
Ethiopia, 133, 218
Eunus, 216
Europe, and nationalism, 208–9
Europeans, as nationality, 155–56
European settlers, 64–77
Eva (Krotoa) (Khoikhoi intermediary), 91–95, 102
Evolution, and dualism, 213

Executions, in prison, 19–20
Eykamma (Khoikhoi warrior), 89

Federation of Free African Trade
   Unions of South Africa
   (FOFATUSA), 43
Feit, Edward, 158–59
Fenton, Norman, 233
First, Ruth, 155, 160
First International Conference on
   the Peaceful Uses of Atomic
   Energy, 38
Fischer, Abram Louis ("Bram"), 52,
   149, 160, 177–78, 179
Fitzclarence, Charles, 113, 114
Fitzherbert, Humphrey, 76–77
FLN, in Algeria, 179–80
Forman, Lionel, 160
Fourth International Organization
   of South Africa, 231
France, 37, 38, 48, 49, 50, 95, 115,
   206
   in Algeria, 179–80, 189, 205
   Community party in, 29, 179
   Huguenots from, 65
Frank, André Gunder, 210
Freedom, and liberation, 205
"Freedom Charter," 159–60
   backers of, 162, 166, 169, 172
French Revolution, 161
French settlers (early), 65–66
Frente de Libertação de
   Moçambique (Frelimo), 195
Freund, W. M., 100

Gabbema, Abraham, 91
Galbraith, John Kenneth, 189
Gama, Vasco da, 68–69
Gandhi, Manilal, 157
Gandhi, Mohandas K. (Mahatma),
   13, 105, 106, 166, 216
   and mobilization of South
   African Indians, 117–21
Garbus, Martin, 16

Gaul, tribes of, 206
Geldenhuys, General Mike, 51, 53
General Law Amendment Act, 177
George V, King of England, 123, 124
Gerhart, Gail, 171, 172, 173, 174
German settlers (early), 64–67
German South-West Africa, 123–
   124, 125
   see also Namibia
German Togoland, 124
German tribes, 206
Germany, 108, 115, 116, 137, 207
   and Thirty Years' War, 66
   see also East Germany, West
   Germany
Geyl, Pieter, 67
Gladstone, Lord, 124–25
Glen Grey Act of 1894, 103
"Goch Street Case," 179
Goens, Ryklob van, 64, 88
Goethe, Johann von, 24
Gogosoa (Goringhaiqua chief), 80,
   86
Gold, 49
   and United States, 59
   value of, 126, 190
Goldreich, Arthur, 55
Gomas, John, 143
Gonaqua, the, 81
Gool, Dr. Goolam, 145
Gorachouqua, the, 80, 86, 88, 92
Goringhaicona, the, 86
Goringhaiqua, the, 86, 88
Goshen (republic), 108
Goske, Isbrand, 96, 97
Goya, Francisco de, 30
Grant, Dr. W. L., 38
Grapow, Dürten, 35–37, 45
Grapow, Jobst, 27, 35, 36
Greece, 219
Green, Peter, 219, 221
Griffiths (of Basutoland), 124
Griqua, the, 73, 101, 102, 106–7
Griqualand, 101

Griqualand West, 101
Groenewald, Pieter, 17–18, 60, 224
   and Breytenbach, 53–58
Guinea, slaves from, 87
Gulag Archipelago (Solzhenitsyn),
   12
Gülich, Gustav von, 67
Gumede, Josiah T., 119, 126, 139–
   140, 141, 143, 153, 157
Guriqua, the, 81

Habash, the, 218
Hadzapi, the, 220
Hafferjee, Dr. Hoosen, 22–23
Hahn, Theophilus, 82, 83
Haiti, 115
Hammond-Tooke, David, 206
Hanbury-Tracy, Algernon, 113
Hancock, W. K., 127
Hamcumqua, the, 81
Hamilton, Angus, 113–14
Hamlet (Shakespeare), 212
Harcourt, Lewis (1st Viscount
   Harcourt), Colonial Secretary,
   125
Harmel, Michael, 138, 156, 160,
   185
Harry (Hadda, Adda, Haddot)
   (Strandlopers leader), 77–78,
   80–86, 88, 91–92
Hendrickse, Kenneth, 25
Henning, Dr. Piet, 48
Here XVII, see Lords Seventeen
Herodotus, 219
Hertzog, J. B. M., 126, 137–38, 140,
   144, 145, 147, 148
Hessequa, the, 95
Hillmann, Michael, 221
Himyarites, of Arabia, 217–18
Hitler, Adolf, 137, 210
Hobson, J. A., 127, 128
"Hoggenheimer," 128
Holism, vs. dualism, 153–55

Holism and Evolution (Smuts), 130,
   131
Holland, 66
   early commercial power of, 67
   seafarers from, 71, 76–77, 78–79
   see also Dutch settlers (early)
Honono, N. I., 150
Hope, Bob, 189
Hottentots, 68, 69, 73, 78, 82, 97,
   98, 208, 220
   see also Khoikhoi
Huguenots, from France, 65
Human, Koos, 30
Huntingford, G. W. B., 219, 220
Hutu, the, 210

ICFTU, 43
Immorality Act, 29
Imperialism (Hobson), 127
Imperialism, and racism, 128
India, 121, 128
Indian Opinion, 119
Indians
   mobilization in South Africa,
      117–21
   as national group in South Africa,
      155
Indonesia, 96
Industrial and Commercial
   Workers' Union (ICU), 137,
   138–39
Industrial Workers of the World,
   132
International Socialist League of
   South Africa, 122
International Universities Exchange
   Fund (IUEF), 180
Iran, 39, 40
*Iron Cow Must Sweat, The (Die
   ysterkoei moet sweet)*
   (Breytenbach), 24
Isandhlwana, battle of, 110, 120
Israel, 40, 67

Israelites (at Bulhoek), 130
Italy, 116, 133

Jabavu, D. D. T., 122, 144
Jabavu, John Tengo, 117, 144
Jabavu, Noni, 193, 196
Jacobins, in French Revolution, 161
Jaffe, Hosea, 150
James I, King of England, 77
Japan, 40–41, 132, 208
Jaynes, Julian, 211, 212
Jeffreys, M. D. W., 81
Jews, in Johannesburg, 128
Johannesburg, 190
  socialism of, 128
  see also Soweto
Johnson, R. W., 49, 176
Johnson, Samuel, 152
"Joktanites," 219
Jones, Daniel I., 122, 133
Jong, Cees de, 26
Jonker, Ingrid, 26–27
July, Jan, 101

Kabyles, in Algeria, 205
Kadalie, Clements, 137, 138–39,
  145
Kaffir wars, 100
Kafka, Franz, 209
Kahn, Sam, 147, 157, 160
Karis, Thomas, 174
Katastrofes (Catastrophes)
  (Breytenbach), 28
Katzen, M. F., 65
Kenya, 216, 219
Kerr, Philip (Lord Lothian), 128–29
Kgogong, Alfred, 185
Kgosana, Philip, 176, 177
Khaile, E. J., 140
Khama (Bechuana chief), 124
Khoebaha (Hamcumqua chief), 81
Khoikhoi, the, 62, 63, 68–71, 93,
  94, 98–100, 220
  diseases among, 96–97

and Dutch settlers, 78–79, 80–
  91, 95
and English, 75–77
speech of, 72–73
Khoisan peoples, 62, 100, 155
Khoi tribes, 63, 207
Khoza, Aaron, 22
Khrushchev, Nikita, 184
Kies, Benjamin, 150
King, Martin Luther, 121
Kissinger, Henry, 48, 49, 204
Kitchener, Lord, 116, 127, 128
Kleinschmidt, Horst, 44
Koekemoer, Joseph, 212
Koestler, Arthur, 211
Koka, Drake, 43, 201
Kolwa, the, 119
Korana, the, 106
Kotane, Moses, 143, 157, 160, 182
Kouevuur (Cold Fire) (Breytenbach),
  30–31
Kraftwerk Union (West Germany),
  37
Kragdadigheid, 165, 166, 173, 200
Kriegler, J. C., 58
Krige, Uys, 26
Kronstadt uprising (Russia), 232
Kruger, Minister of Police J., 21
Kruger, President Paul, 118, 129
Kunene, Raymond, 117, 185
Kuper, Leo, 210

Labour party, 137
La Guma, Alex, 160
La Guma, Jimmy, 140, 142, 143,
  160
Lancaster, Sir James, 71
Land ownership
  and blacks, 103–5
  in Griqualand, 101
Latin America, 210
Lawrence, T. E., 129
League of African Rights (LAR),
  141, 142

League Against Imperialism, 140
Leballo, Potlako Kitchener, 158,
 159, 171, 172, 173, 174, 177
Lee-Warden, Len, 160, 174–75
Legassick, Martin, 141
Legum, Colin, 50, 200
Lembede, Anton, 153, 155, 156–57
Lenin, Nikolai, 127, 161
Lesko, Leonard, 221
Lesotho, *see* Basutoland
Letele, Arthur, 160, 167
"Letter from Abroad to Butcher"
 (from *Skryt*) (Breytenbach), 31–
 32
Levy, Leon, 160
Lewin, Hugh, 19
Lewis, Norman, 44
Liberal Party, 173, 174, 175–77
Liberation, and freedom, 205
Lipheana, Mosi, 101
Lloyd George, David, 115, 126,
 129–30
Lodge, Tom, 175, 176
Loginov, Victor, 40–41
London, Jack, 136
Lords Seventeen, 65, 71, 79, 84, 94,
 97
Lotus (Breytenbach ["Jan Blom"]),
 31
Lucan (Roman poet), 76
Lusaka Accords, 195
Lutuli, Albert, 13, 148, 156, 158,
 159, 160, 170, 177
Lutuli, Martin, 119
Lye, William, 207

Mabelane, Mathews, 22
Mabija, Phakamile, 22, 24
Machel, Samora, 195
Mackintosh, John, 200
Macmillan, Harold, 189
Madagascar, 86, 87, 94, 96
Madzunya, Josiah, 164, 168, 169,
 170, 172–73, 174, 177

Mafeking (Mafikeng), battle at,
 110–16
 see also Barolong, the
Magerman, Arthur, 164, 168
Mahabane, Zaccheus, 148
Mahlangu, S. (APTAC president),
 164, 168–69
Mahlangu, Solomon (ANC militant
 hanged in 1979), 179
Mahomo, Nana, 173
Makgothi, H. G., 158
Makhatini, Johnston Mfanakuti, 32,
 34, 43, 52, 56
Makhatle, Barney, 201
Makiwane, Tennyson, 52
Malagasy (Malayo-Polynesian
 language), 86
Malan, Dr. Daniel F., 137, 144, 165,
 204
Malan government, 157
Malan Purified Nationalists, 153
Malay slaves, 96
Malele, Elmon, 22
Malnutrition, effects on children,
 189
Mandela, Nelson, 148, 155, 160,
 177, 178, 179, 197
Manichees, the, 221
MaNthatisi (Tlokwa warrior
 queen), 106, 107
Manuel I, King of Portugal, 194
Maoists, 179
Mao Tse-tung, 186
Mapikela, Thomas M., 124, 148
Marais, J. S., 98, 100
Maré, Paulus ("Gerry"), 35, 44, 56
Marelana (Pondo chief), 124
Maritz, Gert, 106
Marks, J. B., 145, 156, 160, 179
Marks, Shula, 109, 120
Marsham, Douglas, 113
Martens, Nicholas, 44
Marxism, and class struggle, 161
Marx, Karl, 67

Marxism-Leninism, 57
Maseko, MacDonald, 158
Mashinini, Tsietsi, 201
Maś ūdï (Arab historian and
 geographer), 221
Matabeleland, 107
 see also Rhodesia
Matelief, Cornelis, 71
Materialism, and consciousness,
 212
Mathew, Gervase, 236
Matthews, Joe, 155, 160, 167
Mayisela, Lawrence, 164
Mazwembe, Luke, 21
Mbala, Jim, 114
Mbatha, Dumisani, 21
Mbeki, Govan, 177, 178
McKenzie, Duncan, 120, 121
Mda, Ashby Peter, 153, 155, 171,
 174
Mdloedebe, Elias, 52
Mdluli, Joseph, 21, 23, 224
Medvedev, Roy, 141
Meerhoff, Pieter van, 93, 94
Meerhoff, Pieternell van, 95
Meerhoff, Salamon van, 95
Merriman, John X., 128, 129, 146
Mesopotamia, 211, 216
Mfecane (Difaqane) period, 109, 207
Mfengu, the (Fingoes), 107, 109,
 112, 207
Mgijima, Enoch, 103, 130
Mhudi (Plaatje), 106, 134
Michelbourne, Sir Edward, 72
Middleton, John, 72
Mihajlov, Mihajlo, 186, 203, 212
Miles, John, 50
Milner, Sir Alfred, 110–11, 118,
 125, 126, 127, 128–30, 131
Milner, Lady, 129
"Milner's Kindergarten," 128–29
Modisane, Bloke, 192, 194
Moerdijk, Donald, 35, 36
Moffat, Robert, 107

Mofutsanyana, Edwin, 145
Mohapi, Mapetla, 21, 23
Mokonyane, Dan, 150, 163, 164,
 165, 166, 167, 168, 169, 170,
 171, 172–73
Molema, S. M., 123
'Molotsi, Peter, 173, 215
Molsbergen, E. C. Godée, 78, 79, 94
Molteno, Donald, 147, 157, 174
Mondlane, Eduardo, 195
Monomotapa (kingdom), 81
Montshiwa (Barolong chief), 108
Moodie, Donald, 226
Morand, Charles Albert, 50
Moroka (Barolong chief), 106, 107,
 108, 134
Moroka, Dr. James, 156
Morton, Don, 35, 47, 224
Moshweshwe (Sotho chief), 107,
 207
Moss, Glenn, 44
Mote and the Beam, The: An Epic
 on Sex-Relationship 'Twixt
 White and Black in British
 South Africa (Plaatje), 133
Motor Carriers' Transportation
 Amendment Bill of 1957, 166
Movement for a Democracy of
 Content (MDC), 164, 173
Mozambique, 96, 194–95
Mpande (Zulu king), 109
Mpanza, James "Sofasonke," 162,
 163
Mphahlele, Ezekiel, 15
Msane, Saul, 105, 119, 124, 132
Msimang, Richard, 105
Msimang, Selby, 146
Mswazi (Swazi chief), 207
Mthethwa Confederacy, 206
Muscat, Sultan of, 218
Mussolini, Benito, 116
Muwaffak ('Abbāsid regent), 217
Mvabaza, L. T., 126
Mvelinqangi (First Cause), 154

Mzilikazi (Ndebele warlord), 106, 107, 134, 207

Naicker, Dr. G. M., 160
Nama (Khoikhoi language), 73
Namaqua, the, 81
Namaqualand, 98
Namibia, 38, 39, 59, 73, 99, 180
  see also German South-West
  Africa
Nantes, Edict of, 65
Natal, 109, 124
  Indians in, 117–21
Natal Indian Congress, 118
National Congress of India, 118
National Party, 144, 165, 215
Nationalism, and Europe, 208–209
Nationalities, 155–56
National Union of South African
  Students (NUSAS), 34, 50, 187
Native Life in South Africa
  (Plaatje), 133
Native Services Transport Bill, 170
Natives' Land Act of 1913, 103–5, 124–25
Natives' Representation Act of 1936, 144, 147–48
Natives' Representative Council, 147, 156–57
Ndebele (Matabele), the, 106, 107, 112, 207
Ndlambe (Xhosa chief), 100
Negroes, early references to, 216–217
Neilly, Emerson, 114
Nel, Commandant, 98
Nevinson, Henry W., 87
Ngcayiya, H. R., 126
Ngonomoa (Cochoqua chief), 86, 91, 95
Ngo Sach Vinh, 28
Ngo Thi Hoàng Liên Yolande Bubi, 28, 32–33, 34, 42, 51, 56, 58

Ngqika (Gaika) (Xhosa chief), 99, 100
Ngubane, Jordan, 62, 153, 154, 174
Nguni, the, 81, 82, 109, 206, 207, 208
Nietzsche, Friedrich, 184
Nieuw-Haerlem, 78
1984 (Orwell), 203
Nkatlo, Joseph, 25
Nkosi, Johannes, 143, 144
Noge, Simon, 164
Nokwe, Duma, 155, 157, 158, 160
Non-European Conference (1927), 134
Non-European Unity Movement
  (NEUM), 149–50, 158, 174, 175
Ntshuntsha, Dr. Nanaoth, 22
Nuclear Axis, The (Rogers-
  Červenka), 37–41
Nuclear Conspiracy, The
  (brochure), 41
Nuclear power, production of, 37–41
Nziba, Rosetta, 172
'Nzinga, Queen of the Jagas, 87
Nzo, Alfred, 164, 166

O'Brien, Conor Cruise, 188
Oedasoa (Cochoqua chief), 91, 92–93, 94
Ohlange Institute (Natal), 119–20, 148
Okhela (secret organization), 17, 36, 42, 43, 45, 60
Ólaffson, Jón, 73
Om te vlieg (To Fly) (Breytenbach), 31
Oorblyfsels (Remnants)
  (Breytenbach), 31
"Operation Mayibuye," 178
Opperman, Dirk, 30
Opperman, Gottfried, 63
Orange Free State, 107, 108, 193
Orwell, George, 116, 203

Oxford History of South Africa, 12, 62

Pan Africanist Congress (PAC), 52, 172–77, 179, 215
Pandours, the, 99, 100
Papez-MacLean theory, 211
Pass laws, 23–24, 105, 139
Paton, Alan, 167–68
Pearson, Cyril Arthur, 116
Pelletier, Kenneth, 212
Peloponnesus, the, 219
Periplus of the Erythraean Sea, 217–19, 236
Persian language, 221
Persians, ancient, 216–17
Philip II, King of Spain, 66, 67
Pienaar, Schalk, 33
Pimville, poverty of, 193
Plaatje, Solomon Tshekisho, 103, 104, 116–17, 122–24, 132
    birth of, 106
    on British rule, 105–6, 125–26
    death of, 134
    at Mafeking, 111–12, 114
    writings of, 133
Plessis, I. D. du, 96
Plettenberg, Joachim van, 63
Plutonium, production of, 38–40
Poland, 39, 234
Polley, Reverend James, 44, 45, 56
Pollution, in Soweto, 191–92
Polomé, Edgar, 221
Popper, Karl, 14
Poqo (military wing of PAC), 177
Portugal, 66, 87
    and Mozambique, 194–95
    seafarers from, 68–71
Potgieter, Andries Hendrik, 106, 107
Power structure, and apartheid, 203–205
Pretoria Central Prison, 19, 51
Pretorius, Andries, 109

Pring, Martin, 76
Prins, Marthinus, 23
Prisons, conditions in, 18–24
Progressive Party, 174
Progressive Youth Council, 155
Prohibition of Political Interference Act, 176
Ptolemaeus, Claudius (Ptolemy), 218, 219
Public Safety Act, 157
Public Utility Transport Company (PUTCO), and Alexandra bus boycott, 162–63, 166
"Punt, Land of," 219
Purified National Party, 144
Pynn, John, 77

Qwa Qwa (Southern Sotho "bantustan"), 193
Quaelbergen, Commander, 94, 97
Quellerie, Maria de la, 86

Raath, Heleen, 27
Rabie, Jan, 15, 26
Racial categorizations, terminology for, 12–13
Racism
    and "Coloureds," 149–50
    and CPSA, 136–40, 184–85
    and dualism, 155
    and economics, 126
    and imperialism, 128
    and Indians, 117–21, 149–50
    and Stalinism, 184–86
    see also Apartheid, White racism
Radebe, Mark, 119
Rademeyer, General C. I., 175
Rall, General Gunther, 41
Ramoshana, D. M., 207
Ratshidi, Barolong boo, 112
Raymond, George, 71
"Red Revolt," of miners, 131–32, 136
    see also Witwatersrand mines

Reef, the (Witwatersrand), 190
Reeves, Bishop Ambrose, 167
Rehoboth Basters, 102
Representation of Natives Bill, 147
Resha, Robert, 158, 160, 185
"Resist Apartheid Committee," 158
Revolutionary Action Group
    (RAG), 36*
Rhodes, Cecil, 110, 111
Rhodesia, 36, 43, 182
Ribbentrop, Joachim von, 129
Riebeeck, Jan van, 64, 67, 68, 78–
    80, 82, 84–94, 97, 157, 185
Riley, Megan, 45
Robben Island, 77
Robberson, Wiljam, 90
Robespierre, Maximilien de, 161
Robinson, Sir Hercules, 110, 111
Rogers, Barbara, 37–41, 225
Rohm, Dürten, *see* Grapow, Dürten
Rohm, Dr. Herman, 35, 36
Rommel, Erwin, 151
Rousseau, Leon, 30
Rousset, David, 24, 196
Roux, Eddie, 133, 136, 137, 138,
    139, 140, 141, 142, 143, 169,
    186
Rubusana, Dr. Walter, 123–24
Ruiters, Hazel, 25
Ruskin, John, 119
Russia, *see* Soviet Union
Russian Revolution, 161–62, 181
Russo-Japanese war, 132
Rwanda, 210
Rykov, Aleksey Ivanovich, 142

Saayman, Daantjie, 32
Sabæans, the, 218
Sabotage Act, 177
Sacharias, Jan, 94
Sachs, Solly, 142
Saint-Just, Louis de, 161, 171
Saldanha, Antonio de, 69

Saldanhars, the (Saldanians), 69, 75,
    81, 85
Salisbury, Lord, 111, 115, 208
Sampson, Anthony, 160, 167, 169,
    170
San, the, 62, 63, 82, 83, 95, 220–21
    extermination of, 97–99
Sandawe, the, 220
Sand River Convention, 108
SASM, 200
SASOL II (coal gasification project),
    40
"SASO nine," 59
Satyagraha movement, 117, 121
Saudi Arabia, 40
Sauer, J. W., 104
Schacher (son of Gorachouqua
    chief), 92
Schizophrenia, nature of, 211
Schlichter, Henry, 218
Schoeman, B. J., 165, 166, 170
Schoff, Wilfred, 217–18, 236
Schoon, Marius, 26, 55, 57, 60
Schoor, Willem van, 150
Schuitema, Barend, 35, 42, 43–44,
    45, 46, 47, 52
Schwartz, Martin, 221
Sechuana Proverbs (Plaatje), 133
Seidman, Ann, 190
Seidman, Neva, 190
Sekhukhune (Pedi chief), 64
Sekonyela (Tlokwa chief), 106
Selborne, Lord, 127
Self-consciousness, and
    consciousness, 212–13
Seme, Dr. Pixley Ka Izaka, 122, 143,
    144, 148, 153
Semela, Selby
    arrested, 195
    birth of, 188
    childhood of, 193–94
    in prison, 196–99
    and Soweto uprisings, 200–202
Semitic languages, 219, 220

September, Reggie, 160, 186
Sestigers (Afrikaans writers), 33
Seti I, King of Egypt, 216
Shaka (Zulu king), 109, 206–207,
    208
Shakespeare, William, 212
Shall I Slay My Brother Boer?
    (Stead), 115
Sharpeville massacre, 27, 174
Shaw, George Bernard, 129
Shepstone, Theophilus, 107, 208
Shillinge, Andrew, 76–77
Shoshangane (Tsonga chief), 207
Siam, 208
Sikakane, Joyce, 192
"Silvermine" (radar surveillance
    installation), 41
Simon, William, 49
Simons, H. J., 160
Sisulu, Walter, 155, 157, 158, 160,
    177, 178
Skin color, of Afrikaners, 99–102
*Skryt: Om 'n sinkende skip blou te
    verf* (Breytenbach), 23, 31–32
Slavery, and bloodlines, 100–101
Slaves, importation of, 86–88, 96
Slovo, Joe, 160, 185, 186
Smallpox, and native tribes, 97
Smith government (Rhodesia), 182
Smith, Sir Thomas, 74, 76
Smuts, Jan Christiaan, 105, 115,
    119, 121, 123, 125, 128, 131,
    136, 137, 144, 145, 153, 189
    and Afrikaner nationalism, 129–
    130
    on colour bars, 151–52
    on native races, 146–47
Soaqua (Sonqua), *see* San, the
Sobukwe, Robert Mangaliso, 11, 14,
    34, 155, 159, 172, 173, 174,
    177, 178, 206, 209–10
Sole, Donald Bell, 41, 42
Solidarité (French Communist
    organization), 32, 36, 44

Solzhenitsyn, Aleksandr I., 12
Somalia, 216
Somali language, 221
Sons, Lieutenant, 199
Sontonga, Enoch, 230
Sotho, the, 107, 108, 193, 207
South Africa
    and Angolan civil war, 48–50
    and coal production, 191–92
    economic growth of, 234
    European settlers in, 64–77
    and gold, 49, 126, 190
    and nuclear power, 38–41, 43
    Special Branch, 160, 167
    and strategic nonfuel minerals,
    204
    tribal and clan distinctions, 62
South Africa Act of 1909, 122
South African Atomic Energy Act,
    38
South African Coloured Peoples
    Organization (SACPO), 158,
    159
South African Communist Party
    (SACP), 57, 157–58, 160, 175,
    180–81, 183
    and racism, 184–85
    and Soviet Union, 52
South African Congress of Trade
    Unions (SACTU), 43, 158
South African Indian Congress
    (SAIC), 158, 159
South African Native Congress,
    121–22
South African Native National
    Congress (SANNC), 122, 123,
    124–26, 132–34
South African Party (SAP), 144
South African Students'
    Organization (SASO), 34, 187,
    195, 200
"Southern Africa: A Betrayal"
    (article), 181–82
South Korea, 40

Soviet Union, 20, 36, 115, 116, 203, 204
and Angola, 49
and China, 49, 179, 182–83
and CPSA, 140–43, 153
and French Communist Party, 179
and nuclear power, 39, 40
and racism, 179, 184–86
and SACP, 52
and ANC Youth League, 157
see also Russian Revolution
Soweto, 194
children in, 188–89
crime in, 192–93
location of, 190
and pollution, 191–92
population of, 191
Soweto uprisings, 162, 180, 200–202
Spanish Empire, 66, 67
Spartacus, 216, 221
Special Branch, 167
and Congress Movement, 160
Sputnik I, 189
Stalin, Joseph, 60, 141–42, 153, 161
Stalinism, 175
and racism, 184–86
Standholders' Association, and Alexandra bus boycott, 163
Stead, W. T., 115
Stel, Simon van der, 65, 82, 96, 97
Stellaland, 108
Stellenbosch, University of, 25
Stent, Vere, 134, 137
Stop the War Committee, 115
Story of My Experiments with Truth, The (Gandhi), 119
Strabo (Greek geographer), 207
Strachan, Donald, 101
Strandlopers (Goringhaicona), 69, 80
Strijdom, J. G., 165
Stroewig (policeman), 197, 198, 199

Suppression of Communism Act, 45, 156
Sutu-nguni, the, 62, 63, 82, 97, 99, 109, 117, 154, 155, 189, 206
see also Bantu, the
SWAPO, 180
Swarathle, Shadrock Sello, 23–24
Swart, C. R., 160
Swart, Vincent, 164, 173
Swazi kingdom, 64, 124, 207

Taaibosch, the (Khoikhoi clan), 106
"Tabackteckemans," the (Gorachouqua), 80
Tabata, I. B., 148, 150, 178
Tacitus (Roman historian), 206, 207
Taiwan, 40
Tambo, Oliver, 34, 43, 57, 155, 157, 160, 167, 172, 182, 185
Tanzania, 182–83, 216, 220
Tapscott, Michael, 27
Tasmanians, 98
Tavernier, Jean-Baptiste, 72–73
Taylor, Sergeant Major, 112
Teachers' League of South Africa (TLSA), 150
Terblanche, I. B. S., 175, 176
Terrorism Act of 1967, 16, 45, 47, 48, 58
Terry, Reverend Edward, 72, 74, 76
Theal, G. M., 68, 69, 71, 77, 78, 96
Theebaw (Burmese king), 110
Thema, Selope, 126, 148, 152, 153
Third World countries, 40
Thirty Years' War, 66
Thompson, G. (early traveler), 98
Tip, Karel, 45
t'Jock, Patricq, 90
Tlokwa, the (Mantatees), 106–7
Tolstoy, Leo, 119
Tolstoy Farm, 119
Toussaint L'Ouverture, Pierre, 216
Towerson, Gabriel, 74

Transvaal, 64, 105, 108
  Indians in, 118–19, 121
  provincial conference (ANC), 171
  Uitlanders, 125–26, 128
Transvaal Indian Congress, 119
Treason Trial, 166, 167
  and Congress Movement, 160
Trenndüsenssystem (uranium-
  enrichment process), 38
Trotsky, Leon, 161
Trotskyism, 141–42, 164, 175, 231
Tshazibane, Wellington, 21
Tsonga, the, 207
Tsotsi, Wycliffe, 150
Tswana, the (Bricqua), 81, 106, 108,
  207
Turks, the, 208
Turok, Benjamin, 160
Tutsi, the, 210

Ubiqua, the, 95
Ubuntu (botho), ethical code, 154
Umkhonto we Sizwe (military wing
  of ANC), 43, 177, 179, 182
United Nations (UN), 34, 36
  and FLN, 180
  and South Africa, 151
United South African National
  Party (later United Party), 144
United States, 87, 114, 115, 129,
  161, 189, 204, 207
  and Angola, 49
  and gold, 59
  and nuclear power, 39, 40
  and racism, 205
  and satyagraha, 121
Unlawful Organizations Act, 174
Uranium, production of, 38–40
Uwini (Ndebele leader), 110

van Zyl, Adriaan, 98
van Zyl, Colonel, 55–56
Venter, P. J., 180
Vercingetorix (Gallic chief), 206

Vereeninging, Peace of, 125, 148
Versailles Peace Conference, 126
Verwoerd, Hendrik Frensch, 25,
  126, 128, 175, 185, 189
Victims, selection of, 20–24
Victoria, Queen of England,
  119
Vietnam, 114
Vilikazi, B. W., 43
Visser, Brigadier, 18, 53, 56
Viviers, Jack, 44, 224
VOC, 78, 79, 95, 96, 100
Voetskrif (Breytenbach), 52
Voortrekkers, 101, 106, 107, 109
Vorbeck, Von Lettow, 124
Vorster, Balthazar John, 25, 31, 34,
  46, 49, 54, 126, 128, 177, 196,
  210

Wagenaar (Wagner), Zacharias, 64,
  93, 94, 97, 226
Wallace, Marjorie, 26
Wallerstein, Immanuel, 208
Wankie Affair, 182
War Measure, 145, 151
Washington, Booker T., 120
Waterboer, Andries (West Griqua
  captain), 107
Wedgewood, C. V., 66
Weimar government (Germany),
  137
Wellington, Duke of, 90
Wentzel, E. A., 58
West Africa, 96
  slaves from, 87
West Germany, and nuclear power,
  37–41, 43
West Rand Administration Board,
  191
White racism, beginnings of, 63, 64,
  100, 117–18
  see also Afrikaners
Whyte, L. L., 212–13

Willems, Harman, 90
Wilson, Gordon, 113
Wilson, Monica, 70
Witwatersrand mines, 126, 128,
    190, 192
  workers at, 132
  see also "Red Revolt," of miners
Wodehouse, Sir Philip, 98
Wolheim, Oscar, 174
Wolpe, Harold, 55
Wolton, Douglas, 142, 143
Wolton, Molly, 142, 143
Woods, Donald, 23
Workers' International League, 164
World Council of Churches, 180
World Federation project, 129
World Youth Festival, 158
Wouters, Jan, 96
Wouterssen, Jan, 94
Wreede, George Frederick, 70–71

Xhore (Cory) (Khoikhoi captain), 74,
    75, 77, 80
Xhosa, the, 81, 82, 97, 99–100, 109,
    207

Xuma, Alfred B., 145, 149, 151, 156,
    168

Young, Robert Gordon, 45
Young Communist League (YCL),
    138
Youth League, of ANC, 153, 157,
    158
  Basic Policy, 155–56, 206
  and Communists, 156
Ysterkoei (Breytenbach), 28, 30
Yutar, Dr. Percy, 45–46, 47, 48, 178

Za Hakale ("Zoscales"), 218
Zaijman, Daniel, 95
Zaire, 48–49
Zambesia, 108
Zambia, 182–83
Zander, Ernst, 164
Zandj rebels, 216–17, 221
ZAPU, 182
Zeus, land of, 219
Zululand, 120–21, 206
Zulus, the, 103, 107, 109–10, 117–
    118, 120, 124, 206, 207